MANUAL OF INDIAN BUDDHISM

GRUNDRISS DER INDO-ARISCHEN PHILOLOGIE UND ALTERTUMSKUNDE
(ENCYCLOPEDIA OF INDO-ARYAN RESEARCH)

HERAUSGEGEBEN VON G. BUHLER
III. BAND, 8, HEFT

MANUAL OF INDIAN BUDDHISM

BY

H. KERN

GYAN

Published by

GYAN

Gyan Publishing House
5, Ansari Road
Daryaganj, New Delhi-110002
Phone: 011-47034999, 9811692060
E-mail: books@gyanbooks.com

Distribution Network
gyanbooks.com
India, USA, Canada, UK, Australia, France

ISBN : 978-81-212-2540-3 (HB)
First Published, 1896

2nd Impression 2021

Printed at: Gyan Press, Delhi.

Manual of Indian Buddhism
Author: H. Kern

GRUNDRISS DER INDO-ARISCHEN PHILOLOGIE UND ALTERTUMSKUNDE
(ENCYCLOPEDIA OF INDO-ARYAN RESEARCH)
HERAUSGEGEBEN VON G. BÜHLER.
III. BAND, 8. HEFT.

MANUAL OF INDIAN BUDDHISM

BY

H. KERN.

STRASSBURG
VERLAG VON KARL J. TRÜBNER
1896.

GRUNDRISS DER INDO-ARISCHEN PHILOLOGIE UND ALTERTUMSKUNDE
(ENCYCLOPEDIA OF INDO-ARYAN RESEARCH)
HERAUSGEGEBEN VON G. BÜHLER.
III. BAND, 8. HEFT.

MANUAL OF INDIAN BUDDHISM.

BY

H. KERN.

PART I.

INTRODUCTION.

1. THE SACRED BOOKS.

The sacred lore of the Buddhists is based on the canonical books, a complete collection of which is technically called Tripiṭaka (Tipiṭaka), i. e. the three Baskets: 1. Vinaya, Sūtra (Sutta), and Abhidharma (Abhidhamma). Of all the collections going by that name the Pāli Tipiṭaka, representing the version acknowledged by the orthodox Theras or Vibhajyavādins of Ceylon, is the only one which forms a well arranged whole and is sufficiently known to admit of a critical disquisition into the relative age of its component parts, at least to a certain extent.

The Vinaya, as its very name implies, treats chiefly of Discipline and all questions connected with it[1]. About the development of the Vinaya we find most valuable hints in Prof. OLDENBERG's Introduction to the Mahāvagga[2]. His conclusions are summarized in the following list of successive events in the ancient literary history of Buddhism: 1. The genesis of the Pātimokkha. The earliest beginnings of the Dhamma literature. 2. The formation of the commentary on the Pātimokkha, which is included in the Vibhaṅga. 3. The Vibhaṅga is compiled; the Mahāvagga and the Cullavagga are composed; origin of the main substance of the Suttanta literature. 4. Council at Vesālī (± 383 B. C.). 5. Origin of the legend of the Council at Rājagaha; composition of the closing chapter of the Vinaya. 6. Schisms in the Buddhist community; origin of the Abhidhamma. 7. Council at Pāṭaliputta; the Kathāvatthu.

All these propositions are supported by sound reasoning and seem plausible enough, though a more thorough knowledge of the remains of the *old* Northern versions than we now possess may necessitate us to modify our views in some particulars[3].

The Sutta-Piṭaka, much more extensive and diversified than the Vinaya, may be said, in a loose way, to treat of various subjects more or less related to Doctrine. Its fivefold division into Nikāyas[4] already occurs in Cullavagga

---

[1] The P. Vinaya books have been completely edited by Prof. H. OLDENBERG (1879—83) under the titles of Mahāvagga, Cullavagga, Sutta-vibhaṅga, and Parivāra.

[2] See there p. XV ff.; cp. Introd. to SBE. XIII by Prof. RHYS DAVIDS and OLDENBERG; and Introd. to Dhammapada, SBE. X, p. XXIX ff. by Prof. MAX MÜLLER.

[3] Cp. the criticisms on OLDENBERG's views by MINAYEF Recherches I, 61—67.

[4] To wit: 1. Dīgha-Nikāya; 2. Majjhima-Nikāya; 3. Saṃyutta-N.; 4. Aṅguttara-N. These 4 Nikāyas are also called Āgamas, which is the usual term with the N. Buddhists. 5. Khudda-N., comprizing Khuddaka-pāṭha, Dhammapada, Udāna, Itivuttaka, Sutta-Nipāta,

XI, 1, 8, but the separate works are not mentioned; we only meet with the titles of the two first Suttas of the D. N. At the same passage we are told that the text of the 5 Nikāyas was rehearsed at the first council with the assistance of Ānanda, who bore witness as to the place where, the person concerning whom, and the cause for which each Sutta had been delivered. This account, apart from the legendary character of the first Council, cannot be true, for the opening formula of the Suttantas is *evaṃ me sutaṃ*, which is impossible but in the mouth of one who derives his knowledge of the Master's teaching from oral tradition; no contemporary disciple can speak in such a manner[1]. It may be remarked that the formula is absent from the Vinaya. In general we may assume that the disciplinary rules were elaborated much earlier than the doctrinal writings[2].

About the age of the sundry books in the 5th Nikāya little can be affirmed with any degree of certainty. This much, however, is plain that their contents belong to different periods. To begin with the Jātakas, it will hardly be doubted that many of these popular tales are very old, some of them older than Buddhism itself. It is by no means improbable that from the time of the first expansion of the sect those tales, modified according to the exigencies of the creed, were used by the preaching monks for didactic purposes. It appears from the sculptures at Bharhut and Sānchi that the Jātakas were known as an integral part of Buddhist lore at the time of Aśoka[3].

Whatever may be thought of the relative age of the different Suttantas[4] in the four Āgamas, and of the various compositions in the Khudda-Nikāya, the great bulk of the Sutta-Piṭaka in substance probably existed already in the 3d century B. C. The identification of the titles mentioned in the inscription of Babhra (Bairat) is attended with difficulties, but one Sutta at least, the "Lāghulovāda concerning falsehood" is evidently the same as the "Rāhulovāda on Musāvāda" in Majjhima-N. I. C. 414. It has been pointed out by BÜHLER[5] that the occurrence of the title *pacanekāyika* (**pāñcanaikāyika*) presupposes the existence of a collection of 5 Nikāyas. It is, however, necessary to add that the remark does not apply to all sects; for aught we know, the division of the Sūtra-Piṭaka in 5 Nikāyas is peculiar to the Theravāda[6]. As to the subdivisions of the Nikāyas, there was some disagreement even among the Theravādins themselves[7].

The Abhidhamma-P.[8] is not mentioned at all in CV. This fact is sufficient to warrant the conclusion that it is posterior to the Council of Vesālī,

---

Vimānavatthu, Petavatthu, Theragāthā, Therīgāthā, Jātaka, Niddesa or Mahā-Niddesa, Paṭisambhidā-magga, Apadāna, Buddhavaṃsa, Cariyā-piṭaka. See Saddh. S. p. 27; cp. CHILDERS Dict. p. 507.

1 The authenticity of the Council of R. is maintained by ROCKHILL, Life of the Buddha, p. VII. Cp. MINAYEF, Recherches, ch. II and III.

2 This is also the opinion of WASSILIEF, B., p. 17. About the earliest beginnings of the doctrinal literature cp. OLDENBERG, Introd. p. XXIV.

3 See S. d'OLDENBURG JRAS of 1893, pp. 301—356; HULTZSCH DMG XL and Ind. Ant. XXI, 225 ff.; BÜHLER Votive inscriptions from the Sanchi Stūpas (Epigr. Ind. II, 87); The inscriptions on the Sanchi Stūpas (WZ VII, 291); On the origin of the Indian Brahma Alphabet, p. 17; A. ST. JOHN On the Sāma Jātaka (JRAS of 1894, p. 211); the N. version titled Śyāmaka-Jāt. in Mahavastu II, 210. On the discrepancies of the Bharhut Jātakas compared with the Pāli version, see MINAYEF Recherches I, 140 ff.

4 E. g. the Assalāyana-Sutta (ed. PISCHEL 1880), in which the Indian caste system and the absence of castes with the Greeks are contrasted, cannot have been composed earlier than the 3d cent B. C., but other Suttas may be much older.

5 Op. c. p. 17.

6 Cp. A. BARTH Bull. Rel. de l'Inde, 1893—1894, p. 1. (separate copy).

7 See CHILDERS s. v. *nikāyo*.

8 Consists of seven Pakaraṇas: Dhammasaṅgaṇi, Vibhaṅga, Dhātukathā, Puggala-

a conclusion moreover strengthened by its character. "The compilers of the Abhidhamma books seem to have taken up such subjects, only as are discussed at full length in the Nikāyas, dealing with them more or less in a purely scholastic and technical manner with some variation in regard to the order and arrangement of the numerous details connected with the Buddhist creed"[1]. The edited texts, in fact, consist of a bare enumeration of classifications and definitions, which justifies the use of the term *mātṛkā* as synonymous with *abhidharma* in Northern writings[2]. "The period between the Council of Vesālī and that of Pāṭaliputta", to use the words of OLDENBERG[3] "saw the origin of the schism, and was also the time of the development of the Abhidhamma literature".

The canonical books of the various sects among the Northern Buddhists — to use a more convenient than wholly accurate term — in so far as they have their counterparts in the Pāli canon and do not belong to the *new* canon of the Mahāyānists[4], are but partially known. On comparing, first of all, the Chinese Vinaya of the Mahīśāsakas, a short analysis of which was communicated to OLDENBERG by BEAL, with the extracts of the Tibetan Vinaya of the Mahāsarvāstivādins[4], the editor of the MV. draws the following conclusions[5]: "All of the different versions of the Vinaya are based upon *one* foundation; the arrangement of the material is the same in all; a large portion of the stories interwoven in the text correspond in all[6]. It has been pointed out above, that of the elements which constitute the Vibhaṅga the narrative portions were added last; the addition of these stories was made at an earlier period than that in which the differences of the various schools arose. Even the story of the first two Councils — which is clearly the part of the Pâli Vinaya last composed, is also met with at the exactly corresponding place in the Vinaya of the Mahîçâsakas, and of the Mahâsarvâstivâdinas."

Here it should be observed that both the Mahīśāsakas and Mahāsarvāstivādins are offshoots of the orthodox Sthaviravāda, and may be said to form subdivisions of the orthodox community. It is therefore very natural that their Vinaya bears so close a resemblance to that of the Theras. But from this it does not follow that *all* versions of the Vinaya, those of the different versions of the schismatic Mahāsāṅghikas included, show the same degree of affinity. Apart from the biassed testimony of their opponents that the Mahāsāṅghikas had altered the original redaction and made changes in the Vinaya and the 5 Nikāyas[8], we can adduce a fact that one sect at least of the Mahāsāṅghika party made a peculiar application of the term Vinaya. The Mahāvastu, a book belonging to the school of the Lokottaravādins, a sub-

paññatti (or °paṇṇatti), Kathāvatthu, Yamaka, and Paṭṭhāna. — A compendium of the whole is the Abhidhammattha-Saṅgaha, ed. by Prof. RHYS DAVIDS JPTS of 1884.

1 Words of MORRIS in Intr. to his edition of the Puggala-paññatti, p. VIII.

2 See e. g. Divy. p. 18; 133; BURNOUF Intr. p. 48; 317. Cp. ROCKHILL, L. of B. p. 160.

3 Op. c. p. XXXIV.

4 The term Tripiṭaka, when applied to a collection including Mahāyānist books, is properly a misnomer. In the Vyutpatti § 65 the Tripiṭaka and its subdivisions are duly separated from the Mahāyānist canonical works, the titles of which are given. The Tripiṭaka is not repudiated by the Mahāyānists; it is recognized by them, and stands to their own canon somewhat in the same relation as the Old Testament to the New.

5 According to CSOMA KÖRÖSI in As. Rev. XX, especially p. 45 ff. Cp. JASB I, 1—6, and HUTH, Die Tibetische Version der Naihsargikaprāyaççittikadharmās (1891).

6 Intr. p. XLVII.

7 Cp. JASB I, 1—6. The division in the Tibetan Dulva is: Vinayavastu, Prātimokṣa-sūtra, Vinayavibhaṅga, Vinayakṣudraka, and Vinayottaragrantha. Cp. Vyutp. § 65.

8 Dīpav. V, 32 ff. Bodhivaṃsa, p. 96.

division of the Mahāsāṅghikas, shows after the introduction the following title[1]: "Āryamahāsāṃghikānām Lokottaravādinām Madhyadeśikānān pāṭhena Vinayapiṭakasya Mahāvastu ādi." As the badly arranged contents of this book are merely made up of chapters from the legendary life of the Bodhisattva, of Jātakas, of the praehistory of the Śākya race, etc., without any admixture of matter connected with Discipline, it is strange to find it classed as a Vinaya text[2]. For though the Pāli Vinaya contains narrative parts to a considerable extent, no book of it is wholly made up of subjects which otherwise have a place in the Sutta-Piṭaka[3]. According to Chinese authorities the Mahāvastu is the book that for the Mahāsāṅghikas represents the Abhiniṣkramaṇa-Sūtra of the Dharmaguptas, and the Lalita-Vistara of the Sarvāstivādins[4]. This statement is wanting in precision, for it is only in those portions which deal with the history of the Bodhisattva up to his reaching Buddhahood that it may be said to answer to the compositions just named. Taken as a whole, the Mahāvastu is a work the contents of which are substantially the same as found in the collections of the orthodox sects, but which in its arrangement follows a totally different method, or rather no method at all. It differs in another respect also from the orthodox texts by its invocation of a plurality of Buddhas[5]. It can hardly be doubted that such an invocation, much resembling that of the Vaipulya-Sūtras marks a period posterior to the reign of Aśoka. A comparison of the language and composition of the Mhv. with other documents leaves the impression that the time of its redaction is intermediate between the date of the P. canon and that of the Vaipulyas.

In the absence of other texts our notions regarding the arrangement of the Mahāsāṅghika Scripture must necessarily be very limited. According to Huen Thsang[6] the old canon of the Mahāsāṅghikas was fivefold, divided into Sūtra-, Vinaya, Abhidharma-, Saṃyukta-, and Dhāraṇī- (or Vidyādhara-)Piṭaka. We have no means of estimating the value of this statement.

BURNOUF somewhere[7] remarks that it is strange not to meet with books of Vinaya in the Nepalese collection of HODGSON, and he tries to explain the fact by assuming that in reality the Vinaya is represented by the Avadānas. To this view may be objected that in the Tibetan Do[8] the Avadānas constitute a part of the Sūtra-Piṭaka, as well as in the Pāli canon[9]. The absence of Vinaya texts in HODGSON's collection — barring the Mahāvastu — may be readily accounted for by the condition of Buddhism in Nepāl, where monasticism has long ago ceased to be an institution.

The Sūtra-Piṭaka of the North is preserved in a Chinese trans-

---

1 Mahāvastu (ed. SENART) I, p. 2.

2 A part of the book is downright a Sūtra, viz. the Avalokita-S., which, however, is designated as a Parivāra or Appendix in II, p. 397.

3 The same applies to the Tibetan Vinaya (Dulva), though its character approaches that of the Mhv., because it is not only devoted to recording the rules of the Order, but contains a great number of Jātakas, Vyākaraṇas, Sūtras and Udānas. See ROCKHILL, L. of B. p. VI.

4 SENART, Pref. Mhv. I, p. III; BEAL, Romantic Legend p. V; WASSILIEF, B. p. 114.

5 The invocation is: *Om namah Śrī-Mahābuddhāyātītānāgatapratyutpannebhyaḥ sarvabuddhebhyaḥ*. The theory of the plurality of coeval Buddhas in the different quarters is common to all Mahāsāṅghika sects, according to Kathāv. P. A. XXI, 6, and therefore old, if not originally belonging to the creed.

6 Voy. I, p. 158; III, p. 37.

7 Intr. p. 38.

8 JASB I, p. 384.

9 It is true that the Dīghanikāya preachers did not include the Apadānas in the canon (s. CHILDERS s. v. *nikāya*), but there is no question of the Apad. being incorporated in the Vinaya. Cp. ED. MÜLLER, Les Apadânas du Sud, in Trans. 10th Congr. of Or. I, 165.

lation[1]. Many titles of Sūtras are also known to us from the Tibetan version, some of them in more or less complete translation, e. g. the important Mahāparinirvāṇa-Sūtra[2]. The subject matter of those old Sūtras has passed, more or less modified, into the Vaipulya-Sūtras, forming part of the new or Mahāyānist canon, about which anon.

The Abhidharma books corresponding to those in the P. canon, seven in number, have survived in a Chinese translation. It is not a little curious that in more than one source most of them are ascribed to well known disciples of the Buddha[3]. In how far the original version has been meddled with is a question which can only be solved by those who are able to compare the Chinese translation with the Pāli Abhidharma texts. Works like the Abhidharma-Kośa by Vasubandhu do not belong to the canonical literature.

The Tripiṭaka properly so called, has for a large part yielded the material for the Vaipulya-Sūtras, which if not all of them were composed by the Mahāyānists have at least been adopted by them and incorporated in their new canon. Outwardly the Vaipulya-Sūtras are distinguished from the older Sūtras by a different manner of composition and by the change of idiom. We regularly find in them sections in a redaction in prose, followed by one in verse, the latter being in substance only a repetition of the former[4] or, may be, in some cases the source of the narrative in prose. The idiom of the prosaical part is a kind of Sanskrit; that of the verses, Gāthās, is a veiled Prākrit somewhat clumsily sanskritised as much as the exigencies of the metre permitted. In our opinion, there cannot be the slightest doubt that the prose is a regular translation from a Prākrit text into Sanskrit, a comparatively easy task, whereas a rendering of the Gāthās into Sanskrit would be impossible without entirely remodelling most verses. Why and when has the original idiom been replaced by Sanskrit? At present we can do no more but surmise that the translation was resolved upon in order to meet the wants of the times. It has been the common fate of all Prākrits that they became obsolete, whilst the study and practice of Sanskrit have been kept up all over India as the common language of science, literature and refinement, and as a bond between Aryans and Draviḍas. At what time did Sanskrit reconquer its ascendancy? Of course gradually, but we are not in a position to fix the limits of the period with anything like certainty. We would, however, suggest that the necessity of refounding the Scripture made itself felt shortly before or after the Council in the reign of Kaniṣka.

Some Vaipulyas are, materially, much like the old Sūtras. Whole passages e. g. of the Lalita-Vistara recur almost word for word in the Pāli Scriptures. In the majority of cases works of the same class show more significant peculiarities. In general it may be said that the stock of tradition, common

---

1 The whole divided into 4 Āgamas: Dīrgha-, Madhyama-, Ekottarika-, and Saṃyuktāgama. WASSILIEF, B. p. 115. Whether the Kṣudrāgama, mentioned by Tāranātha p. 42 may be held to be the counterpart of the Khudda-Nikāya, must be left undecided.

2 ROCKHILL op. c. p. 123 ff.

3 WASSILIEF, B. p. 107; BURNOUF, Intr. p. 447; Tāranātha p. 296; Vyutp. § 65. The titles and reputed authors are: 1. Jñāna-prasthāna, by Kātyāyana (al. Kātyāyanīputra); cp. the Pāli title Paṭṭhāna. 2. Dharmaskandha, by Śāriputra; cp. Dhamma-saṅgaṇi. 3. Dhātu-kāya, by Pūrṇa (al. Vasumitra); cp. Dhātu-kathā. 4. Prajñaptiśāstra, by Maudgalyāyana (with WASSILIEF Amṛtaśāstra by Goṣṭha); cp. Puggala-paññatti; 5. Vijñāna-kāya, by Devakṣema (al. Devaśarman). 6. Saṅgīti-paryāya, by Śāriputra (al. Kauṣṭhila). 7. Prakaraṇa-pāda, by Vasumitra. The three last books may or may not be the counterparts of the P. Vibhaṅga, Kathā-vatthu, and Yamaka. Some of these works are also mentioned by Huen Thsang, Voy. I, p. 102; 109; 123. II, 119; 201; 291.

4 BURNOUF, Intr. p. 103.

to all Buddhists, increased among the non-orthodox sects by much additional matter. New mythological beings, such as the Bodhisattvas Avalokiteśvara and Mañjuśrī, make their appearance; a host of Buddhas of the past, present and future are honoured and invoked along with Śākyamuni, whose image, however, far from being effaced, is clad in brilliant majesty more than ever[1].

All Vaipulya texts we know of are qualified as Mahāyāna Sūtras, and constitute the new or Mahāyānist canon[2]. Since we learn from Chinese authorities that the Lalita-Vistara, a decided Mahāyāna Sūtra, properly belongs to the Sarvāstivādins, we must infer that the Mahāyānists did not scruple to adopt such works of the Hīnayāna sects as fitted in with their system, though we cannot help believing that the text must have undergone modifications.

The chronological questions connected with the rise of Mahāyānism are too vast to admit of an incidental treatment. Here it will suffice to note that the Mahāyāna Sūtra Sukhāvatī-Vyūha or Amitāyus-Sūtra is stated to have been translated into Chinese for the first time AD. 148—170[3]. If this notice be exact, and equally the tradition that Nāgārjuna, born about the time of the Council under Kaniṣka, was the founder of Mahāyānism, the Sūtra forenamed must have been one of the very first writings composed or adopted by the new sect. In reality Nāgārjuna may have been one of the most talented and influential leaders of the movement rather than its originator.

To the Mahāyānists is ascribed the introduction of Dhāraṇīs into the sacred texts[4]. How to reconcile this with the statement by Huen Thsang that the Mahāsāṅghikas possessed a Dhāraṇī-Piṭaka from the very beginning of their sect? Unless we repudiate the truthfulness of the report altogether, we are driven to the conclusion that the Mahāyānists did not invent the Dhāraṇīs, but only appropriated them as an integral part of their system. There are, indeed, several indications of a certain connection between the tendencies of the Mahāsāṅghikas and the Mahāyānists, as in the course of this work we shall have occasion to point out. Hence it would be rash to deny the relative trustworthiness of the tradition current in India when the Chinese traveller visited the country. The circumstance that the Dhāraṇīs are visibly accrescences of such texts as the Saddharma-Puṇḍarīka[5], is no decisive argument against the prior separate existence of the formulas.

Of later growth than the Dhāraṇīs, which are exoteric in their character, are the esoteric Tantras. As to the whole Tantric literature, the full development whereof coincides with the decline of Buddhism, we must content ourselves with referring the reader to the authorities on the subject[6].

Besides the division of the whole of Holy Scripture into 3 Piṭakas, the

---

1 Burnouf, Intr. p. 116 ff.

2 The titles of these Sūtras, few of which have been edited, are given in Vyut. § 65; cp. Wassilief, B. p. 145 ff. Some titles also occur in the list of the 9 Dharmas — an elliptical phrase for Dharmaparyāyas — with Hodgson, Ess. p. 13, 49. Cp. The Sanskrit Buddhist literature of Nepal, Rājendralāla Mitra (1882); the Catalogue of the Hodgson Collection by Cowell and Eggeling in JRAS of 1875; do. of the Cambridge Collection by Bendall.

3 Sukhāvatī-Vyūha, ed. Max Müller and Bunyiu Nanjio, pag. IV. — Dates of translation of other books are given in Beal, Buddhist Tripiṭaka, and Bunyiu Nanjio, Catalogue of the Chinese translation of the B. Tripiṭaka, *passim*.

4 For a fuller account see Burnouf, Intr. p. 541 g., Wassilief, B. p. 142; 177 ff.

5 See SBE. XXI, Intr. p. XXI.

6 Burnouf, Intr. p. 522—574; Wassilief, B., p. 144, 184 ff.; Waddell, Buddhism of Tibet, p. 129 ff. Several Tantric works are contained in the Catalogue of the Hodgson Collection by Cowell and Eggeling; cp. Burnouf l. c. and the list in Hodgson, op. c. 38 f. On the influence of Sivaite Tantras on the Buddhist Tantrism of Nepāl see Barth, Rel. of India p. 201.

Buddhists of the South and the North have in common another into Aṅgas, according the subject matter. The Pāli denomination of these Aṅgas, 9 in number, are: 1. Sutta, a connected narrative or a collection of verses on one subject; 2. Geyya, mixed prose and verse; 3. Veyyākaraṇa, exposition; it contains, according to the system, the whole Abhidhamma-Piṭaka, further the Suttas which have no Gāthās, and all the other words of Buddha not included in the remaining eight Aṅgas; 4. Gāthā, unmixed verses; 5. Udāna, enthusiastic utterances in prose or verse; in the system: "Suttas connected with stanzas composed under the inspiration of joy"; 6. Itivuttaka, the collection of 101 Suttas beginning with the words: "Thus has Buddha spoken"; 7. Jātaka, stories of one of the former births of Buddha[1]; 8. Abbhutadhamma, discourses relating to wonderful and mysterious conditions; 9. Vedalla, a kind of Suttas said to be questions put after feeling a pleasant emotion and contentment, whatever that may mean[2].

With the N. Buddhists we sometimes find the same number[3], but more common is the enumeration of 12 kinds of Dharmapravacanas: 1. Sūtra; 2. Geya; 3. Vyākaraṇa; 4. Gāthā: 5. Udāna; 6. Nidāna; 7. Avadāna: 8. Ityukta (wrongly Itivṛttaka); 9. Jātaka; 10. Vaipulya; 11. Adbhutadharma; 12. Upadeśa[4]. This enumeration agrees with that of the Siṃhalese if we deduct Nidāna, Avadāna, and Upadeśa. Nidānas and Avadānas are sufficiently represented in the Pāli canon, but they are not accounted as separate Aṅgas. As to the Vaipulyas, these "treat of several sorts of Dharma and Artha, that is of the several means of acquiring the goods of this world (Artha) and of the world to come (Dharma)". They may safely be identified with the Pāli Vedalla, having nothing but the name in common with the Vaipulya-Sūtras. The Upadeśa, professedly treating of esoteric doctrines, is equivalent to Tantra, which lies outside the pale of original Buddhism.

In connection with the preceding survey we cannot omit touching upon the question of the original language of the holy books. Although "the Pâli version" — to use the words of Prof. OLDENBERG — "has hitherto shown itself to be the most original, if not *the* original version", as regards the contents, "it may with certainty be maintained that in *one* respect, in reference to the *dialect*, it differs from the original text", the fundamental constituent parts of which were undoubtedly fixed in the idiom of Magadha. It is now universally admitted that Pāli does *not* represent that idiom[5], whatever may be the different views about the original home of Pāli. The most plausible view is that Pāli originated in Kaliṅga-Andhra[6]. From an important passage

[1] To the valuable essay "On the Buddhist Jātakas" by S. d'OLDENBURG, already alluded to above p. 2, in JRAS of 1893, p. 301 ff. (originally Russian in Zapiski of 1892) is added a copious bibliographical list of works regarding the Jātakas; other Russian papers of the same author on the Bhadrakalpâvadāna and the Jātaka-mālā are titled "Buddhist Legends" (1894), and "Remarks on Buddhist Art" (1895).

[2] The definitions are found in Sumaṅgala-Vilāsinī, vol. I, pag. 23 ff. Cp. CHILDERS s. vv. and the authors there quoted.

[3] Saddh. Pund. Ch. II, vs. 45, cp. vs. 44.

[4] WASSILIEF, B. p. 109; Dharma-S. LXII, and note; HODGSON, Ess. p. 14; BURNOUF, Intr. 51 ff. — The class of Ityukta is apparently represented by the Sūtra of the 42 Sections (in BEAL's Cat. p. 188), which has traits in common with the Itivuttaka, though the material agreement, as between Sect. 9 and Sutta 100, is slight.

[5] Rightly observed already by LASSEN, Indische Alterthumskunde vol. II, p. 488.

[6] The question is fully discussed by OLDENBERG, op. c. p. XLVII ff. But cp. WESTERGAARD, Ueber den ältesten Zeitraum der Indischen Geschichte, p. 87; and E. KUHN, Beiträge zur Pali-Grammatik, p. 7, where another hypothesis is propounded. — The significant fact that the word *palibodha*, common to Māgadhī and Pali, is replaced by *parigodha* in the Girnar version of Aśoka Edict V, goes far to prove that the home of Pāli is not to be sought for in W. India.

in Culla-Vagga, (V, 33), where we read that Buddha allows every one to study the Buddha-word in his own dialect, we may conclude that at the time when the sacred texts were spread over India "they were certainly not handed over to the different parts of India in the Māgadhī language, but in the vernacular dialect peculiar to the several districts". This being taken for granted, nothing prevents us from supposing that the Northern versions which have come to us in Sanskrit and in a certain sanskritised idiom, although ultimately going back to a Māgadhī original, have passed through an intermediate stage, in other words, that Māgadhī was replaced by other local dialects. Now the course of events in India and its literary development have been such that we can readily understand how at a certain period it was thought advisable to sanskritise the sacred texts as much as possible. The more scientifically Sanskrit was learnt by the Buddhists, the more correct their writings. Some renowned names in mediaeval Sanskrit literature belong to authors of the Buddhist persuasion. The steadily growing ascendancy of Sanskrit is visible even in Ceylon, for, not to speak of later inscriptions, we learn from Fa Hian[1] that the Vinaya-Piṭaka and other texts of the Mahīśāsakas in the island were in Sanskrit.

2. LITERATURE SUBSIDIARY TO THE CANON. WORKS ON LEGENDARY AND SEMI-HISTORICAL SUBJECTS. RELIGIOUS POETRY.

The sacred books have naturally given rise to a subsidiary literature in the form of commentaries, manuals, treatises, and the like[2]. The mass of that literature, both in the S. and the N., is so immense that only a very few of the most noteworthy productions can here be treated of.

Beginning with the South, we first have the Aṭṭhakathā, a body of commentaries on the various parts of the Tipiṭaka[3]. According to Simhalese tradition the Aṭṭhakathā was fixed at the first Convocation, and rehearsed at the two following Councils; it was introduced by Mahendra along with the holy texts into Ceylon, and translated by the same into Simhalese; it was not put to writing before the reign of Abhaya Vaṭṭagāmani, in the last century B. C., and retranslated into Pāli by Buddhaghoṣa about A. D. 420[4]. It is easy to see that those statements are a mixture of dogmatical fiction and truth. This much is well ascertained that there existed a collection of commentaries of semi-sacred character under the name of Aṭṭhakathā in the time when the Dīpavaṃsa was written, about A. D. 300, but we are in the dark about the relative age of its various portions, and we possess as yet no sufficient data for making out what has been added or changed after A. D. 300, either by Buddhaghoṣa or by others. The story in the Mahāvaṃsa according to which Buddhaghoṣa translated the whole Aṭṭhakathā is in conflict with some

[1] Record (LEGGE), p. 111. The doubts entertained by Prof. OLDENBERG (op. c. p. XLIII) are, apparently, based upon the assumption of the Theravāda being the only B. sect in the island.

[2] The MSS of Pali sacred books and their commentaries in the India Office Library have been described by OLDENBERG in JPTS of 1882 (pp. 59—85); a list of the collection in the Bibliothèque Nationale has been published by L. FEER, ib. pp. 32—37; see in that same number of the Journal the lists by FRANKFURTER, and by L. DE ZOYSA; the Bibliography of texts in FRANKFURTER's Handbook XV—XVIII; of translations, XIX.

[3] The titles enumerated in CHILDERS s. v. *Aṭṭhakathā;* Saddh. S. p. 56; MINAYEF Recherches I, 258, from the Gandhavaṃsa.

[4] Dīp. XX, 20; Mahāvaṃsa, p. 205 ff. Sum. Vil. I, p. 1. Saddh. S. p. 52 ff. HARDY, E. M. p. 171; cp. M. of B. p. 509 ff.

well established facts. The commentary on the Thera- and Therīgāthā titled Paramattha-Dīpanī, and some other commentaries have been composed by Dhammapāla of Kāñcipura, and not by Buddhaghoṣa[1]. Further it should be noted that Buddhaghoṣa in his Samanta-Pāsādikā quotes the Dīpavaṃsa by name. The Aṭṭhakathā being professedly older then the chronicle, his work cannot have been a simple translation, or he must have found those quotations in his original and in that case some portions of the Aṭṭhakathā must have been posterior to the chronicle.

Notwithstanding some doubts about the absolute correctness of the Simhalese accounts, we may hold that the principal Pāli commentaries on canonical works are due to Buddhaghoṣa, as well as the Visuddhimagga[2], a kind of cyclopaedia of the Buddhist creed. Another work that has been characterized as "a short encyclopaedia of the Buddhist theology and cosmology" is the Sārasaṅgaha[3]. The commentary on the treatise Kathāvatthu[4] contains much about the tenets of the various sects.

A dogmatical treatise in the form of dialogues between king Milinda[5] and the Buddhist sage Nāgasena is the work titled Milinda-Pañha[6]. Date and source of the work are uncertain, but for various reasons it must be posterior to the beginning of our era, and have been composed in the North of India, though all quotations from Scripture in it are from the Pāli canon[7].

Writings belonging to the class of compendiums, and containing repetitions of passages from more ancient works with more or less apocryphal additions, are the Anāgatavaṃsa or History of future Buddhas[8], the Saddhamma-Saṅgaha, and the Mahābodhivamsa, which is a translation of a Simhalese original[9]. The same applies to the Rasavāhinī, a collection of 103 tales[10], the Dāṭhāvaṃsa[11] and the Chakesadhātuvaṃsa[12]. A much used compendium of ecclesiastical acts is titled Kammavācā[13], whereas the chronicles Dīpavaṃsa, Mahāvaṃsa and Sāsanavaṃsa deserve a special notice on account of their being so highly important for the ecclesiastical history of Ceylon. Interesting notices on Pāli books and authors are contained in the Gandhavaṃsa[14].

Among the poems in the praise of Buddha we have the Pajjamadhu[15]. Another religious poem of didactic character is the Saddhammopāyana[16].

---

[1] Cp. ED. MÜLLER in the Pref. to his edition of the Param.-Dīp. and the authorities quoted above.

[2] Cp. HARDY, M. of B., p. 512. For an abstract of contents by CARPENTER, see JPTS for 1890, and cp. A. C. WARREN in Trans. 9th Congr. of Or. I, 392.

[3] See K. E. NEUMANN „Des Sārasaṅghaho erstes Kapitel", text and translation (Leipzig 1891), p. 6.

[4] Kathāvatthuppakaraṇaṭṭhakathā, ed. by MINAYEF JPTS of 1889.

[5] The Skr. form of Milinda, identified with Menandros, is Milindra in Kṣemendra's Avadāna-Kalpalatā No. 57, vs. 15. Not unlikely Minara in Tāranātha, p. 23, is another form of the same name.

[6] Ed. by TRENCKNER (1880); transl. by Prof. RHYS DAVIDS in SBE. XXXV (1890).

[7] The question has been discussed by Prof. D. RHYS DAVIDS in the preface to his translation. On two Chinese translations of the work see E. SPECHT and S. LÉVI in Trans. 9th Congr. of Or. I, 518—529.

[8] Ed. by MINAYEF in JPTS of 1886.

[9] See STRONG in his ed. p. VIII, where the question of authorship and date is dealt with.

[10] The four first tales ed. by SPIEGEL in his Anecdota Palica (1845); others by KONOW in DMG of 1889, p. 297 ff.; the 7th Chapter by PAVOLINI (1894).

[11] Ed. by RHYS DAVIDS in JPTS of 1884; by M. C. SWAMY (Lond. 1874).

[12] Ed. by MINAYEF in JPTS of 1885.

[13] See CHILDERS s. v.

[14] Ed. by MINAYEF in JPTS of 1886. Cp. the same, Recherches I. 257.

[15] Ed. by GOONERATNE in JPTS of 1887.

[16] Ed. by MORRIS in JPTS of 1887.

Works bearing on philological inquiry, grammars, dictionaries and grammatical papers, are here passed in silence[1].

The literary activity of the Northern schools of Buddhists was not inferior to that of the Theravādins, but the ancient texts have only survived in translations or have come to us much altered, if they have not wholly perished. The oldest of the surviving commentaries and treatises are posterior to the Council under Kaniṣka, and all that Huen Thsang tells us[2] concerning commentaries on Vinaya, Sūtra and Abhidharma being composed at that occasion is nothing else but an echo of the universal Buddhist tradition about the legendary first Council. From nearly that period may date the Vibhāṣā, a commentary on the Abhidharma; it is at any rate anterior to the Abhidharma-kośa by Vasubandhu, who flourished in the 6th century of our era and wrote many other exegetical works on Mahāyāna texts[3]. The Abhidharmakośa was again commented by more than one author. To Asaṅga is ascribed a Yogaśāstra or Yogācāryabhūmi-śāstra along with other works of a philosophical character[4]. Dignāga wrote a work on logic, the Pramāṇa-samuccaya. Similar works of a more or less polemical character are numerous, but as long as we cannot examine the contents their enumeration is of little use, the more so as the absurd legends about their authors must deter us from entering deeper into the subject. Some celebrities and their works we shall have occasion to notice in Part V, hereafter[5].

The N. Buddhists have excelled in various kinds of what may be classed as devotional and edifying literature, so that a high rank must be assigned to not a few of their literary productions on account of the tasteful reproduction of subjects derived from the sacred lore or the lives of Saints. Works as the Buddhacarita of Aśvaghoṣa[6], the Jātaka-mālā of Ārya Śūra, the Avadāna- kalpalatā of Kṣemendra are noble compositions in every respect. The collection of legendary and semi-historical lore, known under the title of Divyāvadāna, though less refined in language and style, is no less attractive. This valuable collection must have been reduced to its present state in a period after Kaniṣka, for the Dīnāra repeatedly occurs in it as the name of an *Indian* coin; yet the constituent parts of it are undoubtedly, for a large part, anterior to A. D. 100, abstraction made of the idiom, which may have been modified. The books of legends called Bhadrakalpāvādana and Avadāna-śataka are only known from extracts and translations[7].

[1] A good bibliographical list, up to 1883, is found in FRANKFURTER's Handbook XX, XXI. For a short description of some valuable works in Siṃhalese, see HARDY, M. of B. p. 518. Several Pāli commentaries, treatises etc. are enumerated in Saddh. S. Ch. XI, and in Gandhavaṃsa.

[2] Voy. vol. p. 172.

[3] WASSILIEF, B. p. 210; 215; 222. Voy. I, p. 115; II. p. 274. Tār. *passim*. Cp. MAX MÜLLER, India 302; 308 f.

[4] Voy. I, 114; 118. It is strange that Huen Thsang fathers upon him also an Abhidharmakośa, perhaps identical with the Abhidharmasamuccaya in Tār. p. 112.

[5] Further notices on renowned mediaeval scholastic writers are found in WASSILIEF, B. p. 200—222. For the commentaries in the Tibetan collections, see CSOMA KÖRÖSI, As. Res. XX, p. 400 ff. — Dictionaries and similar works which will be referred to in the course of this Manual need not to be specified here.

[6] Ed. by COWELL. For the Chinese transl. see BEAL, SBE. vol. XIX. The first Ch. has been edited by S. LÉVI with a French transl. in JA of 1892. Cf. A. BARTH Bull. Rel. de l' Inde of 1894, p. 16 (separ. copy); LEUMANN, Some Notes on Açvaghosha's Buddhacarita in Wien. Zeitsch. VIII, 193.

[7] See S. d'OLDENBURG in Zapiski of 1894; and for the latter work see FÉER, Le livre des Cent Légendes in JA of 1879; his transl. in Ann. Mus. Guimet XVIII. A similar collection in Chinese are the "Contes et Apologues Indiens" (1860), from which STANISLAS JULIEN has published a specimen.

The published specimens of religious poetry bear the stamp of having been productions in the palmy days of mediaeval Sanskrit literature. The Bodhicaryāvatāra by Sāntideva, a poem breathing a truly pious spirit, ranks foremost[1]. Almost as elegant in form, but wholly wanting in originality and warmth of feeling is the poem Śiṣyalekha by the grammarian Candra-Gomin[2]. Hymns to Sākyasiṃha, Avalokiteśvara etc. are known only from Catalogues[3] or occasional quotations.

3. TIME OF RISE OF BUDDHISM. INDIAN THOUGHT AND IDEALS AT THAT TIME.

Owing to the unsettled state of Indian chronology we cannot with full certainty fix the absolute date of the Nirvāṇa[4]; yet we may confidently assert that the rise of Buddhism nearly coincides with the close of the Upaniṣad period. From the very tenets of Buddhism it is evident that the theories of the Vedānta had reached their full development, albeit not in the scholastic form of the Brahma-Sūtras. The practices of the Yoga, which though dogmatically no integral part of the Vedānta are not repudiated or disapproved by the Vedāntins, were scarcely less developed in the days of Buddha than later in the time of Patañjali, the author of the manual titled Yoga-sūtra. The doctrine of Karman, of metempsychosis, was already so deeply rooted in the popular conscience that Buddhism has retained it notwithstanding its standing in the most glaring conflict with Buddhist psychology, which denies the existence of soul altogether[5].

The spiritual aspirations and the views of human life as entertained by the more serious Indians at the rise of Buddhism are, at first sight, extremely gloomy. What strikes us most, is the emphatically pronounced dread — *saṃvega*, as the Buddhists like to call it — of the miseries of life, of old age and death; a dread intensified by the belief in perpetual rebirth, and consequently of repeated misery. All sects — barring the Sadducees of the epoch — agree in the persuasion that life is a burden, an unmixed evil. All accordingly strive to get liberated from worldly existence, from rebirth, from Saṃsāra. All are convinced that there are means to escape rebirth, that there is a path of salvation, that path consisting in conquering innate ignorance and in attaining the highest truth. But what is the highest truth? Here the views go asunder. Some, as the Vedāntins, affirm that truth in the highest sense[6] of the word is the essential unity of the highest soul, *paramātman*, with the individual soul, *pratyagātman* or *jīvātman*. Others, as

[1] Ed. by MINAYEF in Zapiski vol. XV, p. 156—225; partial French transl. by L. DE LA VALLÉE POUSSIN in Museon of 1892. Noteworthy as an indication of the influence of contemporary Hinduistic sentiments is such a passage as we read section 2, vs. 8: *parigrahaṃ me kurutāgrasattvāḥ, yuṣmāsu dāsatvam upaimi bhaktyā.* Cp. A. BARTH in Bull. Rel. de l'Inde, (p. 20 separ. copy).

[2] Ed. by MINAYEF, with a valuable introduction, in Zapiski IV, p. 29—52; Tibetan text added by IWANOWSKI.

[3] E. g. No. 29—32 in the Catal. of COWELL and EGGELING. Cp. BURNOUF, Intr. p. 557. Specimens of prayers also published by MINAYEF Zapiski II, 130, to Avalokiteśvara; 233, to Buddha; the latter ascribed to the king Harṣadeva.

[4] The knotty questions connected with Buddhist chronology will be dealt with hereafter, in Part V.

[5] Dīgha-N. I, p. 34; Pugg.-P. p. 38. More about this in the sequel.

[6] We avoid using the term "real truth", because reality for the majority of Indian sects is the reverse of truth in the highest sense, of *sat*, τὸ ὄντως ὄν; it being only a relative, practical truth, and passing into a more illusionary appearance, *māyā*.

the Sāṅkhyas, proclaim that the soul is essentially different from matter, by which it is clogged, though it remains essentially undefiled and eternal[1]. The Buddhists, denying the existence of any thing like a soul, necessarily reject the notion of *paramātman*, and see the highest truth in the formula of the 4 Ārya-satyāni.

The Indian view of life, in the mystical and transcendental systems of the Vedānta and Buddhism, as well as in the rationalistic Sāṅkhya, Yoga, Nyāya, is not seldom considered pessimistic. That qualification is true in a restricted sense, the Indians being pessimists only halfway. Just as they have no objection to the most tragic situations in their dramas, provided the final be a happy one, so they admit of all sorts of dreariness in human life, but at the same time they believe that it is possible, and that by a comparatively easy method, to get rid of the nuisance called existence and rebirth: they have only to follow some one of the infallible teachers of the path to salvation, of whom there was no lack in India. There, too, the rule holds good that the supply is proportionate to the demand.

PART II.

LIFE OF BUDDHA.

The history of Buddha, such as may be extracted from the canonical writings, is so marvellous that all who are standing outside the pale of Buddhism reject, more or less, its truthfulness. A few of the unbelievers have gone to such lengths as to see in that history the remoulding of an ancient myth. Others, less radical, are of opinion that it will be possible by stripping the tale of its miraculous and mythical elements to find out the historic nucleus. Those are apt to believe that by the aid of their critical manipulations they can produce an image which is extremely like the original. Without denying the worth of critical disquisitions or entering into the merits of the different reconstructions of the traditional history, we must limit ourselves in the following pages to a condensed account of the principal feats in the career of the Sublime Being whom all Buddhists acknowledge and revere as their Lord, Bhagavat, as the fountainhead of all Dharmas; who, according to his own words, throughout myriads of ages had prepared himself, out of charity, before becoming a Buddha, to free sentient beings from the misery of existence. The history of *that* Buddha may be said to be true in an ideal sense. To a certain extent we agree with Spence Hardy[2] that "we must be content with the legend in its received version", though we would not subscribe to what he adds: "with all the accumulations it has gathered in successive ages", because these supposed accumulations are found in the sacred books, which are not separated from the epoch of Nirvāṇa by ages[3].

---

[1] For more particulars, here out of place, concerning the speculations of the Upaniṣads and the Sāṅkhya, we refer the reader to the exposition in Barth's Religions of India, p. 64—86. Cp. Oldenberg, Die Religion des Veda und der Buddhismus, in Deutsche Kundschau of Nov. 1895; Jacobi, Der Ursprung des Buddhismus, GGA. 1896.

[2] M. of B. p. 139.

[3] There is nothing like a connected biography of the Buddha in the canonical books. The Lalita-Vistara erroneously considered as such, is in reality the narrative of

1. DESCENT FROM HEAVEN. CONCEPTION. BIRTH. CHILDHOOD. ADOLESCENCE[1].

After having exercised the 30 Pāramitās in anterior births the Bodhisattva destined to become an omniscient Buddha was born in the Tuṣita heaven. At the request of the deities, urging him to release mankind, he made, before giving his assent, 5 necessary examinations: 1. of the time of his appearance; 2. of the continent; 3. of the country; 4. of the race and family; 5. of the mother who should bear him, and the time when her life should be at an end[2]. He saw that the proper time had arrived; that all Buddhas are born in Jambudvīpa, in the country Madhyadeśa[3]; that the Buddhas are born either in the caste of Brahmans or of Kṣatriyas; the latter being predominant, he resolved upon becoming the son of Suddhodana, the king of the Sākya clan in Kapilavastu; finally he saw that the queen Mahā-Māyā should be his mother, and that she would die seven days after his birth[4]. He left Nandanavana, Indra's paradise, and was conceived in the womb of Mahā-Māyā.

It was then, on the last day of the Āṣāḍha festival[5] in Kapilavastu that Māyā had a dream, in which she saw how the Bodhisattva who in the shape of a white elephant was wandering on the Gold Mountain approached her from the North, and entered — so it seemed — her womb. So the Bodhisattva was conceived[6].

When the Queen the next morning told her dream to the King, he summoned Brahmans, interpreters of dreams, who declared that she had conceived a son destined to become either a universal Monarch or a Buddha.

During the time of gestation, four celestials guarded the Bodhisattva and his mother, to shield them from all harm. When the time of her confinement drew near, Māyā wished to visit her parents at Devadaha (Devahrada). On

---

the heroical career of the Bodhisattva from his descent on earth to the time when, after valiantly doing battle and vanquishing the Fiend, he proclaims his Kingdom of Dharma. It has the character of an epic on the Bodhisattva. The same applies to the Chinese texts enumerated by BEAL, SBE. XIX, p. XVI ff. The genuine portion of Aśvaghoṣa's Buddha-carita is nearly coextensive with Lal. V. The complete biographies, known to us, are compilations of canonical accounts, but as compositions comparatively modern; thus the originally Pali source of Bigandet's Life or legend of Gaudama; the Simhalese Pūjāvaliya; the Tibetan Life by Ratnadharmarāja, transl. in extract by SCHIEFNER; ROCKHILL's Life of the Buddha, derived from the Byah-Hgyur and Bstan-Hgyur; the Bhadrakalpavadāna.

1 The following narrative is mainly based upon Intr. Jāt. I, p. 47 ff. (transl. by RHYS DAVIDS, 1880; by CHALMERS 1895). For comparison's sake references are given to Lal. V.; Mhv. I, 142 ff. and 197 ff., II, 1 ff. HARDY, M. of B. p. 140 ff. BIGANDET I; p. 20 ff. ROCKHILL, L., of B. p. 14 ff. and other sources of information.

2 It is the Buddha himself who is the authority for his abode in, and descent from the Tuṣita heaven; Aṅg. N. II, p. 130, and, according to CHALMERS, also Acchariyabbhuta-S. No. 123 of Majjh. N. (JRAS of 1894, p. 386).

3 The Buddhist Madhyadeśa, for the boundaries of which see MV. V, 13, 12, lies to the east of Madhyadeśa properly so called. It is, in reality, the Pragdeśa. It is geographically impossible that in any period of Indian history Eastern Hindustān was looked upon as the central region of the Aryan Indians.

4 The reason why she *must* die, is stated Jāt. I, p. 52; cp. BIGANDET I, p. 27, and Mhv. I, 199 = II, 3. A different reason adduced Lal. V. 112. A third account, the mythical base whereof is but slightly veiled, is found Buddhac. II, vs. 18.

5 Lal. V. p. 63 the conception takes place at fullmoon day of Vaiśākha, the moon standing in Puṣya (Tiṣya); Mhv. gives the same asterism, omitting the name of the month.

6 The conception is represented in the Bharhut sculpture Pl. XXVIII, inscribed *Bhagavato okamti*. Cp. MINAYEF Recherches I, 146.

her arriving at the Lumbini Grove, she felt a desire to enter the wood. Seeing a holy Sāl iree, she stretched out her hand to take hold of a branch, which bent down of its own accord, and whilst she held it, she was delivered, in standing position and holding the branch. The child was received by the 4 Guardian gods of the quarters, and from their hands by men, but he, descending from their hands, stood erect on the ground, looked in all directions, and, after making 7 steps, exclaimed triumphantly: "I am the foremost of the world". — The child was brought to Kapilavastu.

On the same day with the Bodhisattva were born Yaśodharā, the mother of Rāhula[1], Channa (Chanda), Kāḷudāyin (Kālodāyin, Udāyin), the horse Kanthaka (Kaṇṭhaka), and Ānanda[2]; at the same time sprung into existence the Bodhi tree, and the four treasure vases.

Northern sources name as born at the same time 4 kings who will play a part in the history of the Buddha, viz. Bimbisāra, Prasenajit, Pradyota, and Udayana[3].

The birth of the Bodhisattva caused great rejoicing in the heaven of the Thirty-three gods. The Seer Kāla (al. Asita) Devala, who happened to witness those rejoicings, and on enquiry was informed of the happy event, went to Śuddhodana and expressed the wish to see the child. The infant was brought, but instead of worshiping Devala, put its feet on the matted hair of the Seer, who, rising from his seat bowed respectfully to the child, and the king, following his example, prostrated himself before his son. The Sage prophetically foresaw that the child one day would become a Buddha, but that himself would die before that time. This afflicted him and he wept. In order to secure to one of his relatives the blessing he was be deprived of, he went to his nephew Nālaka[4], and recommended him to become a recluse, as in the house of Śuddhodana a son was born, who in 35 years would become a Buddha. Nālaka, accordingly, took up the life of a Śramaṇa, heard afterwards the Master, entered the Order, reached Arhatship, and finally extinction[5].

Five days after his birth the Bodhisattva received the name of Siddhattha (Siddhārtha[6]). Among the Brahmans attending the ceremony there were eight renowned soothsayers, who were asked by the King to prognosticate the future destiny of his son. Seven of them were not able to make out whether the Prince would become a universal Monarch or a Buddha. Alone the eigth, young Koṇḍañña (Kauṇḍinya) predicted that the latter alternative would infallibly prove true. This Koṇḍañña was the very same who afterwards as one belonging to the group of Five (Pañcavaggiya; in N. sources: Bhadravargīya) took the vows.

The King, anxious to prevent his son from forsaking the world, asked what would move the Prince to flee from wordly enjoyments. The answer was: four ominous sights: an old man, a sick man, a corpse, and a monk.

---

1 Also called Bimbā, Bodhi-V. p. 20, and in N. sources Gopā, e. g. SCHIEFNER Tib. L. p. 236; 245. Lal. V. 155; cp. 270, where she is called Yaśovatī.

2 The cousin of the Buddha and the son of Amṛtodana, according to N. sources; e. g. SCHIEFNER, Tib. L. p. 264; ROCKHILL, L. of B. p. 13. Curiously BIGANDET I, 36 has the same statement, against the common S. tradition; see RHYS DAVIDS, B. p. 52. In Mhv. II, 157 Ananda's mother is Mṛgī (virtually identical with Kisā Gotamī).

3 SCHIEFNER, Tib. L. p. 235; ROCKHILL, L. of B. p. 16.

4 So, too, Mhv. II, p. 33, but Naradatta Lal. V. 135; 127.

5 Cp. Nalaka-S. in S. Nip. p. 128.

6 In N. works also Sarvārthasiddha. The new born child is brought to the temple, where the idols — or as another account has it — the goddess Abhayā — bow down at his feet; Lal. V. chap. VIII; Mhv. II, 26; ROCKHILL, op. c. p. 17.

Śuddhodana forthwith took all possible precautions that none of those sights should meet the eye of Siddhārtha.

While the child grew up, surrounded by a brilliant retinue, under the special care of his aunt and stepmother, Prajāpatī (the Matron) Gāutamī, it happened on a certain day that the King went out to the Ploughing festival, and the Prince was brought to the field by the nurses, who prepared for him a couch under the shade of a Jambutree. Attracted by the spectacle of the King handing the golden plough, the nurses left the Bodhisattva alone, who, seeing no one by him, rose up, seated himself crosslegged, and exercised the first degree of Meditation. Meanwhile the shadow of the trees had turned, but that of the Jambutree had not changed. As the nurses returning saw both miracles, they informed the King, who came in all haste and prostrated himself before his son, saying: "This is my second homage to thee, darling".

There is a tale in the North that the Prince, when he first went to school, perplexed the schoolmaster, Viśvāmitra, by his miraculous faculties[1].

On reaching the age of 16 years Siddhārtha was married to Yaśodharā, the daughter of Suprabuddha[2], his own cousin.

Many feats of prowess were achieved by the Bodhisattva, when a youth. He was an uncomparable archer, had herculean strength, and was an expert in all arts. In all contests he showed himself superior to all other Śākyas, among whom Devadatta, and it was then that the seed of jealousy was planted in the proud heart of Devadatta[3].

2. FOREBODINGS OF THE FUTURE. FLIGHT FROM KAPILAVASTU. RENUNCIATION OF THE WORLD.

Time passed on, and the Bodhisattva lived in luxury and all kinds of enjoyments[4].

On a certain day the Prince ascended his chariot, and drove with his charioteer Channa (Skr. Chanda, Chandaka)to the pleasure gardens. The gods, knowing that the time was approaching when he would attain supreme Enlightenment, resolved to show him the 4 ominous sights. One among the gods assumed the form of an old, decrepit man. The Prince asked Channa:[5] "What man is this?" "He is an old man", was the answer, "and every living being is doomed to become like him". With emotion in his mind, the Prince quickly returned home, and Śuddhodana on being informed of the reason of that speedy return, felt his anxiety increase, and doubled the guard surrounding the palace.

On another day the Prince saw, under the same circumstances, a sick man produced by the power of the gods. He put the same question, and on

---

[1] This undoubtedly apocryphal tale occurs Lal. V. Chap. X; cp. SCHIEFNER, Tib. L. p. 236. It is curious that in Mil. P. p. 236 Sabbamitta, a name synonymous with Viśvāmitra, is mentioned as a preceptor of the Prince.

[2] Of Mahānāman in Mhv. II, 48; of Daṇḍapāṇi in Lal. V. p. 179. In S. texts Daṇḍapāṇi is the brother of Suppabuddha; HARDY, M. of B. p. 137. The latter is the father of Māyā, in some N. sources, but in Mhv. I, 356 Māyā is the daughter of Subhūti. Cp. RHYS DAVIDS, B. p. 52.

[3] Lal. V. Chap. XII; Mhv. II, 74 ff.; Tib. L. p. 237; ROCKHILL, L. of B. p. 21. Cp. HARDY, M. of B. p. 153. D. is in Pali texts the brother of Yaśodharā and a son to Suppabuddha; HARDY, M. of B. p. 231. His mother is Godhī, e. g. CV. VII, 3, but in Tib. L. p. 237 Devadatta, wife to Amṛtodana.

[4] Cp. Lal. V. Chap. XIV; Buddhac. Chap. III, vs. 26 ff. and V, 16 f.

[5] The compiler of Intr. Jāt. I, 59 here refers to the Mahāpadāna.

hearing the answer, turned back in agitation. The King multiplied the means of enjoyments for his son, and again doubled the guards.

Sometime after the Bodhisattva, when driving to the gardens, met with a corpse. The answer, given by his charioteer moved him more than ever. Quickly he returned to the palace, and the King redoubled his precautions.

On a fourth occasion the Bodhisattva on his drive to the gardens saw, by the instrumentality of the gods, a monk. The decent deportment of the person made a deep impression on his mind, and when he heard that the man was an ascetic, he forthwith felt a strong inclination to renounce the world[1]. Now he drove on to the gardens, and there spent the day. After taking a bath he seated himself on the resting sto : to be clothed.

At that moment Śakra felt that his throne became hot, a certain foreboding of danger to his dominion. Conceiving that the Bodhisattva at midnight of that very day would leave the palace and carry out the Great Renunciation, he ordered Viśvakarman to go to the gardens, and adorn Siddhārtha with heavenly attire.

Viśvakarman obeyed the order, came into the presence of the Prince, and disposed in a divine manner the folds of the latter's hairdress. Thus arrayed in all his splendour, the Bodhisattva ascended his chariot. Just at that time he received the message that Yaśodharā had been delivered of a son[2], on hearing which he said: "Rāhula has been born, a bond has come into being." Hence the name of Rāhula was given to the child by order of Śuddhodana.

When the Prince was entering the town with great magnificence, a young lady, Kisā Gotamī[3], was contemplating from the upper storey of her palace the entrance of the Bodhisattva, and exclaimed:

Happy, indeed, is the mother,
Happy, indeed, is the father,
Happy, indeed, is the wife,
Who possesses such a husband!

On hearing those words, the Bodhisattva became meditative, and as his mind was already estranged from evil passions, he perceived that real happiness can only be gained by quenching the fire of love, hatred and delusion. "She has given me a good lesson", quoth he, "I will search for the peace of Nirvāṇa[4], and this very day leave my family and renounce the world." Then detaching from his neck a collar of great value, he sent it to Kisā Gotamī as a token of gratitude.

---

1 Jāt. I, p. 59 adds the remark: "The preachers of the Dīgha-N. say that he saw all the 4 signs on the same day". This has nothing to do, as ROCKHILL op. c. p. 22 supposes, with the Prince riding on horseback to the fields and seeing some poor ploughing labourers; this scene falls between the third and the forth ominous sight in Buddhac. V, in ROCKHILL's source afterwards.

2 In Mhv. II, 159, and Tib. L. p. 240 (cp. Bhadrak. II) it is not the birth, but the conception which took place in the night of the Prince's flight. No date is given Buddhac. II, vs. 46, where Rāhula is marked by the epithet *Rāhusapatnavaktra*. Cp. the fact that in Tib. L. p. 245 Rāhula's birth coincides with the defeat of Māra at the time of a lunar eclipse on fullmoon day in Vaiśākha. The same moment gave birth to Ānanda, the son of Amṛtodana. In Bhadrak. IX, Rāhula is born six years after his conception, as in Tib. L.

3 Her story is told Par. Dīp. 195 ff.; Therīg. 213—223. Cp. Dhp. p. 118; 289; 387; Aṅg. N. I, 14, 5. In Mhv. II, 157 and Bhadrak. XXXV, she is called Mṛgī, the mother of Ānanda; in a confused Tibetan account something like Mṛgajā, with ROCKHILL, L. of B. p. 23; not named Buddhac. V, 24.

4 The term rendered by "happy" in the stanza, is *nibbuta*, and Nirvāṇa is synonymous with *nibbuti* (*nirvṛti*). See CHILDERS s. vv.

When Siddhārtha, after retiring to his apartments, lay reclined on his couch, a crowd of fair damsels began to sing, play and dance to divert him, but he took no pleasure in the spectacle and fell asleep. The damsels, disappointed, lay down to sleep. A short time after the Prince awoke and, looking around, saw the loathsome appearance of the sleeping women[1]. He felt more and more disgusted, and the desire to accomplish the Great Renunciation (Abhiniṣkramaṇa) arose in him with double force. He rose, called his charioteer, and gave order to saddle his horse[2].

While Channa was saddling the courser Kanthaka, the Bodhisattva went to the room of Rāhula's mother. He opened the door and saw Yaśodharā sleeping, with one of her hands upon the head of the child. Fearing that her awakening would be an obstacle to his going away, he silently left the palace[3]. As soon as he came out, he went to his gigantic white steed, bestrode it, and ordered Channa to take hold of its tail[4]. The city gate was opened by the power of the guardian deity, and so the Bodhisattva escaped.

At that moment Māra the Fiend appeared in the air, with the intention to prevent the Bodhisattva to become a Buddha, by promising him in a week the dignity of a universal Monarch. But the Prince, not aiming at worldly sovereignty, remained deaf to the Tempter, who, baffled in his design, maliciously followed him, as a shadow the body, waiting for an opportunity[5].

It was on the full moon day of Āṣāḍha[6] when the Prince left the city. At a certain distance he turned the face, at the spot where would be erected the shrine of "Kanthaka's Return"[7]. His progress through the country went on in great pomp and glory, a host of heavenly beings attending him with lighted torches, and the sky being replete with flowers from Indra's heaven "as with the drops of rain at the beginning of the rains"[8].

After going with such a splendid retinue 30 Yojanas the Prince arrived at the river Anomā[9]. He sprang with his steed over the river, lighted, and said to Channa: "Here take my ornaments, and return with Kanthaka. I am going to become an ascetic".

Thereupon the Bodhisattva thought: "These long locks of mine are unbecoming a Śramaṇa". He took his sword, cut off his hair, and flung it together with the crest jewel towards the sky, saying: "If I am destined to become a Buddha, let it stand in the air; if not, let it come down on the ground!" The tuft of hair with the jewel went up and remained suspended in the sky, where Śakra received it in a golden casket, to place it in the Shrine of the Crest jewel (*Cūḷāmaṇi*) in the Heaven of the 33 gods[10].

---

1 For a fuller description see Jāt. I, p. 61 and Lal. V., p. 251, with the misogynic effusion p. 252. Cp. Buddhac. V, 43 ff. Mhv. II, 159.

2 N. writings insert an episod describing how the Prince as a dutiful son, before departing, asks his father's leave; Lal. V., Chap. XV; Mhv. II, 141; cp. Buddhac. V, vs. 27—38. The episode contains powerful passages, but is hardly appropriate.

3 Intr. Jāt. I, p. 62 adds the notice that according to a Jāt. commentary "Rāhula was at that time seven days old", but rejects that view as not being found in other commentaries. Quite different again several N. traditions, see note above p. 16.

4 The horse measured 18 cubits from the neck to the tail.

5 Lal. V, p. 257 it is not Māra, but Chandaka who tries to deturn the Prince from his design. Cp. Mhv. II, 160, and again 165. Cp. WINDISCH Māra und B. p. 205.

6 I. e. the date of his conception.

7 *Kanthakanivattana.* This shrine not mentioned Lal. V. 277, but another erected on the spot where Chandaka took leave, (*Chandakanivartana*).

8 In Madhyadeśa the rains set in about the end of June.

9 Slightly different Mhv. II, 164, where the place Anomiya is apparently the same as Anupiya in the country of the Mallas. Cp. Lal. V. p. 277.

10 The name of the Caitya in Lal. V. p. 278 is *Cūḍāpratigrahaṇa.* The relic is

Again the Prince thought: "These fine Benares clothes do not befit a Śramaṇa". At that moment the Mahābrahma angel Ghaṭīkāra, who in the days of yore had been the friend of the Bodhisattva, when the latter was Gyotipāla [1], provided him with the right requisites of a Śramaṇa, the 3 robes etc. The Bodhisattva put on his new dress, and bade Channa to go back with the salutations to his parents. The charioteer obeyed, but the horse Kanthaka, unable to bear his grief, died of a broken heart. After his death he was reborn as a deity of the same name in heaven [2].

3. WANDERING LIFE. ASCETISM. CONTEST WITH MĀRA. TRIUMPH. ATTAINMENT OF BUDDHAHOOD.

The Bodhisattva having thus entered upon the life of a recluse spent a week in the mango grove of Anupiya. Thence he travelled in one day to Rājagṛha, the capital of Magadha, where he begged his food. At this sight the inhabitants were struck with wonder, not knowing whether he was a deity, a mortal, or any other being. The King, Seniya (Śreṇya, Śreṇika) Bimbisāra, observing the Great Man (*Mahāpuruṣa*) from his palace tower, ordered his servants to go and ascertain the nature of the stranger. The men found the Bodhisattva, who after having got sufficient food had left the city, at the foot of the Pāṇḍava Rock, eating, not without an effort, his coarse meal. The messengers returned, and related all to the King, who quickly went to the place where the Great Man was sitting, and offered him his whole kingdom, but the latter rejected that generous offer, saying that he had abandoned all in the hope of attaining supreme Enlightenment, whereupon Bimbisāra asked the favour that his kingdom should first of all be visited by the Buddha [3].

On leaving the King, the Bodhisattva went forward, and in due course came to Āḷāra Kālāma and Uddaka, son of Rāma, two renowned teachers of philosophy [4]. He learned from them the successive degrees of ecstatic meditation (*samāpatti*), but soon discovering that it was not the way to Enlightenment, he resolved to apply himself to the Great Effort (Mahāpadhāna) [5]. To effect his purpose, he went to Uruvelā (Uruvilvā). Now it came to pass that the Pañcavaggiyas, i. e. the 5 mendicants, Koṇḍañña and the rest, met with him, and resolved to stay with him, persuaded as they were that erelong he would become a Buddha.

After six years of exertion the Bodhisattva resolved to practise the most profound meditation (*dhyāna*) and to perform the most rigid penance. By

---

figured as placed in the Sudhammā Devasabhā, and called *Bhagavato Cūḍāmaho* Pl. XVI of Bharhut; cp. CUNNINGHAM p. 189 of his text.

[1] For the history of the two friends, see Mhv. I, 319 ff. and cp. Mil. P. p. 221 ff. Dhp. p. 349. — In Mhv. II, 195; Lal. V. 276; Buddhac. VI, vs. 60, the B. changes his dress with the *kāṣāya* of a hunter or a Devaputra who had assumed the shape of a hunter.

[2] The death and deification of the steed is more amply told in Mhv. II, 189 ff. According to this source, and Lal. V. p. 282 K. died after his having returned to Kapilavastu. Cp. about his blissful state in heaven Vimāna-V. p. 81.

[3] A fuller account of this story is found S.-Nip. p. 71 and commentary. The poetical version Lal. V. 297 ff. is much longer.

[4] About the two teachers, see the Buddha's own account, Majjh. N. I, p. 80 ff. Cp. Lal. V. 319 ff. — In the N. books the course of events is somewhat different; see Lal. V. 294; Mhv. II, 195; Buddhac. X—XII; the N. names of the teachers are Ārāḍa Kālāma, and Udraka (mistakenly Rudraka) Rāmaputra.

[5] The system is set forth in the Mahāpadhāna-S. in Dīgh. N.; cp. Ang. N. II, p. 16, and CHILDERS s. v. *padhānaṃ*.

carrying his fasting to excess, he became as thin as a skeleton, and at last so weak that one day he fainted and fell down[1]. Some gods said: "The Śramaṇa Gautama[2] is dead; others, however, remarked: 'Such is the state of Arhats'". And, indeed, not long afterwards he recovered from his swoon[3].

As he perceived that mortification was not the way to Enlightenment, he resumed his former diet, which caused the Five friars to loose faith in him. Hence they left him, and went to Ṛṣipatana (Isipatana) in the Deer-park near Benares.

At that time there lived in Uruvelā a girl named Sujātā, the Chieftain's daughter[4]. On the fullmoon day of Vaiśākha she rose early to make an offering to a holy tree and milked the cows. Seeing many miracles, she joyfully sent her servant girl Pūrṇā (Puṇṇā) to clear the place under the holy tree.

Now in the latter part of the previous night the Bodhisattva had seen 5 dreams, by which he got the certainty that in the course of that day he would become Buddha. At daybreak he went in quest of his food and sat down at the foot of the holy tree, lighting up the East with his radiance. Pūrṇā saw him shining, the whole tree goldcoloured by the rays issuing from his body. She ran back to her mistress, who, after pouring milk-rice in a golden vessel, went to the tree, and presented the golden vessel to the Great Man. And at that moment disappeared the earthen pot given him by Ghaṭikāra. He went with the golden vessel to the bank of the river Nairañjanā (P. Nerañjarā), to a place called Well-established (Supatiṭṭhita), where innumerable Bodhisattvas had bathed on the day of their awaking to Enlightenment. After taking a bath he dressed himself in the garb of an Arhat worn by numberless Buddhas, and, sitting down Eastward, ate all his food, divided into 49 portions, as he would have no other nourishment during the next 7 weeks. Having finished his meal, he flung the golden vessel into the stream with the following asseveration: "If on this day I am to become a Buddha, let this vessel ascend the stream; if not, let it go down". And, lo, it went up to a great distance, when it sunk down to the abode of the Nāgaking Kāla. On striking against the vessels of the three last Buddhas, it produced a sound, by which Kāla became aware of the rise of a new Buddha[5].

In the evening the Great Man marched toward the tree of Enlightenment. He met on his march with a grasscutter, Svastika (Sotthiya), who offered him 8 bundles of grass. He accepted the offering, and, after taking a survey of the quarters, he went to the East, the seat of all Buddhas, facing the West. There he scattered the handful of grass on the ground, where a seat

---

1 Buddha himself describes his severe penance and subsequent exhaustion in Majjh. N. I, p. 80; p. 245 ff. Cp. Lal. V. 319 ff.; SENART Not. Ep. 3 (statue). — The Dhyāna alluded to is termed *appānaka* Majjh. N. l. c.; *āsphānaka* Lal. V. 314; 324; Mhv. II, 125.

2 This is the first time the B. is so termed in Jāt. Intr., whereas in Lal. V. he is addressed by that name by Ārāḍa. As to the origin of the name, see BURNOUF, Intr. p. 155. The Buddha is also known as an Āṅgirasa, the Gautamas being a sub-division of the Āṅgirasas. One of his other appellations is Ādityabandhu, the Śākyas forming a *gens* of the great tribe of Sun-descendants. Cp. S. Nip. p. 73: Ādicca nāma gottena, Sakkiyā nāma jātiyā.

3 Another tradition describes the grief of Māyā on hearing the (false) report of her son's death; Lal. V. 314 ff.

4 Her father's title is *senānī*, *senāpati*, and otherwise *gopādhipa* or *grāmika* (i. e. village head) in Jāt., Mhv., Lal. V., Buddhac. In this last non canonical source her name is Nandabalā XII, 106, but Sudatā XVII, 9. The name Balā also occurs Lal. V. 331. The story of her offering, the subsequent march of the B., and his victory is twice told, Mhv. II, 264 ff. and 299 ff. Cp. Lal. V. Chap. XVIII—XXI; Buddhac. p. 106 ff.

5 Cp. Mhv. II, 265; twice repeated, with variations, p. 307 and p. 400.

of 14 cubits was formed. Then he uttered the following asseveration: "Let my skin, my nerves and bones waste away, let my life blood dry up, I will not leave this seat before attaining perfect Enlightenment"[1].

It was at that moment that Māra[2] thinking: "Prince Siddhārtha wishes to escape from my dominion", summoned his hosts to do battle. Himself mounted on the elephant Mountain-girdled (Girimekhala) led the attack, which was so dreadful that the gods attending the Bodhisattva were seized with terror and fled. The Great Man alone remained undaunted, putting his trust in the Pāramitās. Thereupon Māra caused violent winds to blow, followed by a rain of rocks, weapons, glowing ashes, charcoal. All in vain[3].

Seeing all his attempts baffled, the Fiend approached the Great Man, and summoned him to vacate his seat. "Māra!" was the reply, "you have not devoted your life to benefit the world, to attain wisdom. This seat does not belong to you". Enraged at these words, Māra cast his discus weapon at the Great Man, but it became a garland of flowers. Again the host of Māra renewed the attack, but the rocks they hurled down at him, were turned into nosegays. Sure of his triumph, the Bodhisattva exclaimed: "The seat belongs to me", and turning to the Fiend, he defied him to adduce a witness for his merits. Māra pointed to his followers, who with a roar testified to their master's liberality. In his turn the Fiend asked: "As to you, Siddhārtha, who is witness to your having bestowed alms?" Then the Bodhisattva called up the Earth to be his witness, and she replied with such a roaring voice that the hosts of Māra were discomfited, and the elephant Girimekhala fell down on his knees to pay homage to the Great Man. The army of the enemy fled in all directions, whereas the gods exultingly shouted: "Māra is defeated! The Prince Siddhārtha has prevailed!" The Nāgas and other celestial beings approached the seat of Enlightenment, chanting songs of victory.

The sun was still above the horizon when the Great Man defeated the army of his foe[4]. In the first watch of the night he arrived at the knowledge of his former states of existence (*pūrvanivāsa, pubbenivāsa*); in the second watch he acquired the heavenly eye (*divyacakṣus, dibbacakkhu*); in the 3d the knowledge of the series of causes and effects[5].

While he was mentally revolving the 12 causes (Nidānas) in direct order and in reverse order[6], the whole universe shook 12 times to its foundation, and the most extraordinary phaenomena were seen, even as at his birth.

---

1 Cp. the stanza in Lal. V. p. 362.

2 *Māro pāpimā*, the usual name of the Fiend in P., originally, it appears, synonymous with the *Mṛtyuḥ pāpmā* in Vaidic texts, has with the Buddhists become the incarnation of Evil. His connection with Death is further exemplified by his being identified with *Maccurāja*, in Therag. vs. 411. For *pāpimā* Mhv. has *pāpīmān*, along with *pāpīyān* (e. g. II, 264; 268); the latter form being used in Lal. V. A wellknown synonymous term both in S. and in N. texts is Namuci. His identification with Smara is founded upon his being the ruler of the highest Kāmaloka; hence he is termed Kāmeśvara, Lal. V. p. 427; *kāmadhātau Māraḥ pāpīyān adhipatir īśvaro vaśavartī*, p. 375. Cp. Buddhac. XIII, vs. 2. See also Windisch Māra und B. p. 184 ff.

3 According to Lal. V. p. 404 Māra, after his first unsuccessful attack, sends his daughters to tempt the B. He repeats his attempt in a later period, in which the P. texts place it, as we shall see below. Other transpositions occur Mhv. II, 322 and Buddhac. XIII, vs. 2 ff.

4 In Mhv. II, 417 the army is defeated at sunrise.

5 *Pratītyasamutpāda*, P. *paticcasamuppāda;* the system, as developed MV. I, 1; Lal. V. Chap. XXII; Mhv. II, 285 and 346, will be expounded in Part III below. — Bigandet's source adds the conception of the 4 Āryasatyāni; likewise Lal. V. 447; Mhv. II, 345. The 4 truths or axioms are fully set forth Majjh. N. I, p. 48.

6 Cp. MV. I, 1; for the stanzas there cp. also Mhv. II, 88; 416 ff.

Amid these wonders the Bodhisattva attained Omniscience, and he uttered the joyful song[1] common to all Buddhas.

4. THE FIRST SEVEN WEEKS OF BUDDHAHOOD. PREACHING OF THE LAW AND CONVERSION OF THE 5 MENDICANT FRIARS. OTHER CONVERTS. TEMPTATION BY MĀRA. THE THREE KĀŚYAPAS. SERMON ON BURNING. MEETING WITH BIMBISĀRA. CONVERSION OF SĀRIPUTRA AND MAUDGALYĀYANA.

After reaching perfect Enlightenment, the Lord Buddha remained sitting on the same seat, realizing the bliss of Deliverance, and thinking of his generous acts in his previous existence as Viśvantara (Vessantara[2]). Some deities, seeing that he did not leave his seat, felt a doubt whether he had fulfilled his daytask, but the Master, knowing their thoughts, rose into the air, performed a magical[3] feat, and thus dispelled their misgivings. Thereupon he took his stand a little to the North-East, looking during a week with unblenching eyes at the spot which became the "Shrine of the Unblenching one". Between that spot and his seat he shaped a walk, stretching from East to West, which he spent a week in walking to and fro. That walk became known as the "Jewel shrine of the Walk". In the fourth week the gods made to the Northwest a Jewelhouse. There he spent a week, going through the whole Abhidharma-Piṭaka.

After having spent four weeks near the Bodhi tree, he went in the fifth week to the Goatherd's Banyan tree, and sat there scrutinizing the Dharma[4]. It was at that time that Māra, who always followed the Master to discover a flaw sat down overcome with sorrow after his defeat. His three daughters, Desire, Pining and Lust[5], on hearing the reason of his affliction, promised that by their charms they would overcome the Saint. So they approached the Lord and tried to seduce him, but he paid not the slightest attention to them. At last he said: "Go away! Suchlike endeavours may have success with men who have not subdued the passions, but the Tathāgata has done away with affection, hate and illusion", and he recited two stanzas (Dhp. vss. 179, 180). Baffled in their attemps the daughters returned to their father.

The Lord, after spending there a week, went to Mucalinda[6]. There he

---

[1] See Intr. Jāt. I, p. 76; the dogmatic interpretation in the comment on Dhp. vs. 153 f. An explanation of the "train of thought" is found in Prof. RHYS DAVIDS, B. pp. 100—112. — The Udāna in Mhv. II, 285 contains in plainer words the same idea.

[2] His last birth but one. The story of V. is the most favourite of all the Jātakas and forms the subject of dramatic performances in Burma and Tibet; WADDELL, Buddh. of Tib. 540—551. Cp. HARDY, M. of B. 116 ff. Fa Hian's Rec. 106.

[3] *Yamaka-pāṭihāriya.* Yamaka, a term which has given rise to various remarks, is, if we are not mistaken, a conundrum, a veiled expression for *yoga* in the sense of "jugglery, magic"; *yamaka*, double, being nearly synonymous with *yoga*, conjunction, and wholly with *yuga*, a couple.

[4] The account of the Lord's stations in MV I, 1—5 is different; viz. 1. Bodhi tree; 2. The Goatherd's Banyan tree; 3. Mucalinda; 4. Rājāyatana tree; 5. Goatherd's Banyan tree; cp. Majjh. N. I, p. 167. In Lal. V. 488 ff. the sequel is: 1. Bodhi terrace (Bodhimaṇḍa); 2. the Long Walk, extending over the whole universe; 3. B. looks with unblenching eyes to the Bodhimaṇḍa; 4. He goes the Short Walk from the Eastern to the Western Ocean; 5. Mucilinda; 6. the Goatherd's Banyan tree; 7. Tārāyaṇa tree.

[5] Their names in P. are: Taṇhā, Aratī, Ragā; see more about them S. Nip. p. 157; Saṃy. N. I, p. 124; Aṅg. N. I, 3. In Lal. V. 490 they occur as Tṛṣṇā, Arati, Rati; in Buddhac. XIII, 3 Tṛṣ, Prīti, Rati. The episod is wanting in MV.

[6] Lal. V. 491: Mucilinda. It occurs as the name of a mountain, a lake, a Nāga, and a tree.

was shielded during a rainshower by the coils and hoods of the Nāga king. After a week he went to the Rājāyatana tree[1], where he remained another week.

On the last day of the seven weeks, whilst the Lord was sitting at the foot of the Rājāyatana, it came to pass that two merchants, Tapussa and Bhalluka[2], were travelling from Utkala (Orissa) to Madhyadeśa, with 500 carts. A deity, who had been a bloodrelation of those merchants, stopped their carts, and exhorted them to offer cakes of barley and honey to the Lord. The merchants followed the advice, went to the presence of the Buddha, and said: "O Lord! out of mercy to us accept this food!"[3] The Tathāgatha had no vessel to receive those offerings, but the Guardian deities of the four quarters forthwith came from heaven, and presented him each with a bowl of sapphire. He refused. Then they offered him four other bowls of bean-coloured stone, which he accepted, putting the four bowls one in the other with the word of command: "Let them become one". He now took the food and ate it.

When the Lord had finished his meal, the merchants, prostrating themselves, made profession of faith with the words: "We take refuge in the Buddha and in the Law; take us, o Lord, from hence forward lifelong as lay devotees (Upāsaka)!" The two merchants thus became the first lay devotees, by pronouncing only two articles of faith[4], since at that time the Congregation (Saṅgha) did not yet exist. After their profession of faith they besought the Master to bestow upon them something which in the sequel they might worship. And he gave them a few hairs of his head. These were afterwards deposited by the merchants as relics in a shrine, which they erected in their native city[5].

Then the Tathāgata rose up and returned to the Goatherd's Banyan tree. The thought arose in him that the Law he had mastered was too profound and subtle to be preached to others. But Brahmā Sahampati, knowing that the world would be lost, if the Buddha continued unwilling to reveal the Law, repaired to the place where the Lord was sitting and urged him to show the way of salvation in so eloquent words that finally his request was granted[6].

The Buddha now pondered in his mind to whom he should first reveal the Law. He thought of Āḷāra, but by the suggestion of a deity he became aware that his former teacher had died a week ago. Then he thought of Udraka, but on an intimation by a deity he came to the conclusion that Udraka had died last night[7]. Now his thoughts turned to the 5 mendicant

---

1 Corresponding to Skr. *rājātana*. *Tārāyaṇa* of Lal. V. may be a corruption of a supposed Prākrit *rājāyana*.

2 Lal. V. has Trapuṣa and, like MV., Bhallika, two brothers, as with BIGANDET I, 108. *Tapassu* in Intr. Jāt. is certainly wrong. The event takes place earlier in MV. I, 4, but equally near the Rājāyatana. On the redaction of the episod in Mhv. see MINAYEF Recherches I, 158.

3 The formula MV I, 4 is: "that it may be to our weal and happiness for long time!" Lal. V. 495 has *anukampām upādāya*, exactly as Jāt. Intr.

4 They became *upāsakā dvevācikā*.

5 About the conflicting claims of the Burmese and the Siṃhalese to the possession of these relics see Prof. RHYS DAVIDS, Birth stories p. 110, note. It may be added that a town in Bactria raised the same claim; Voy. I, 66. Cf. MINAYEF Recherches I, 161.

6 More amply and poetically told MV. I, 5; Majjh. N. I, 167 ff. Saṃy. N. I, 136 ff. Lal. V. 514 ff. The agreement between the S. and the N. tradition is here very close. We only remark that for P. Brahmā Sahampati Lal. V. has usually Śikhī Mahābrahmā; yet Sahāmpati occurs e. g. p. 69; 342 (cp. Vyutp. § 163), and Sahapati p. 49.

7 Cp. for this part of the narrative and the sequel Lal. V. 523 ff. Buddhac. XV, 87 ff. ROCKHILL, L. of B. p. 37 ff.

friars, who had for a while so faithfully attented him. Discovering in his mind that they were living in the Deerpark near Benares, he took the resolution to go thither and inaugurate there the dominion of the Law[1]. He lingered a few days more near the Bodhi tree, and departed on the full moon day of Āṣāḍha[2].

On his way he met the Ājīvaka monk Upaka, who struck with his prepossessing exterior, asked him to what order of monks he belonged, and who was his master. Whereupon the Lord, proclaiming his own omniscience and superiority, declared his intention to proceed to Benares to inaugurate the dominion of the Law, and to beat the drum of Immortality (Nirvāṇa) in this world that is groping in darkness[3].

On the evening the Master arrived at the Deerpark[4]. When the Five monks saw him from afar, they said one to another: "Brethren[5], here comes the Sramaṇa Gautama, who has returned to a good life and forsaken all earnest striving. We will not receive him with marks of reverence, but as he is of a good family he deserves the honour of a seat". Such was their agreement, but when the Lord came nearer, they involuntarily rose and respectfully welcomed him. Not knowing that he had became a Buddha, they addressed him by his name or by "Reverend". But the Lord said: "Do not, o monks, address me thus; I am a Tathāgata. I will preach you the Law by following which you will attain, even in this life, at the highest degree of holiness".

After persuading them to be attentive, the Master preached his first discourse, in which he set forth that one who renounces the world should shun two extremes: the pursuit of worldly pleasures, and the practice of useless austerities[6]; that it is the middle course, discovered by the Tathāgata, which leads to wisdom and Nirvāṇa. That middle course, as he proceeded to unfold, is the eightfold Path[7]. Further he gave an exposition of the 4. Axioms or Certainties (Āryasatyāni): suffering, the cause of suffering, the suppression of suffering, the path leading to that suppression. During that exposition Koṇḍañña (Kauṇḍinya) came to true insight, and understood[8] that whatever has an origin is destined to have an end. Thereby he acquired the fruit of

---

1 And: "begin to turn the wheel of the Law". Both translations of *dharmacakram pravartayitum* are admissible. Yet it must be noticed that the Buddhists usually take the expression in a symbolical sense, and so they did anciently, as is proved by the representations of the wheel at Bharhut, Pl. XIII and XXXI. Cp. Ep. Ind. II, 322. A third meaning results from such epithets as *dvādaśākāra* — an allusion to the 12 Nidānas and perhaps to the 12 Aṅgas — and *sūkṣma*, *gambhīra*; viz. that of "the whole circle of the Law". In such a connection, *dharmacakram vartayati* or *pravartayati* may be rendered with "unfolding the whole of the Dharma".

2 The date of his conception and of his entering upon a wandering life. The "few days" must be a week, for it is eight weeks between full moon day of Vaiśākha to full moon in Āṣāḍha.

3 See the Gathās MV I, 6; Majjh. N. I, p. 169; Lal. V. 526. — Concerning Upaka cp. BURNOUF Intr. 389; FEER, Etudes Buddhiques pp. 15—17.

4 The legend about the origin of the name in Mhv. I, 359 ff. presupposes the Prākṛit form *dāya*, not the Skr. *dāva*.

5 *Āvuso*, properly "Sir, Reverend". It is not exactly indeclinable, as CHILDERS has it, but the vocat. case, also used in addressing a company, of *āyasmat* (*āyuṣmat*); see e. g. S. Vibh. IV, 8, 8. The form of the case agrees with Vaidic-*vas*, as in *adrivas*, *bhagos*.

6 Cp. BEAL SBE. XIX, 174.

7 *Aṣṭāṅgiko* (*āryāṣṭ°*) *mārgaḥ*, *aṭṭhāṅgiko maggo*, viz. right views, r. thoughts, r. speech, r. actions, r. living, r. exertion, r. recollection, r. meditation, MV. I, 6, 18; Dīgh. N I, p. 157; Majjh. N. I, p. 47 ff.; Saṃy. N. II, p. 106; Lal. V. 540 ff. Kāraṇḍ. V., 46. Cp. Vyu. § 44; Dharma. S. L.

8 Hence his surname Añña- or Aññāta-Koṇḍañña, in ungrammatical Skr. Ājñāta-Kauṇḍinya. Cp. Jeta-vana instead of Jetṛ-vana. A correction has Ājñāta K. Vyu. § 47.

the first stage on the path to Nirvāṇa[1], and at the time he received ordination. The next day Vappa (Vāṣpa) was converted, and on the three following days Bhaddiya (Bhadrika), Mahānāmān and Assaji (Aśvajit) successively[2]. On the fifth day the Master preached to all of them the discourse "On the inanity of all physical and mental phaenomena" (*Anattalakkhaṇa-Suttanta*), in consequence whereof the 5 monks became in their minds freed from all impurity. Thus there were at that time six Arhats.

In those days there was in Benares a young man, named Yaśas (P. Yasa), a wealthy banker's son. Once it happened that he saw the same spectacle of sleeping female musicians as Siddhārtha had witnessed in the night of his flight. Disgusted, he fled the house and directed his steps to the Deerpark. There the Lord saw him, and perceiving his predisposition to become a saint, he called him, established him in the fruition of the first stage on the path to Nirvāṇa, and on the next day in Arhatship[3].

Soon afterwards the father of Yaśas became a convert as lay devotee. He was the first Upāsaka making profession of faith by taking refuge in the threefold formula (*tevācika*). The mother of Yaśas and his wife became likewise lay devotees; not long after 54 friends of Yaśas took orders, and attained to Arhatship, so that there were then 61 Arhats all in all.

After the rainy season and its solemn close (*pravāraṇā, pavāraṇā*), the Master sent out the 60 in different directions with the words: "Go forth, O monks, wandering and preaching". He himself went to Uruvelā. On his way thither he overcame the temptations of Māra[4] and converted the Bhaddavaggiyas[5].

At Uruvelā there lived three brothers, hermits with matted hair and fireworshippers (Jaṭilas), known by the name of Uruvela-Kassapa (Uruvilvā-Kāśyapa), Nadī-K., and Gayā-K. By performing many miracles[6], the Tathāgata converted the three brothers, with their disciples. Accompanied by all of them, he went to the hill of Gayāśīrṣa (P. Gayāsīsa), and delivered there his sermon on Burning (Āditta-pariyāya), in consequence of which all his hearers were established in Arhatship[7].

After staying for some time near Gayāśīrṣa, the Master wandered with his numerous followers, wending his way to the Supatiṭṭha Shrine in the Laṭṭhivana (Yaṣṭivana[8]) near Rājagṛha, in order to redeem the promise he had made to Bimbisāra.

When the King heard that the Buddha had arrived, he hastened with a great number of Brahman householders to the Yaṣṭivana, and prostrated himself before the feet of the Lord — those feet, marked by the figure of a wheel and emitting a flood of light. As the Brahmans stood in doubt whether

---

1 Sotāpattiphala; see Childers s. vv. *maggo* and *sotāpatti;* cp. Bigandet I, p. 153.

2 The formula of ordination is: "Come, O monks! well proclaimed is the Law, lead a holy life that an end may be put to suffering!"

3 The scene of the story of Yaśas is laid in Kusinārā SBE. XIX, 180, but Beal's Rom. Leg. agrees with MV.

4 MV I, 11 and 18; cp. Rockhill, L. of B. p. 39. No mention of it in Jāt. Intr. p. 82.

5 Different from the N. five Bhadravargīyas = S. Pañcavaggiyas. Yet a Tibetan source has the same story of the 60 young men of "the happy band" or Bhadravarga; see Rockhill, L. of B. p. 40.

6 Details about those miracles are found MV. I, 15—20; cp. Tib. L. 250 ff. SBE. XIX, 184.

7 MV. I, 21. SBE. XIX, 186.

8 Schiefner, Tib. L. p. 254 has: "Rohrhain des festen K'aitja". Whether "Rohrhain" is intended for a rendering of Yaṣṭivana is doubtful. If so, Y. and Veṇuvana would seem to have been identified, or confounded. The name of the Shrine is obviously Supratiṣṭha, answering to P. Supatiṭṭha. Cf. Rockhill, op. c. p. 42, note.

the Great Śramaṇa was the pupil of Uruvelā-Kāśyapa, or the reverse, the Lord penetrating their feelings, summoned the Sthavira to give testimony anent his conversion, whereupon Kāśyapa declared that he had renounced the worship of Fire, and exclaimed: "The Lord is my master, I am his disciple". Then he rose into the air, and by that wonder fully convinced the crowd that he had yielded to the Tathāgata. But the Lord said: "Not now only have I subdued Kāśyapa; in the past, too, he was subdued by me", and on that occasion he told the Mahā-Nārada-Kassapa Jātaka, winding up with a discourse on the 4 Axioms. On the conclusion the King with almost the whole of the assembly was established in the fruition of the first stage on the path to Nirvāṇa, and made profession of faith. Before taking leave he invited the Lord to dinner for next day.

The following morning, when the Master with his disciples entered Rājagṛha, there appeared in front of him a young Brahman — in reality Śakra, who had assumed that shape — singing the praises of Buddha, the Law, and the Congregation in the most lofty strain[1].

When the King of Magadha had received his guests, he presented to the Saṅgha whose chief is the Buddha in the most formal way, by pouring water over the Master's hand, the Bambu grove (Veṇuvana, P. Veḷuvana). The Buddha accepted the grant, and took up his abode in the grove with his company[2].

At that time there lived at Rājagṛha a heterodox wandering ascetic (*paribbājaka*), Sañjaya, who had many disciples, amongst whom Śāriputra (Sāriputta) and Maudgalyāyana (Moggallāna)[3]. On a certain morning Śāriputra saw Aśvajit on his begging round, and, impressed by the Sthavira's deportment, he asked him who was his teacher. Aśvajit answered that his Master was the Great Śramaṇa of the Śākya race, and added that he was not yet able[4] to give a detailed exposition of the doctrine, the essence of which, however, was contained in the following formula:

> Of those things (conditions) which spring from a cause
> The cause has been told by Tathāgata;
> And their suppression likewise
> The Great Śramaṇa has revealed[5].

Immediately on hearing this verse Śāriputra was established in the fruition of the first stage on the path to Nirvāṇa, and he repeated the formula to Maudgalyāyana, who likewise became a convert. Both left their teacher Sañjaya. Maudgalyāyana attained Arhatship in a week, Śāriputra in a fortnight, and they were elevated by the Buddha to the rank of his two Chief Disciples. That distinction excited the jealousy of the other disciples, but the Master proved by references to parallel cases under former Buddhas how their discontent was unfounded[6].

1 MV I, 22; Intr. Jāt. p. 84; S. Nip. vv. 405—424. Cp. WINDISCH op. c. pp. 234—303.

2 Cp. ROCKHILL op. c. p. 43; SBE. XIX, 193.

3 Śāriputra or Śārisuta, also called Upatiṣya (Upatissa); another name of Maudgalyāyana is Kolita; see MV. I, 24; Dhp. p. 120; Tib. L. p. 255, where the history of the two friends before their becoming pupils to Sañjaya is told. Śāriputta Dhp. l. c. is the son of the Brahmanwoman Sārī; Tib. L. agrees, but confounds the birds *śāri* and *sārikā*. The origin of the names Upatiṣya and Kolita is differently told ll. cc. For Śāradvatīputra, synonymous with Śāriputra, see Tib. L. l. c. and BURNOUF Intr. p. 312. Cp. ROCKHILL op. c. p. 44 and the references there given.

4 Notwithstanding his being an Arhat.

5 An able discussion on the purport of this *confessio fidei* is found in HODGSON's Ess. p. 111.

6 Dhp. pp. 125 ff. Cp. ROCKHILL op. c. p. 115; SBE. XIX, 196.

5. VISIT TO KAPILAVASTU. ORDINATION OF RĀHULA AND NANDA. BUDDHA'S RETURN TO RĀJAGṚHA. CONVERSION OF ĀNANDA AND OTHER ŚĀKYAS. ANĀTHAPIṆḌIKA. VIŚĀKHĀ.

During the Tathāgata's stay in the Bambu grove, the news reached Śuddhodana that his son had become a Buddha, and was dwelling near Rājagṛha[1]. The old King despatched one of his courtiers with a large retinue to bring his son to Kapilavastu. The envoy departed and arrived at the Bambu grove, when the Master was engaged in preaching. The effect was that the courtier and all his followers attained to Arhatship and asked to be ordained. Their request was complied with, and as Arhats become indifferent to worldly matters, they failed to deliver the King's message.

Śuddhodana repeatedly sent other envoys, but the same thing happened to all his messengers nine times over. At last he thought of Udāyin the Black[2], who was born on the same day as the Bodhisattva and had been his playmate. Udāyin undertook the task, but on the condition that he should be allowed to become a monk. The King agreed to the stipulation, the noble man went off to Rājagṛha, heard the Master preaching and, like his predecessors, obtained Arhatship[3].

The Master had spent the time of Retreat during the rains near Benares; then went to Uruvelā, where he stayed 3 months. On the full moon day of Pauṣa he went to Rājagṛha, remaining there 2 months, so that 5 months had elapsed since he left Benares, and the cold season (*hemanta*) had past, a week after Udāyin's arrival[4]. Now on the full moon day of Phālguna, when the spring in all its loveliness had set in, Udāyin conceived that it was the fit time for the Buddha to visit his family. He went to the Lord, and painted him in glowing colours[5] the pleasantness of the spring-season, the right time to undertake a journey. When the Master asked to what purpose he so sweetly lauded travelling, Udāyin answered: "o Lord, your father desires to see you; deign to pay him a visit". "Well", said the Buddha, "I will do so".

Accompanied by a great number of monks, the Tathāgata left Rājagṛha with the intention of reaching Kapilavastu in two months. But Udāyin went instantly through the air, and made his appearance before Śuddhodana, to whom he announced his son's slow approach. The King, exceedingly pleased, supplied him with a meal, and gave him at the same time a bowl filled with the choicest food for the Buddha. The Sthavira, after throwing the bowl into the air, rose himself up into the sky, caught the portion of food, and presented it to the Master.

Every day the Sthavira brought food in the same manner. He moreover never failed to extol the great qualities of the Buddha in the presence of the Śākyas, on account of which meritorious act the Lord assigned to him the first place among those who knew to propitiate his family.

Meanwhile the Śākyas made preparatories to receive their relative, and at his approach went out to meet him at the Banyan garden. In their pride

[1] In Tib. sources the event is placed much later; Śuddhodana hears the tidings from Prasenajit, King of Kosala; Tib. L. p. 16; Rockhill op. c. 51.

[2] Kaḷudāyin; in N. writings Kalodāyin, which may mean: Rising in time.

[3] The account in Tib. L. 262 is slightly different; the letter from the King to his son is evidently a late invention. The interview between father and son in SBE. XIX, 218 ff.

[4] This reckoning presupposes a period of Retreat of three months. Cp. Childers s. v. *vasso*.

[5] Therag. vv. 527—536, making only 10 stanzas instead of 60, as Intr. Jāt. p. 87 has it.

they were unwilling to prostrale themselves before him, but by a miracle the Lord forced them to do so[1]. The King, seeing that miracle, bowed down before his son. That was his third homage.

Then the Lord came down from the sky, and caused a shower of rain, which only wetted those who liked it, and no others. To the astonished crowd the Teacher said: "Not now only a rain falls on my relatives, formerly also the same took place", and on this occasion he related the Viśvantara Jātaka[2].

The next day the Tathāgata entered Kapilavastu to go his begging round. The mother of Rāhula, moved by curiosity, looked out from the high palace to see her former husband, and she beheld him in his monk's habit more glorious than he ever was in his princely state. She glorified him, the Lion of Men, and informed the King that his son was begging in the streets, in the dress of a monk. Śuddhodana went to meet the Buddha, and tried to persuade him that begging was unworthy of the descendant of an illustrious royal race, but his son replied: "Yours, o King, is that lineage of kings, but mine is the lineage of Buddhas, from Dīpaṃkara down to Kāśyapa. These and all other Buddhas have been in the habit of living on alms". Then he uttered an edifying stanza, after which the King obtained the fruition of the first stage on the way to Nirvāṇa. A second stanza had the effect that Śuddhodana reached the second stage[3]. Afterwards he was established in the fruition of the third stage, on hearing the Dharmapāla Jātaka[4], and at the moment when he was dying he attained to Arhatship.

On having become a saint of the first degree, the King conducted the Lord with the assembly of monks to the palace, where they partook of a savoury meal. After dinner all the women came and paid their homage to the Lord, except the mother of Rāhula. Then Buddha, flanked by Śāriputra and Maudgalyāyana, went to her apartments, and no sooner had she seen him, than she threw herself at his feet. When Śuddhodana praised her and dilated upon her virtuous behaviour, the Lord observed that her good conduct was not to be wondered at, since formerly, too, she watched over herself, and he told the Canda-kinnara Jātaka[5].

On the second day Nanda, the son of Śuddhodana[6] and the Matron Gautamī was to celebrate his inauguration as crown prince and his marriage to Janapada-Kalyāṇi (the Beauty of the Land). The Buddha entered the house, and led him away to the Banyan garden. Nanda's bride impatiently waited for the return of her bridegroom, but in vain, for on the third day Nanda, much against his will, was compelled by the Buddha to become a monk[7].

---

1 According to Dhp. p. 334 the Lord produced in the sky a jewel path on which he moved to and fro, preaching the Law. In Intr. Jāt. p. 88 the wonder performed is the same as the one at the foot of the Gaṇḍamba tree. Somewhat different again in Tib. L. 263. The essential trait in all is the walking in the sky.

2 He was thinking of the same immediately after his Enlightenment; see p. 21.

3 The two stanzas are Dhp. vss. 168 f.

4 Jāt. Nr. 447; a N. version in Mhv. II, 77. This event took place after Rahula's Ordination.

5 Jāt. Nr. 485; represented in a *basrelief* of Bharhut Pl. XXVII. Other Jātakas referring to Yaśodharā in her former births are found Mhv. II, 68—94; 166; the Kinnarī-J. pp. 94—115 is different from the Canda-k. J., but agrees in substance with Divy. 441 ff.; Bhadrak. XXIX; Avad. Kalp. LXIV.

6 In Bhadrak. XXXV Nanda and Nandika are sons to Dhautodana, a name which must be synonymous with Śuddhodana.

7 Cp. Tib. L. 265, where the bride is Sundarika; with ROCKHILL op. c. 55: Bhadrā. In the story of Ānanda's temptation with BIGANDET I, 187 J. K. is represented as the wife of Ānanda. The story itself recurs Tib. L. 267, but refers to Nanda; so, too, in

On the seventh day the mother of Rāhula, on seeing the Buddha enter the palace, said to her son: "Look, Rāhula, that monk there is thy father; go and ask thine inheritance". The boy went up to his father, and said: "Monk, give me my inheritance". But the Tathāgata, wishig to make Rāhula the heir of a spiritual inheritance, ordered Sāriputra to confer on the boy the novice ordination (*sāmaṇera-pabbajjā*). This was done, much to the spite of Śuddhodana, who complained of what had happened, and obtained from his son the boon that in the sequel no one should be ordained without the consent of the parents[1].

From Kapilavastu the Master returned to Rājagṛha, where he took his abode in the Śītavana[2].

After the depart of the Buddha, but before his arrival at Rājagṛha, whilst he was staying at Anupiya in the country of the Mallas, many conversions took place in Kapilavastu. The chief converts were Anuruddha, brother to Mahānāma, Bhaddiya, Ānanda, Bhagu, Kimbila and Devadatta. With the intention to become monks, these Śākian princes followed by Upāli the barber, went in the direction of Anupiya. At some distance from Kapilavastu they doffed their fine dresses and gave them to Upāli, who at first accepted them, but on afterthought resolved to follow the princes. As soon as they came into the presence of the Master, they asked admission into the Congregation, and, in order to curb their own pride, they requested that the barber should be first ordained. Their demand was granted[3].

At the time when the Lord was at the Śītavana, there came to Rājagṛha a wealthy merchant, Sudatta, surnamed Anāthapiṇḍika, from Śrāvastī. He heard from a friend in whose house he was lodging that the Lord Buddha had arisen, which moved him to go the next morning to the Śītavana. Then he heard the preaching of the Law and became a Srotaāpanna. On the following day he bestowed a great donation on the Saṅgha having the Buddha for its head, and invited them to come to Śrāvastī.

In order to prepare for a worthy reception, Anāthapiṇḍika returned to Śrāvastī, where he bought from the prince Jeta the Jetavana park for 18 Koṭis of goldpieces[4]. There he erected a splendid monastery, in the midst a private room (*gandhakuṭi*) for the Master, and all around separate dwellings for the senior monks, cells etc.

On the day when the Lord approached the city, he was received with great pomp, and, on entering the precincts of the monastery, he was asked by the merchant: "What, o Lord, shall I do with this Vihāra?" The reply was: "Give it to the Saṅgha present and future". And Anāthapiṇḍika, pouring water over the hands of the Buddha, pronounced the solemn formula of

---

HARDY's M. of B. p. 205. In Bhadrak. XXXV Sundara and Sundarānanda appear synonymous with Ānanda. The bride seems to be identical with the Janapada-Kalyāṇī Rūpa-Nandā Dhp. Comm. on vs. 150; cp. Therīg. vs. 82, and her history Par. Dīp. 80 ff.

1 MV. I, 54. Cp. Intr. Jāt. 91; Tib. L. 265.

2 P. Sītavana; Skr. also pleonastically Śītavana-śmaśāna, a cemetery, Divy. 264, 268; Tib. L. 258.

3 More amply told CV. VII, 1; Dhp. pp. 139 ff. Cp. HARDY M. of B. 227 ff. Tib. L. 264; 266; ROCKHILL op. c. 53 ff. Cp. Bhadrak. XXXV. From CV. VII, 2 it would appear that Buddha went from Anupiya to Kauśāmbī, but BIGANDET I, 183 agrees with the Tib. tradition. — The Skr. names are Aniruddha, Mahānāman, Bhadrika, Bhṛgu; Kimbila is wanting.

4 CV. VI, 4; Saṃy. N. I, p. 210; Intr. Jāt. p. 92; Bodhiv. p. 42; HARDY M. of B. 218; Tib. L. 258; ROCKHILL op. c. 47; BEAL SBE. XIX, 201 and 230. The N. form of the surname is Anāthapiṇḍada; in the Bharhut sculpture Pl. XXVIII and LVII Anadhapeḍika; for the inscription below the sculpture see CHILDERS in Academy of 1874, p. 586; 612.

donation. The Master accepted the gift with thanks and celebrated in stanzas the advantages of a monastery[1].

In those days Śrāvastī was the residence of Prasenajit (P. Pasenadi), king of Kosala, and brother in law to Bimbisāra[2]. There lived also a rich merchant, Migāra[3], whose son Pūrṇavardhana (Puṇṇavaddhana), became the husband of the virtuous Viśākhā[4], the daughter of Dhanamjaya and Sumanā from Bhaddiya in Aṅga-land[5]. When she was seven years of age, it happened that the Buddha visiting Bhaddiya, perceived her predisposition to become a convert. In course of time her family migrated to Sāketa, and from this place she went, at the age of sixteen, to Śrāvastī as the bride of Pūrṇavardhana. After her marriage she rendered signal services to Buddha and the Congregation; she was the means of converting her father-in-law, who previously was an adherent of the naked Jains, in consequence of which she was surnamed "the mother of Migāra". Another merit of hers was the erection of the monastery of Pūrvārāma (Pubbārāma) near Śrāvastī, which in splendour was inferior only to the Vihāra built by Anāthapiṇḍika. Though these occurrences must have taken place several years after the story of Anāthapiṇḍika they are here briefly alluded to[6].

6. ĀMRAPĀLĪ. JĪVAKA. BUDDHA'S JOURNEY TO VAIŚĀLĪ. DISPUTE BETWEEN ŚĀKYAS AND KOḶIYAS. DEATH OF ŚUDDHODANA. ADMISSION OF NUNS INTO THE ORDER. CONVERSION OF KHEMĀ.

Once upon a time, when the Tathāgata spent the rainy season near Rājagṛha, at the Kalandaka-nivāpa[7] in the Bambu grove — it may have been the second or third retreat or later — it came to the notice of Bimbisāra that there was in Vaiśālī a famous courtezan, named Āmrapālī (Ambapālī, Ambapālikā[8]). Being jealous of that city and wishing to emulate with it, he resolved to produce in his own kingdom some courtezan who in accomplishments would be superior to Āmrapālī. Such a person was found in the girl Sālavatī. After some time she became pregnant by Abhaya, the son of the King. She was delivered of a boy, who according to the custom of courtezans was exposed, but accidentally the Prince discovered the infant, and though unaware that it was his own son, he took the boy to the palace, called him Jīvaka, and gave him a careful education[9].

[1] The same stanzas, according to CV. VI, 1, were uttered on another occasion, at the donation of 60 Vihāras by a merchant of Rājagṛha.

[2] A sculpture referring to Prasenajit in Bharhut Pl. XIII; cp. CUNNINGHAM p. 90.

[3] Skr. Mṛgāra; Divy. 44; 77; wrongly Mṛgadhara Tib. L. 270.

[4] In Dsanglun Chap. 28 she is named Anurādhā, the asterism following on Viśākhā; Tib. L. l. c.

[5] The name of the place is Bhadramkara in Divy. 123 ff. The father of Dhanamjaya, Meṇḍaka, also excelled in virtue, as in fact the whole family. For the story of Meṇḍaka or Meṇḍhaka see MV. VI, 34; Divy. l. c.

[6] For a fuller account see Dhp. pp. 230 ff. MV. VIII, 15; Divy. 44, 77, 466; HARDY M. of B. 220 ff. Tib. L. 270; ROCKHILL op. c. 70 ff. More references in ED. MÜLLER's Glossary (JPTS of 1888) s. vv. Migāramātā and Visākhā.

[7] The N. Kalandaka-nivāpa, e. g. Divy. 262; and Kalandaka-nivāsa.

[8] Her history and prehistory is told in Par. Dīp. 207 ff., commenting the highly poetical stanzas ascribed to her, Therīg. vv. 252—270. Cp. ROCKHILL op. c. 64; Tib. L. 253, where she is represented as the mother of Prince Abhaya by Bimbisāra. In Pāli sources, the Comm. on Therag. vs. 64, and Par. Dīp. 207, she has a son, the Thera Vimala-Koṇḍañña by Bimbisāra; in the former passage her name is indicated by the conundrum Dumavhayā, the king's by Paṇḍaraketu. Abhaya's conversion told Majjh. N. Nr. 58.

[9] The story of Jīvaka is told MV. VIII, 1; Majjh. N. I, pp. 368 ff. Cp. ROCKHILL l. c. and Tib. L. 253, where J. is the son of Bimbisāra, procreated in adultery.

When Jīvaka, surnamed Komārabhacca[1] had reached the years of discretion, he went to Takṣaśilā to study medicine under a renowned professor. After seven years of study he was perfectly skilled in the art and dismissed as such by his teacher. In course of time the young physician had occasion to show his eminent skill; he cured — not to speak of other cases — Pradyota the Cruel, King of Ujjayinī, as well as Bimbisāra, who appointed him to his physician in ordinary.

On a certain day the Buddha happened to be troubled with constipation. Jīvaka was called and by applying a most delicate purgative succeeded in healing within short the Lord from his disease[2].

It was not only by this happy cure that Jīvaka rendered himself useful to the Master; he presented him also two magnificent pieces of cloth he had received from Pradyota in acknowledgment of his medical services. The Lord accepted this gift, and, assembling the monks, gave them permission to wear a dress presented by laymen, but also, if they pleased, a cloth of rags[3].

During his stay in the Bambu grove in the third rainy season, the Lord received a deputation from the Vaiśālians, imploring him to deliver them from a frightful pestilence which desolated their country. In vain they had sought relief by recurring to the 6 heretical teachers[4], and now they besought the Buddha to save them. The Master willingly acceded to their demand, and proceeded on a road, prepared by order of the King, to the Southern bank of the Ganges. On the Northern side of the river he was most respectfully received by the Licchavi nobles. No sooner had he set foot in the country, than the malign spirits that caused the disease fled away and the sick were restored to health. Having entered the city, the Tathāgata uttered the Ratana-sutta[5] and made numberless converts. After receiving many pious gifts he returned to Rājagṛha[6].

Three consecutive rainy seasons were spent by the Lord in the Bambu grove; in the fifth he sojourned near Vaiśālī in the Kūṭāgāra hall of the Mahāvana[7]. In that period there arose a dispute between the Śākyas and the Koḷiyas about the water of the river Rohiṇī, which owing to an unusual drought was not sufficient to irrigate the fields on both sides of the river. The quarrel rose high, and a battle would have ensued, had not the Buddha, perceiving by his divine eye what was going on, hastened through the sky

---

1 This answers to a Skr. Kaumārabhṛtya, but in Divy. 270 and 506 modified to Kumārabhūta. Komārabhaṇḍa, occasionally occurring in P. texts, looks like a misread Komārabhacca. ROCKHILL's rendering of Tib. *Gdzon-nus-gsos* l. c. is quite fanciful; the words clearly point to "therapeutics of children", i. e. Kaumārabhṛtya; see JÄSCHKE Tib. Engl. Dict. s. vv.

2 Albeit the Lord had conquered death and disease by his having eradicated their ultimate cause, viz. *avidyā*, the consequences of his former *karman* were not completely destroyed. Hence he was liable to human infirmities.

3 According to HARDY M. of B. 249, these things occurred in the twentieth year.

4 More about these worthies anon.

5 The visit to Vaiśālī is told more circumstantially and with some variations in Mhv. I, 253; HARDY M. of B. 236; cp. Tib. L. 285, where the event is placed much later, in the reign of Ajātaśatru. — The Ratana-Sutta (ed. CHILDERS, JRAS of 1870, p. 318; FRANKFURTER, Handb. 85) has its counterpart in Mhv. I, 290 ff (Svastyayana-Gāthā).

6 Among the donations mention is made Mhv. l. c. of the Salavana. It was presented by Gośṛṅgī, who had sent a parrot to invite Buddha to dinner; the same is told Tib. L. l. c. of Āmrapālī.

7 The succession of places where B. is said to have spent the Retreat is differently given; we follow the order in BIGANDET. A really historical chronology is out of question. — Mahāvana is characterized in BIGANDET I, 204 as a forest of Sāltrees; thus it appears to be identical with Sālavana, the donation of Gośṛṅgī.

to the place where the parties stood ready to fight, and moved them to lay down the arms. The eloquent discourse which he delivered at that occasion had the effect that he made many converts[1].

A short time after the event the Buddha got the notice that his father was seriously ill. Without delay he flew with some of his followers through the sky to Kapilavastu. Having come into the presence of the patient, he preached to him the instability of all things, so that Śuddhodana reached the fourth stage, that of Arhatship, and, paying for the third time in his life homage to his son, he entered Nirvāṇa.

After the death of her husband, the Matron Gautamī[2] desired to forsake the world and embrace a religious life. Therefore she went to the Lord, who was then sojourning in the Banyan garden, and asked to become a nun. But the Buddha refused, because he would not admit females into the Order, and returned to Vaiśālī.

Far from giving up her design, the widowed Queen and many other ladies cut their hair, put on yellow robes and went on foot to Vaiśālī. When these ladies, covered with dust, with swollen feet, and bathed in tears arrived at the Kūṭāgāra hall, they were seen by Ānanda, who, having ascertained the object of their journey, went to the Master and pleaded in their favour. At first the Buddha was unwilling to admit women into the Congregation; at last, however, at the instances of Ānanda, who remembered him of the motherly care of Gautamī, he gave his consent, but on the condition that the Matron should submit to 8 duties of subordination (*garudhamma*). Gautamī gladly promised to keep those duties[3], whereupon she with all the other ladies became nuns.

Although the Master thus had ceded to the entreaties of Ānanda, he was fully aware of the dangerous consequences attending on the admission of women. "If no women had been admitted into the Order", said he to Ānanda, "the Good Law would stand 1000 years, but now chastity and holiness will not last long, and the Law will only stand 500 years". His misgivings proved true by the subsequent events: the ladies, even Gautamī, were now and then fretful, and some time afterwards, when the Lord sojourned at Śrāvastī, some nuns moved the indignation of the public by their scandalous behaviour[4].

From Vaiśālī the Tathāgata went to Śrāvastī, where he spent the 6th rainy season. At the end of the Retreat he removed to Rājagṛha. Whilst he was staying in the Bambu grove happened the conversion of Khemā, wife to Bimbisāra. In the pride of her beauty she had never deigned to see the Lord, but on a certain day, when she was taking her recreation in the Bambu grove, she was brought by a contrivance of the King into the presence of the Master, who, to cure her from her vanity, produced by his miraculous power a female beautiful as a Nymph from heaven. While she was gazing on that apparition, he made it pass through the stages of youth, middle age, old age, and death. By that frightful sight Khemā was prepared to hear the lessons of the Master, and on hearing him utter some stanzas[5] she at once

---

[1] Dhp. p. 351; Jāt. V, p. 412. Cp. HARDY M. of B. 307.

[2] For details concerning G. see ED. MÜLLER in Par. Dīp. p. XI.

[3] As to those duties and the whole story of the admission of G. see CV. X, 1; cp. HARDY E. M. p. 157; M. of B. 312; ROCKHILL op. c. 61. The institution of the Order of nuns took place in the 7th year according Tib. L. 268, nearly agreeing with the chronology in BIGANDET.

[4] Instances of indecent conduct are related CV. X, 9—27.

[5] Par. Dīp. p. 133, vss. 66—70; cp. Dhp. vs. 347.

attained the first stage, or as others say, Arhatship[1]. Before her Arhatship she was tempted by Māra, but she happily overcame the temptation[2].

7. THE HERETICAL TEACHERS CONFOUNDED. BUDDHA GOES TO HEAVEN AND EXPOUNDS THE ABHIDHARMA TO MĀYĀ. DESCENT AT SĀṂKĀŚYA. CIÑCĀ. DISSENSION IN THE CONGREGATION. BUDDHA'S STAY IN THE WILDERNESS. RETURN. PARABLE OF THE LABOURER. FURTHER EVENTS. PUNISHMENT OF SUPRABUDDHA.

Among the opponents of the Lord stood foremost six chiefs of heretical sects (Tīrthikas, Tīrthyas, P. Titthiyas) to wit: Pūraṇa Kassapa, Makkhali Gosāla, Ajita Kesakambalin, Pakudha Kaccāyana, Nigaṇṭha Nātaputta, and Sañjaya Belaṭṭhiputta[3]. Each of these teachers had numerous adherents, which did not prevent them from being jealous of the success of the Lord — the Śramaṇa Gautama, as they were went to call him —, and everywhere, oft by foul means, they tried to thwart him. One of them, Sañjaya had been the teacher of Śāriputra and Maudgalyāyana before they became disciples of the Buddha. Both he and the other Tīrthikas had proved powerless against the pestilence in the country of Vaiśālī, so miraculously removed by Buddha.

During the stay of the Lord near Rājagṛha it happened that a wealthy merchant of that place came in possession of a piece of sandal wood[4]. He had a bowl carved out of that piece, put it in a balance, and raising it to the top of a series of bambus he said: "If any Śramaṇa or Brahman be possessed of miraculous faculty, let him take down the bowl". The 6 heretics, conscious of their lack of miraculous faculty, went in succession to the merchant and tried to get from him the bowl, but he refused. At that time Maudgalyāyana and Piṇḍola-Bhāradvāja saw the bowl and incited each other to fetch it down. Then Piṇḍola-Bhāradvāja[5] rose up into the sky, took the bowl and moved thrice round the city, to the astonishment of the public. When it came to the notice of the Lord what had happened, he rebuked P. Bhāradvāja for such a display of superhuman power for the sake of a paltry wooden bowl. "This will not conduce", said he, "either to the conversion of the unconverted, or to the advantage of the converted". And he prohibited the monks in the sequel to display before the laity their superhuman power of working miracles. This prohibition did not imply that the Lord himself should refrain from working miracles, nor that his disciples were bound, under all circumstances, not to display their superhuman faculty. Very soon it would

[1] Par. Dīp. p. 126 ff. with the quotation from Apadāna there; cp. Dhp. p. 412.

[2] See the beautiful verses Therīg. 139 ff. Saṃy. N. V, 4, 2 ff.; cp. CAROLINE FOLEY, Women Leaders of the Buddhist Reformation, p. 3—10. The same story of conversion is told of Nandā; see above p. 28. Apparently another person is Kṣemā, daughter to Prasenajit, in Avad. Śat. VIII, 9.

[3] In N. writings, Divy. XII and Mhv. I, 253, the names are Pūraṇa-Kāśyapa or Kāśyapa Pūraṇa, Maskarin Gośālīputra, Ajita Keśakambala, Kakuda Kātyāyana, Nirgrantha Jñātiputra, and Sañjayin Vairaṭṭīputra. Their tenets are described in Sāmaññaphala-S. (Dīgh. N. I, Nr. 2; transl. BURNOUF, Lotus p. 448); cp. ROCKHILL op. c. p. 99 ff., in the Chinese version by Bunyiu Nanjio there p. 255; on Gosāla Maṅkhaliputta's doctrine viewed from the Jaina standpoint, see LEUMANN there p. 249.

[4] CV. V, 8; transl. SBE. XX, 78. Cp. ROCKHILL op. c. 69, where the man's name is Jyotiṣka, probably the Jotiya of Dhp. p. 231.

[5] This person was still living in the last years of Aśoka's reign, according to Divy. p. 399.

appear that in order to confound the obstinate Tīrthikas, a grand display of miraculous power by the Lord would be required.

The heretics, finding no encouragement for their tricks from Bimbisāra, went to the King Prasenajit in Śrāvastī, in the hope there to be more successful[1]. The Buddha, knowing what was going on, and remembering that Śrāvastī was the very place where all former Buddhas had shown their greatest miracle, travelled to that capital and took his abode in the Jetavana. A few days after his arrival the great show would be performed in the presence of Prasenajit, the six Tīrthikas, and an immense crowd. The Master created in the sky an immense road from the Eastern to the Western horizon, and after ascending it he began performing a series of inimitable wonders; first appeared a reddish gleam, then a flood of light, glittering as gold, which spread over the whole world — phenomena similar to those which the world saw when he took possession of the seat of Enlightenment. From his elevated place he preached the Law to mortals, and the people who heard him came to understand the four Axioms.

The six heretical teachers were confounded, and quite powerless, so that the Lord in full justice could declare: "The fire-fly shineth as long as the Sun doeth not shine, but as soon as the great luminary hath risen, the worm is overpowered by the rays and shineth no more"[2]. An attempt of Pūraṇa-Kāśyapa to annul the effects of the Lord's miracles and teaching was utterly unsuccessful, and in despair he tied a large jar to his neck, threw himself into the river, was drowned, and went, as he deserved, to the lowest of hells, Avīci.

It is a fixed law that all Buddhas after performing their great miracle resort to the heaven of the 33 gods. After producing a shadowy likeness of himself, the Tathāgata vanished, and went to heaven, in order to expound the Abhidharma to his mother Māyā[3]. Since every day he had to go his begging round on earth, he created a likeness of himself, that had to continue the teaching of the Abhidharma during his own temporary absence.

During three months the Lord stayed in heaven. When he was about to descend, Sakra ordered Viśvakarman to construct a triple ladder, the foot of which was put near the town of Sāṃkāśya (P. Saṅkissa). Flanked by Brahma on the right, and by Śakra on the left, the Tathāgata descended, and came down near Sāṃkāśya, on the spot where all Buddhas set their feet when descending from heaven. A celebrated shrine has been erected on that very spot[4].

From Sāṃkāśya the Buddha went to the Jetavana near Śrāvastī. The Tīrthikas, more angry than ever at his increasing fame and the loss of their own profits, now tried to obtain by slander what they could not effect by fair means. For that purpose they induced a young woman, Ciñcā[5] by name, who was a lay devotee of their sect, to accuse the Sramaṇa Gautama of having had carnal intercourse with her. The wily woman succeeded, by feigned visits to the Jetavana, to arouse the suspicion of the public, and contrived a means to assume the appearance of a person in a state of pregnancy.

1 Divy. XII; (transl. BURNOUF Intr. pp. 162 ff.); cp. ROCKHILL op. c. 79; BIGANDET I, 216 ff.

2 Cp. the expression Dhp. p. 338: Titthiyā suriyuggame khajjopanakasadisā ahesum.

3 BIGANDET I, 221 ff. Cp. Tib. L. 272.

4 BIGANDET I, 225 ff.; Divy. 401; Tib. L. 273; ROCKHILL op. c. 81; Fa Hian, Rec. pp. 47 ff.; Voy. II, 237 ff. The ladder is represented at Bharhut Pl. XVII, central compartment.

5 Ciñca-Māṇavikā.

In the ninth month she rendered herself at evening time to the place where the Master was in the act of preaching. There, in the presence of the assembly, she accused the Buddha of being the cause of her pregnancy, and required that he should provide a place for her approaching confinement.

The Tathāgata, interrupted in his teaching, answered with a roaring voice: "Sister, whether thy words be true or not true, nobody knows but myself, and thou". And in that very moment, lo! Śakra followed by four angels who were transformed into young mice came to the spot. The mice gnawed through the strings by which the wooden globe designed to give the appearance of pregnancy was fastened, and so the globe fell to the ground, crushing the feet of the wicked Ciñcā. Hooted at and pursued by the indignant people, she at once disappeared in the midst of flames rising from the depth of the earth, and descended to the bottom of the hell Avīci[1].

The eighth Retreat was held at the Crocodile-hill[2] in the Deerpark of the Bhesakalā-forest in the Bharga country[3]. At that time the Prince Bodhi, having just finished the palace Kokanada, sent a young Brahman to invite the Master with the disciples to dinner. The invitation being accepted, the palace was spread over with white cloth down to the last row of steps, and the Prince went out to meet his guest. The Buddha came near, but stopped at the lowest step and refused to proceed farther. He cast a significant glance at Ānanda, and the latter said to the Prince: "Let this cloth be removed, Prince. The Lord will not tread on a strip of cloth, for he has compassion on the meanest thing". Then the cloth was removed, the Tathāgata went up to the palace, and sat down to partake of dinner with his followers. After finishing his meal, he edified the assembly by a discourse, and lay down the rule that the monks were forbidden to tread on cloth. — From Bharga country the Buddha set out for Śrāvastī[4].

According to a S. tradition[5], the Lord spent the ninth Retreat at Kauśāmbī, in the Ghositārāma[6]. During his stay in this place there arose deplorable dissensions among the brethren. One of the monks had infringed unintentionally a point of discipline, and was therefore accused by another. The former protested. Some brethren took the part of the defendant, others that of the accuser, and the dispute became more and more vehement. The Master tried repeatedly to allay the strife; he told the beautiful story of

---

[1] Dhp. p. 338; Jât. IV, p. 187. Fa Hian, Rec. p. 60. Cp. FEER JA of 1895, pp. 200 ff.

[2] Śiṃśumāra-giri, P. Sumsumāra-gira. *Sumsumāra* is given as an equivalent of *kumbhīla*, and the corresponding word in Skr. is decidedly *not* Delphinus Gangeticus in Suśruta I, 205, for the animal has feet.

[3] Tib. L. 316 has for Bhesakalā "the Deerpark of the Yakṣa Bhayaṃkara"; and for Pāli Bhagga wrongly Vagga. — In BIGANDET the 8th Retreat immediately follows on the abode in Śrāvastī, but CV. V, 21 the B. comes from Vaiśālī.

[4] CV. V, 22.

[5] BIGANDET I, 234.

[6] I. e. Ghoṣita's garden. Ghoṣita, in N. texts also Ghoṣila, is one of the three ministers of Udayana (P. Udena), King of the Vatsa country, in the capital Kauśāmbī (Kosambi). Udayana is a popular personage in Indian fable lore. As to the Buddhist version of his story see Dhp. pp. 155 ff.; Divy. pp. 528 ff.; Tib. L. 269, 276; his three wives were Sāmavatī, Vāsuladattā, and Māgandiyā or °ndikā, N. Śyāmavatī, Anupamā (apparently = S. Māgandiyā), the daughter of the heterodox Makandika, and, as known from other sources, Vāsavadattā. It was Ghoṣita who presented the garden to Buddha. Dhp. p. 167; Fa Hian, Rec. p. 96, where LEGGE's Ghochira should be Ghoṣila; cp. BEAL SBE. XIX, 245. The name of the garden in N. sources is usually Ghoṣāvatārāma; Tib. L. 276, 316. — Concerning the unbeliever Māgandiya see Mil. P. 313; Majjh. N. I, 502 ff.; Dhp. 162; S. Nip. p. 157.

Dīghāvu, the son of Dīghīti, King of Kosala[1], but all his wisdom and kind remonstrances were in vain. At last disgusted with such a state of things, and judging that good counsels would be squandered on such fools, he left their company, but not before uttering in the midst of the assembly some suitable stanzas[2]. Thereupon he repaired to the village of Bālakaloṇakāra, with the intention to devote himself to a hermit's life. After a meeting with the venerable Bhagu he proceeded to the Eastern Bambu park (Pācīna-Vaṃsadāya), where Anuruddha, Nandiya and Kimbila were living in the most perfect unity and concord. They cordially welcomed their Master, who gladdened them with a sermon, and then went farther to Pārileyyaka. There, dwelling in the Rakkhita grove, at the foot of a Bhadrasāla tree, he felt all the happiness of a solitary life.

Near that place, there lived a noble elephant who had experienced much inconvenience from the herd of elephants in his train. Therefore he had left the herd and came to Pārileyyaka. He approached the Lord, provided him with food and drink, and enjoyed his calm life, now that he lived remote from the crowd of elephants which had given him so much trouble. The Buddha fully understood the feelings of the animal, and gave vent to his feeling of sympathy in a stanza[3].

After dwelling for sometime at Pārileyyaka, the Lord went to Śrāvastī. In the meanwhile the seditious monks of Kauśāmbī had received such signal marks of disrespect from the laity in that city, that they resolved upon going to Śrāvastī to have the question settled before the Master. Both contending parties having arrived at Śrāvastī laid the case anew before the Lord, who by pronouncing a lawful decision restored the concord in the Saṅgha[4].

During the eleventh Retreat the Tathāgata sojourned near Rājagṛha. One day, when he was in the district of the Southern hills (Dakkhiṇāgiri) at the village of Ekanālā, he saw the Brahman Bhāradvāja superintending the labourers in his fields[5]. On perceiving the Buddha, the Brahman said: "O Śramaṇa, I plough and sow, and by doing so find my subsistance. Do thou also plough and sow to live upon". The Lord replied: "I, too, O Brahman, plough and sow, and by doing so find my food". The Brahman, surprised at that answer, said: "I do not see, reverend Gautama, that you have a yoke, ploughshare, goad or bullocks. How can you then say that you, too, are a labourer?" Then the Lord said: "Faith is the seed I sow; devotion is the rain; modesty is the ploughshaft; the mind is the tie of the yoke; mindfulness is my ploughshare and goad. Truthfulness is the means to bind; tenderness, to untie. Energy is my team and bullock, leading to safety and proceeding without backsliding to the place where there is no sorrow".

The Brahman was so much impressed by the parable that he became a convert and made profession of faith.

---

1 MV. X, 2; Jāt. III, 212, 489; Dhp. pp. 104 ff.

2 MV. X, 3; cp. Dhp. vv. 3—6; 328—330; S. Nip. Khaggavisāṇa-S. vv. 11, 12. Cp. the Khadgaviṣāṇa Gathās Mhv. I, 357—359.

3 A detailed account of the dissensions in Kauśāmbī is contained in MV. X, 1—4; Dhp. pp. 103 ff. Cp. Jāt. III, p. 489. The Pārileya elephant is made mention of in Jāt. Mālā XIX, 36.

4 MV. X, 5; an account with some traits wanting in MV. occurs Dhp. p. 107, agreeing with BIGANDET I, 236.

5 Sam. N. VII, 2, 1, and with some variations S. Nip. No. 4; cp. Prof. RHYS DAVIDS, B. p. 134.

In the twelfth rainy season the Lord stayed near the town of Verañjā[1]. A certain Brahman there came to visit him and became a believer. On the invitation of the Brahman Buddha spent at Verañjā the whole season, at the end of which period he took leave of the hospitable convert, and travelled all over the country as far as Soreyya near Takṣaśilā; thence to Sāṃkāśya, Kanauj, Prayāga, where he crossed the Ganges, directing himself to Benares. From this city he travelled to Vaiśālī, where he took his abode in the Kūṭāgāra hall[2].

The thirteenth Retreat was held in Śrāvastī and Cālikā; the following rainy season was spent in the Jetavana[3], where Rāhula, then 20 years old, received the Upasampadā Ordination. In the same year the Master visited Kapilavastu.

During his stay in the Banyan garden he had to endure a grave insult from his father-in-law, Suprabuddha[4]. One day as the latter was informed that the Tathāgata was about to go his begging round in a certain quarter of the town, he went out, after intoxicating himself with liquor, planted himself in the middle of the street, barring the passage to the Buddha and vilely abusing him. The Master, quietly glancing at Ānanda, uttered the prediction that in a week Suprabuddha should be swallowed alive by the earth. Suprabuddha laughed at that prediction, and imagined that he might easily avoid his doom by remaining during a week in the tower of his palace, but he should experience that no place on earth can afford shelter to the author of a wicked deed[5]. On the fatal day the earth burst open under his feet, and he sunk in the abyss down to the bottom of the Avīci hell as a punishment for his wickedness[6].

8. THE YAKṢA OF ĀḶAVĪ. APPOINTMENT OF ĀNANDA. CONVERSION OF AṄGULIMĀLA. MURDER OF SUNDARĪ. ANĀTHAPIṆḌIKA'S DAUGHTER.

The Lord returned from Kapilavastu to the Jetavana monastery[7]. Hence he proceeded to Āḷavī, where he succeeded in converting a cruel Yakṣa who was in the habit of devouring the children of that place. When the Buddha came in his presence, the monster received him with contempt and threats, but gradually overcome by the meekness and patience of the Master, he felt softer feelings spring up in his breast, and at last he said: "I will ask you, Śramaṇa, some questions. If you are not able to solve them, I shall tear out your heart or fling you into the Ganges". The Lord quietly allowed

1 In Skr. the town is called Vairantī; Vairantya, P. Verañjo, being the Adj. Vairantās, in plur., is the name of the people and country in Avad. K. L., 27.

2 S. Vibh. I, 1; 4.

3 Thus BIGANDET I, 240. In N. traditions Buddha spent the 12th rainy season in the Pūrvārāma; the 13th in the Jetavana; the 14th in the Śiṃśapā grove near Naḍikā; Tib. L. 315.

4 So HARDY M. of B. p. 152 and p. 339, but, curiously enough, he is called p. 134 the father of Māyā, just as in Tib. L. p. 234.

5 Dhp. vs. 128.

6 Suprabuddha was one of the five persons thus punished for a heinous crime against the Buddha or against one of the latter's disciples, the four others being Devadatta, the youth Nanda, the Yakṣa Nandaka, and Ciñcā; Mil. P. 101.

7 It is perhaps to this period that we should refer the conversion of the Brahman Pokkharasādi, in N. texts wrongly sanskritized to Puṣkarasārin, instead of Pauṣkarasādi. See Ambaṭṭha-S. and Tevijja-S. (Dīgh. N. III and XIII); S. Nip. p. 112; cp. ROCKHILL op. c. 82 and especially the interesting Śārdūlāvadāna in Divy. pp. 611–659; BURNOUF Intr. 205 ff.

the Yakṣa to put the questions and immediately solved them to the satisfaction of the enquirer, who became a believer and mended his life[1]. Afterwards on the spot of that conversion a monastery was erected[2].

From Āḷavī the Master went to Rājagṛha, where he spent the 17th rainy season in the Bambu grove. The time of Retreat being over, he resumed his preaching all over the country, and came, after a short stay at Śrāvastī, again to Āḷavī. The 18th season was spent on a hill near Cālikā; the following again in the Bambu grove; the 20th in the Jetavana[3]. It was in this year that Ānanda was appointed as the Lord's waiter[4]. Another event of importance in that period was the conversion of Aṅgulimāla or Aṅgulimālaka, a famous robber and murderer in Kosala. Undaunted by all evil reports, the Buddha went to the abode of the robber in the forest, and by his equanimity succeeded in conquering the fierceness of the cruel Aṅgulimāla, who not only became a convert, but in a short time attained Arhatship, much to the wonder of the brethren[5]. The Master, however, showed them how Aṅgulimāla by eradicating his sinful propensities had so rapidly reached perfection.

During the stay of the Lord in the Jetavana another attempt was made by his heretical opponents to blacken his reputation. They hired some bravoes to murder the nun Sundarī. The crime was perpetrated, and the body of Sundarī thrown into a thicket near the Jetavana monastery. When the corpse had been found, the Tīrthikas intimated that no other but Gautama could be the author of the crime, but by an accident the real culprits were found out, and the heretics put to shame[6].

About that time the pious Anāthapiṇḍika gave his daughter[7] in marriage to the son of a friend of his in Aṅga. As that friend was an adherent of the naked ascetics, Anāthapiṇḍika, fearing lest his daughter would be shaken in her convictions, gave her a retinue of female attendants to support her in the true faith. When the young wife had come to her new home, she was required by her father-in-law to pay her respects to the naked ascetics. Disgusted at the sight of these heretics, the young woman refused even to look at them, which much exasperated her father-in-law, but by keeping firm and by continually extolling the glorious virtues of the Buddha and the Saṅgha, she excited in her mother-in-law and other ladies of the town the eager desire to see the Lord and to hear him preach the Law.

The Lord, who in the early morning surveys with his allseeing eye the whole of Jambudvīpa, perceived what was happening in Aṅga land. At once

1 For these questions and answers see Samy. N. X, 12; S. Nip. I, 10. Cp. the account in BIGANDET I, 246, and the variation in HARDY M. of B. 261 ff.

2 Āḷavī is the Skr. Āṭavī, and undoubtedly the place designated as the "Wood-village" in Tib. L. 315, with a monastery where B. is said to have spent the 29th rainy season. It was situated between Kosala and Magadha. The monastery may be identified with the Aggāḷava Shrine near Āḷavī, Samy. N. VIII and CN. VI, 17, cp. 21, where we read that the Lord went from Āḷavī to Rājagṛha.

3 BIGANDET I, 248 ff.

4 P. *upaṭṭhāka*, in Skr. Buddhist writings *upasthāyaka;* in other works *upasthāyin*, *upasthāyika*, *upasthātar*. Cp. ROCKHILL op. c. 88.

5 A more detailed account in BIGANDET I, 254; HARDY M. of B. 249 ff. Cp. Dhp. 147; 337; 434; Mil. P. 410. The story of A. has so many traits in common with the Āḷavaka Yakṣa's that it is not strange to see how Tib. L. 315 ascribes to Aṅgulimāla — this must be meant by the Tib. *Lag-rgyud* "Handreihe" — the erection of a monastery at Āṭavī.

6 Ud. p. 43; Avad. K. L., 26, 70, where she is termed a *parivrājikā*. To her are ascribed Therīg. vv. 312—337; her history Par. Dīp. 228 ff.

7 Two daughters of his, Subhadda the Great, and S. the Little, are mentioned Intr. Jāt. p. 93.

he flew in the company of 500 disciples through the sky and alighted in the courtyard of the merchant's house. All the inmates rejoiced to behold the Master and his disciples. Attentively they listened to his preaching, and the whole family along with many other people became converts. After leaving Anuruddha in Aṅga to complete the work of conversion, the Buddha reverted to Śrāvastī[1].

After the narrative of the occurrences in the 20th rainy season there is in the history of the Master "an almost complete blank"[2]. For a period of 23 years a summary of the Buddha's proceedings is wanting, although various incidents may be held to fall within that period. In the Tibetan Life of Śākyamuni there is something like a chronological arrangement of events, but not a few of them belong, according to the Southern compilations, to earlier years.

9. DEVADATTA AND AJĀTAŚATRU. CONVERSION OF AJĀTAŚATRU. DESTRUCTION OF THE ŚĀKYAS.

A new period of stirring events, — whatever may be thought of their historical character — may be said to date from the death of Bimbisāra and the accession to the throne of his parricidal son Ajātaśatru. This took place when the Buddha had reached the age of 72 years.

Already long before that epoch enmity had sprung up in the breast of Devadatta against the Lord, whose growing fame and influence filled him with jealousy[3]. By his supernatural power he won the favour of the Prince royal, Ajātaśatru, and by that mighty protection he hoped one day to become the leader of the Congregation of monks.

Some time afterwards, when the Lord, sojourning in the Bambu grove, was preaching the Law, Devadatta rose from his seat, and reverentially made the proposal that the Lord, on account of his age, should leave the leadership of the Congregation of monks to him, Devadatta[4]. But on this request he received, three times over, a flat refusal. From that moment Devadatta harboured evil designs against the Lord.

In consequence of what had happened, the Master ordered the monks that Devadatta should be publicly denounced as one who had proved false, and whose words and deeds were not to be recognized as issuing from the Buddha, the Law, or the Congregation.

The act of denunciation was carried out by Śāriputra, accompanied by a number of monks. The exasperated Devadatta went to Ajātaśatru Vaidehīputra and incited him to kill Bimbisāra. "Do you kill your father, and become king", said he, "and I will kill the Lord and become Buddha". The Prince lent the ear to the instigation of the traitor, and was about to carry his murderous plan into effect, when he was detected and brought before

1 A remarkable Northern version of the story, in which Anāthapiṇḍika's daughter is named Sumāgadhā, occurs in Tib. L. 283.

2 BIGANDET I, 260.

3 For a fuller account of the growing enmity of Devadatta, his wicked deeds and punishment, we refer the reader to CV. VII, 1—4; Dhp. pp. 139 ff. HARDY M. of B. 318 ff. Tib. L. 278; cp. ROCKHILL op. c. 83 ff. BEAL, SBE. XIX, 246 ff. Cp. also Saṃy. N. I, p. 154; Aṅg. N. II, p. 73 = CV. VII, 2. 5.

4 This happened according to Tib. L. 278 in the 25th rainy season. The reason adduced by D. that the Buddha was so old, is significant, as he himself was of the same age. *Sapienti sat.*

the King, who magnanimously abdicated and gave over the kingdom to Ajātaśatru[1].

Then Devadatta went to Ajātaśatru to secure for himself the Prince's support in his design to deprive Gautama of life. Having got the consent of the ruler, the traitor hired 16 men to murder the Buddha. But when the bravoes saw the Lord, they felt themselves so overawed that they fell at his feet, confessed their sinful intention and became converts. One man returned to Devadatta and declared that it was impossible to deprive the Lord of life. Devadatta now took to another means to accomplish his criminal design. He watched the moment when the Lord was walking in the shade below the Gṛdhrakūṭa mountain and hurled down a large piece of rock to crush his enemy. But two mountain peaks came together and stopped that rock, so that only a splinter caused the Lord's foot to bleed. Then the Master, looking up, said to Devadatta: "Foolish man! great is the demerit you have produced for yourself", and to the monks: "Devadatta has here committed one of the deadly sins that bring with them immediate retribution"[2].

When the monks heard of the nefarious attempt of Devadatta, they were much affected and made loud recitations to protect the Lord, but he allayed their fears, saying: "It is impossible that one should deprive the Tathāgata of life by violence. The Tathāgatas reach extinction in due and natural course".

A last attempt on the Lord's life was made by Devadatta by means of the elephant Nālāgiri, whom they maddened and then let loose in the carriage road of Rājagṛha. No sooner had the infuriated animal come into the presence of the Lord, than he was pervaded by a sense of benevolence issuing from the Buddha, and lowered his trunk. Some edifying words of the Master were sufficient to wholly subdue the elephant, that took up the dust from off the Lord's feet, sprinkled it over his head and quietly retired[3].

After these events Devadatta made an attempt to stir up discord in the Saṅgha[4]. He persuaded Kokālika, Kaṭamoraka-tissaka, Khaṇḍadevī-putta, and Samuddadatta[5] to go with him to the Buddha in order to request that a life of more severe ascetism should be prescribed for all members of the Congregation, viz. to live as hermits in the woods; to beg lifelong for food, without ever accepting an invitation; to clothe themselves in cast off rags; to dwell at the foot of trees; to abstain from fish and meat. The Master refused to accede to these demands, and declared that he left liberty to those who wished to live in such a manner, but that he would not make those rules obligatory for all monks.

Devadatta, who had expected this refusal, made it a pretext for agitating against the Lord. He gained over to his party 500 Vṛjian monks from Vaiśālī, who having recently entered the Congregation, were ignorant of the

---

1 We know from other sources that Bimbisāra was murdered by Ajātaśatru; Dīgh. N. I, p. 85; Divy. p. 280; HARDY M. of B. p. 318; Tib. L. 284; ROCKHILL op. c. 89—91.

2 *Ānantariya-* or *ānantarika-kamma*, coinciding with five of the six *abhiṭhānas*. They are *mātughāta*, *pitugh.*, *arahatagh.*, *lohituppāda*, and *saṅghabheda*; S. Nip. p. 40; cp. CHILDERS s. vv. *pañcānantariyakammaṃ* and *abhiṭhānaṃ*. The corresponding Skr. terms of the 5 Anantaryāni are given Vyu. § 122; WASSILIEF B. 240 has Ānantarīya. — Any one guilty of such a crime, should not be ordained, and, if he is a monk, be expelled; MV. I, 64—67.

3 Cp. ROCKHILL op. c. 93; BEAL SBE. XIX, 247.

4 Saṅghabheda. The tale — supposing it has an historical basis — is misplaced, since all connection between Devadatta and the Master was broken off.

5 Evidently the same as the 5 Śākyas Kokālika, Katamoraga, Tiṣya, Khaṇḍadravya, and Sāgaradatta of Tib, L. 266. Whether Khaṇḍadevīputta is identical with Khaṇḍadeva in Saṃy. N. I, 5, 10; II, 3, 4, is not clear.

rules, and thus he created a schism. After he had gone with these followers to the Gayāśīrṣa hill, it happened that he was preaching and saw Śāriputra with Maudgalyāyana in the assembly. On the erroneous supposition that they had joined his party, he invited Śāriputra to deliver a sermon, as he himself felt tired and wanted to sleep. Śāriputra and Maudgalyāyana now addressed the assembly and prevailed upon the 500 schismatics to return to the Buddha. When Devadatta, roused from his slumber by Kokālika, heard what had happened, the hot blood issued from his mouth.

The wickedness of Devadatta could not remain unpunished, and the Master accordingly declared to his disciples that the man who had thus been swayed by his bad passions was doomed to remain for a Kalpa in states of suffering and punishment[1]. And he, once so wise and virtuous, so bright with glory, went down to the deepest of hells, to be reborn after a Kalpa as a Pratyekabuddha, named Aṭṭhissara, or as others say, Devarāja[2].

King Ajātaśatru, having killed his father, felt the pangs of conscience. In his anxiety and doubts, he consulted the six Tīrthikas, the adversaries of the Lord, but their teachings disappointed him. Then on the advice of Jīvaka, the physician, he went to the great spiritual physician, the Tathāgata, and owing to the words of wisdom he heard from the Master's lips he became a convert to the true faith[3].

During the reign of Ajātaśatru, in the 7th year, the Śākya-race met with a sad fate. King Prasenajit of Kosala had a son Viḍūḍabha, by Vāsabhakkhattiyā, the natural daughter of Mahānāman, the successor of Śuddhodana in Kapilavastu, and of a slave girl. It was by deceit that Vāsabhakkhattiyā had been affianced by the Śākyas. When the trick afterwards was discovered, and Viḍūḍabha had been slighted by the Śākyas, he resolved to take revenge. With the assistance of the commander-in-chief Dīgha-Kārāyana he dethroned his father Prasenajit, who fled from Śrāvastī and died soon afterwards. Viḍūḍabha now marched against Kapilavastu, in consequence of which the whole Śākya clan was exterminated. He himself, however, miserably perished, along with his Kosala company, by a sudden flood[4].

In the N. version of the story Viḍūḍabha is named Virūḍhaka, his mother Mālikā[5], and the commander-in-chief Dīrgha-Cārāyaṇa. In spite of other variations, the main features of the tale are the same[6].

---

1 *Āpāyiko nerayiko.* There are 4 Apāyas: *naraka*, hell, purgatory; *petaloka*, the world of spectres; *asuraloka*, the world of demons; *tiracchāna*, the state of brute; see Childers s. vv. In Lal. V. 238 the number of Apāyas is three.

2 Mil. P. 111; Dhp. p. 148; Beal SBE. 248; Rockhill op. c. 107; Hardy M. of B. 328. Fa Hian, Rec. p. 60, saw in Śrāvastī the very spot where Devadatta went down to hell. How he came in Śrāvastī is left unexplained in the N. traditions, which, indeed, represent him as continuing his wicked attempts after the conversion of Ajātaśatru. Aṭṭhissara means "the Lord of 16" (of course *kalās*).

3 Sāmaññaph. S. in different versions; cp. above p. 32, note. The reappearance there of Pūraṇa-Kāśyapa, notwithstanding his previous death, has nothing in it to surprise us. For what kind of *historical* value the Buddhist authorities attach to such tales, is egregiously exemplified by the fact that the six heretical teachers reappear on the scene in the days of Nāgasena and the King Menander — as busy and mischievous as ever; Mil. P. pp. 4 ff.

4 Jāt. IV, pp. 144 ff. Dhp. pp. 216—225; cp. Hardy M. of B. 283.

5 Schiefner, Tib. L. 287: Mālinī. Both renderings of Tib. Phreṅ-can are admissible, *phreng* answering to Skr. *mālā*.

6 Tib. L. l. c.; Rockhill op. 75—79; 112—122. Mālikā, the flower girl — the spelling in the texts is Mallikā — is not unknown to the Pāli writings as one of Prasenajit's queens, but she is not the mother of Viḍūḍabha. For her history see Jāt. III, 405 ff. Cp. IV, 437; Ud. V, 1; Mil. P. 115; 291; Saṃy. N. III, 1, 8; Dhp. p. 317; M. of B. 285. Another Mallikā is the wife of Bandhula; Jāt. IV, 148; Dhp. 218. A

10. EVENTS IN THE LAST YEAR. AJĀTAŚATRU AND THE VṚJIANS. BUDDHA LEAVES RĀJAGṚHA. JOURNEY TO PĀṬALIGRĀMA. CROSSING OF THE GANGES. ĀMRAPĀLĪ. ILLNESS OF BUDDHA. STAY AT VAIŚĀLĪ. DEATH OF ŚĀRIPUTRA AND MAUDGALYĀYANA. MEAL AT CUNDA'S AND CONSEQUENT SICKNESS. ARRIVAL AT KUSINĀRĀ. INSTRUCTIONS TO ĀNANDA. CONVERSION OF SUBHADRA. PARINIRVĀṆA. CREMATION OF THE CORPSE. PARTITION OF THE RELICS[1].

When the Lord had reached his 79th year and was sojourning on the Gṛdhrakūṭa near Rājagṛha, Ajātaśatru intended making war upon the Vṛjians of Vaiśālī. Before carrying his designs into the effect, he sent the Brahman Varṣakāra to the Buddha with his respectful greetings and the humble demand to be informed anent the issue of his undertaking. When the envoy had come into the presence of the Tathāgata, and delivered his message, the Master asked Ānanda whether the Vṛjians were living in concord, and whether they were virtuous and religious in their conduct. On the satisfactory answer of Ānanda, the Buddha turned to Varṣakāra and said: "So long as the Vṛjians behave themselves in such a laudable way, their prosperity will increase and not decline". Then Varṣakāra intimated his conviction that the King of Magadha would be powerless against the Vṛjians and departed.

One day, after explaining to his disciples the merits of morality, mental concentration (*samādhi*) and wisdom, the Master said to Ānanda: "Come, Ānanda, let us go to Ambalaṭṭhikā"[2]. And the Lord went with a large company of monks to that place. After staying there for a short time, he proceeded to Nāḷandā, where he took up his abode in the Pāvārika Mango grove, repeating the lessons he had given on the Gṛdhrakūṭa.

From Nāḷandā the Lord proceeded to Pāṭali-grāma. There he pronounced in the rest house to the laity a discourse on the merits of the five moral precepts. Before leaving the village he predicted that one day it would become the mighty city of Pāṭaliputra, but at the same time that three great dangers would befall it[3].

When the Lord came to the Ganges, the river was brimming. Whilst some were looking for boats, others for rafts, the Buddha vanished and at once stood with the whole company of monks on the opposite bank. He continued his journey to Koṭigrāma, further to Nādikā, everywhere repeating his discourse on morality, mental concentration and wisdom. From Nādikā he continued his journey to Vaiśālī, where he sojourned at the Mango grove of Āmrapālī, teaching and exhorting his disciples[4].

When the courtezan Āmrapālī heard that the Lord had arrived and was

---

similar, though not the same figure is Mālinī, reborn as the daughter of Kṛkin, Mhv. I, pp. 300 ff.

[1] Chief source of the following narrative is the Mahāparinibbāna-S. ed. by CHILDERS JRAS of 1874—1876; transl. by Prof. RHYS DAVIDS in SBE. XI, in whose Intr. p. XXXV the parallel passages are collected; Chinese versions mentioned p. XXXVI ff. For the Tibetan versions see ROCKHILL op. c. p. 123 ff. Cp. BEAL SBE. XIX, 250 ff. BIGANDET II, 1—95; HARDY M. of B. 343 ff. WINDISCH Māra und B. pp. 43—86.

[2] Between Rājagṛha and Nālandā; see ED. MÜLLER in JPTS s. v.

[3] At that time Sunīdha (answering to a Skr. Sunītha) and Varṣakāra were building a fortress to check the Vṛjians; MPN. I, 26; MV. VI, 28; Ud. VIII, 6. Cp. ROCKHILL op. c. 127, note.

[4] To this period may be referred the question of Viśuddhimati to the Master in the Grove of Āmrapālī, related Mhv. II, 293.

staying in her Mango grove, she went with a splendid train in her carriage to near the entrance of the grove, where she alighted to proceed on foot to the place where the Master was. After hearing his edifying lessons, she invited him with the monks to come next day to her house in order to take the meal. The invitation was accepted. On the same day the Licchavi grandees came with the same invitation, and when the Tathāgata told them that he refused because he had already accepted the invitation of Āmrapālī, they could not but acknowledge that they were outdone by the courtezan.

On the following day Āmrapālī entertained her distinguished guests, and, after the meal, she presented her grove to the Congregation having for its chief the Buddha[1].

From Vaiśālī[2] the Master went to a village in the neighbourhood of that city, Beluva, where he spent his last Retreat. There a severe illness befell him, but by a strong effort of his will he recovered soon; yet he felt that now at the age of 80 years his end was approaching. One day after the rainy season he walked with Ānanda to the Cāpāla Shrine. He intimated to his disciple that, if he desired he could through his miraculous power remain in the same existence for a Kalpa, but Ānanda, whose heart was possessed by Māra, did not understand the hint and did not beseech the Master to remain for a Kalpa. Not only Ānanda, the Buddha himself was tempted by Māra, urging him to pass away from existence. The Tathāgata replied that he would not die until his law should be firmly established, and when the Fiend remarked that the Law was already established and widely spread, the Lord answered: "Be content, Fiend, the final extinction of the Tathāgata shall take place ere long. At the end of three months hence the Tathāgata will die"[3].

After staying at that place some time, explaining to Ānanda many matters connected with the Law, the Master proceeded to the Kūṭāgāra hall in the Mahāvana. There, too, he was untired in exhorting and teaching the disciples. The same he did in the following stations of his journey.

It was about this time — if we may trust a N. tradition — that Śāriputra died, and immediately after Maudgalyāyana[4]. A S. account assigns to their death nearly the same date, a week after the Buddha had spent the rainy season in Beluva[5]. According to another N. tradition again, the two chief disciples died shortly after a visit to Devadatta in hell[6].

When the Buddha had reached Pāvā, he resided there in the Mango grove of Cunda, the smith. This man invited the Master to do him the honour of partaking of a meal at his house next day. The invitation was accepted, and the smith prepared the meal, consisting of rice with cakes and

1 In MV. VI, 30 it is to Koṭigrāma that the courtezan came to invite the Buddha. The transposition is, perhaps, due to the consideration that he could not properly sojourn in the grove of Āmrapālī, before having received it in donation. Cp. BEAL op. c. 252. The grove is mentioned Fa Hian Rec. p. 72.

2 MV. VI, 31 contains the meeting of Buddha with Siṃha (Sīha), the generalissimo of the Licchavis, and the conversion of the latter, but this event probably belongs to a former period, though in BEAL op. c. 258 it likewise immediately follows on the meeting with Āmrapālī; cp. Tib. L. 268.

3 Cp. the redaction in Divy. Chap. XVII, where the Lord is represented as staying in the Kūṭāgāra hall near the bank of the Monkey tank (Markaṭahrada). Cp. BEAL op. c. 267; WINDISCH l. c.

4 Tib. L. 289.

5 BIGANDET II, 9—26. There is much confusion in that account; should we read there Vaiśālī and Mahāvana for Śrāvastī and Jetavana?

6 ROCKHILL op. c. 110.

pork. When the Lord had come and was seated, he took for himself the pork, leaving to the disciples the other food. After the dinner he desired Cunda to bury what was left of the pork, because no one in the world could digest such food except the Tathāgata. Soon after it the Buddha was seized with a violent attack of dysentery. On his way to Kusinārā[1] he felt extremely weak, and, wishing to sit down, he commanded Ānanda to spread out the robe for him, and to fetch him some water to drink. Ānanda went to the stream which had just become muddy by passing carts, and found it to his astonishment clear and limpid[2]. Gladly he returned to the Master, who drank of the water.

At that time it happened that a young Malla, Pukkusa[3], a disciple of Āḷāra Kālāma's, passed the road from Kusinārā to Pāvā. On seeing the Lord, he approached him, and recorded how on a certain occasion Āḷāra had proved by his example what incredible degree of composure and power of abstraction can be reached by one who has renounced the world. The Tathāgata, having heard the story, told a much more wonderful case from his own experience, so that Pukkusa declared that now he had lost his faith in Āḷāra, and became a convert to the true faith. Forthwith he directed somebody to fetch a pair of pieces of gold cloth. When the pair was brought, Pukkusa offered both pieces to the Lord, who took one for himself, the other for Ānanda[4].

After this occurrence the Master proceeded to the river Kakutthā, where he took a bath. Then he crossed the river and went on, preaching, to the Mango grove, and thence to a grove in the Malla country, the Upavartana of Kusinārā, on the other side of the Hiraṇyavatī. There between the twin Sāl trees a couch was spread by Ānanda, with the place for the head to the North, and the Lord laid himself down on his right side, like a lion, with one leg resting on the other[5].

The last hours before the Lord's Parinirvāṇa were spent by him in useful counsels and instructions to Ānanda. Among other topics he spoke of the four places which the pious believer ought to visit with feelings of holy reverence: the place where the Tathāgata is born; the place where he has reached perfect Enlightenment; the place where for the first time he proclaims the Law; the place of his final extinction. He dilated on the merits of pilgrimage[6] to those places and declared: "They who shall die on such a pilgrimage, shall be reborn after death in the happy realms of heaven".

On the question of Ānanda what ceremonies were to be performed after his demise, he answered that the disciples should not trouble themselves about it, because there were enough believers in the highest classes of society who would not fail to honour the remains of the Tathāgata, in the same manner as one honours the remains of a Cakravartin. And he described to Ānanda the ceremonies performed after the death of a Cakravartin. He added that

---

1 Skr. Kuśinagara, °nagarī, and Kuśanagara; see Pet. Dict. s. vv.

2 It is doubtful whether this stream is the Kakutthā or Kukutthā, as HARDY M. of B. 356; BIGANDET II, 39, and ROCKHILL op. c. 134 have it. We shall meet with the K. anon as the river where Buddha bathed; cp. Ud. VIII, 5. In Tib. L. 291 it is the Hiraṇyavatī where he bathes.

3 Cp. Tib. L. 291. The "young" Malla must have been at least 65 years of age, his teacher having died 45 years ago.

4 A little further on, vs. 52 of the text, the Buddha is said to be clad with both robes; herewith agrees Tib. L. 291.

5 This is the posture of the images which represent Buddha's Nirvāṇa. — Cp. for this passage and the sequel BEAL SBE. XIX, 286 ff.

6 Cp. Aṅg. N. II, p. 120.

four kinds of men are worthy of a Stūpa: a Tathāgata; a Pratyeka-buddha; a disciple of the Tathāgata; and a Cakravartin[1].

After these instructions Ānanda was painfully affected by the thought of his impending separation from the Master, and weeping he went into the Vihāra[2], but the Lord sent for him, comforted him, and praised his virtues in the presence of the brethren.

When the Lord had finished his discourse, Ānanda emitted the opinion that it would hardly become the dignity of the Tathāgata to die in so small a town situated in a waste tract of country, and that one of the 6 great cities, Campā, Rājagṛha, Śrāvastī, Sāketa, Kauśāmbī, or Benares[3], would be a fitter place. But the Master showed him that Kusinārā, being in former times the royal city of Kusāvatī, was the most becoming place. Thereupon he ordered Ānanda to go and inform the Mallas of Kusinārā that in the last watch of the night the final extinction of the Tathāgata would take place, and to invite them not to let pass the opportunity of seeing the Tathāgata in his last moments. The Mallas, on receiving the message, hastened to the place where the Lord was lying, and were admitted in his presence.

Now there lived at that time a heretical monk, named Subhadra (Subhadda). Having heard that the Śramaṇa Gautama should attain to final extinction in the last watch of the night, he felt a longing to visit the Buddha. He went to the place where Ānanda was and asked for admittance. The disciple refused, out of care for the Master, but the latter ordered him to admit Subhadra, who was not come to annoy him, but from a desire of enlightenment. Subhadra accordingly came into the presence of the Lord, and after hearing an edifying discourse, more especially on the eightfold Path and the four stages of the path to Nirvāṇa, became a convert. He was the last disciple whom the Lord himself converted. In a very short time Subhadra reached Nirvāṇa[4].

The last moments of the Tathāgata were taken up with exhortations to keep faithfully to the rules of the Order, which after his demise would be to them in his stead. Further he gave indications concerning their future behaviour, and asked them whether there was any one among the brethren who had some lingering doubt as to the Buddha, the Law, the Congregation, or the four stages. There was none, as the Master knew full well beforehand.

Then the Lord spoke these words to his brethren: "Now, monks, I have nothing more to tell you but that all that is composed is liable to decay. Strive after salvation energetically!" These were the last words of the Tathāgata[5].

Thereupon the Lord entered into the first stage of meditation (Dhyāna); from that he passed into the second, the third, the fourth, successively. Out of the fourth stage he entered into the stage of the infinity of space; thence into the stage of the infinity of thought; thence into the stage of nothingness; thence into the stage of neither consciousness nor unconsciousness; finally into the stage in which consciousness has wholly passed away[6].

Then Ānanda said to Anuruddha: "The Lord is dead, Anuruddha!"

---

1 In Aṅg. N. I, p. 77 only two: a Tathāgata and a Cakravartin.

2 It is not clear what is here meant with this term.

3 The 6 cities, though not named, also occur in Tib. L. 291. Cp. ṣaṇṇagarī, Vārtt. on Pāṇini VIII, 4, 42.

4 It is likewise said in Tib. L. 293 that Subhadra dies immediately after having attained Arhatship; so, too, Voy. II, 339. Cp. ROCKHILL op. c. 138.

5 Somewhat different in Voy. I, 341.

6 These stages are also represented as certain immaterial worlds. Cp. Tib. L. 292.

"No, Ānanda, the Lord is not dead: he has reached the stage of complete unconsciousness".

Now the Lord passed from the stage of complete unconsciousness into that of neither consciousness nor unconsciousness; thence into the stage of nothingness; thence into that of the infinity of thought; thence into that of the infinity of space; further into the 4th, 3d, 2d, 1st stage of meditation, successively. Then again he passed into the 2d stage, thence into the 3d, thence into the 4th stage of meditation. And immediately on passing out of that stage he was extinguished.

The death of the Lord was attended with an earthquake and thunder-strokes. Brahmā Sahampati and Śakra, as well as Ānanda and Anuruddha uttered appropriate stanzas. Some of the monks who were not yet completely emancipated from passion wailed and lamented: "Too soon has the Lord died! Too soon has the Light gone out in the world!" But others, more advanced, bore their loss with resignation, because they knew that all composite things are impermanent.

At the end of the night Anuruddha sent Ānanda to inform the Mallas of the Master's decease. When the Mallas, who then were assembled in the Council hall heard the tidings, they, with their wives and children, gave marks of deep sorrow, and ordered the attendants to gather in Kusinārā perfumes, garlands, and all sorts of musical instruments. When the mourning crowd had come to the spot where the body of the Lord lay in the Sāla grove, they past the day in paying honour to the remains of the Tathāgata with dancing, hymns and music. This was repeated on the following days until on the seventh day the corpse was carried by 8 Malla chieftains, among a rain of heavenly Mandārava flowers, to the shrine called Makuṭa-bandhana, where the funeral pile was raised.

When four Malla chieftains tried to set the pile on fire, they were not able to do so. In their amazement they asked Anuruddha the cause of that unexpected case. He informed them that the pile would not be set on fire until the arrival of Kāśyapa the Great, who was just travelling on the road from Pāvā to Kusinārā, with a company of monks. And, in fact, Kāśyapa was coming, as he had heard from an Ājīvaka monk, who had picked up a Mandārava flower, that "the Śramaṇa Gautama" died a week ago. Kāśyapa hastened to the spot where the funeral pile had been raised, and there he with his company ceremoniously walked thrice round the pile, and bowed down at the feet of the Lord[1]. No sooner had this act of piety been performed, than the pile caught fire of itself[2].

As soon as the fire had consumed the body of the Tathāgata, with exception of the bones, and a rain from heaven had extinguished the flames, the Mallas paid honour to the relics with dancing, singing and music, with garlands and perfumes.

When Ajātaśatru heard the tidings that the Lord had departed this life, he forwarded a claim for obtaining the possession of a portion of the relics. The Licchavis of Vaiśālī asked for themselves the same prerogative, likewise the Śākyas of Kapilavastu[3], the Bulis of Allakappa, the Koḷiyas of Rāmagrāma, the Mallas of Pāvā, and a Brahman of Veṭhadīpa, all of them promising to

---

[1] BIGANDET II, 88 has some details regarding the feet of Buddha; cp. Mhv. I, 67, where the feet are described as *cakravaralakṣitau*.

[2] A Northern account closely agreeing in Mhv. I, 64 ff.

[3] These had been exterminated by Viḍūḍabha, but in Buddhist writings the dead are apt to reappear as often as their presence is needed. The revival of the famous six Tīrthikas is a similar case in point.

erect a Stūpa over the relics. At first the Mallas of Kusinārā were unwilling to give away any part of the relics, but by an impressive speech of the Brahman Droṇa (Doṇa), who reminded them how the Buddha had always taught forbearance, and by his counsel to divide the relics into eight equal portions, so that Stūpas should rise everywhere to spread the belief in the Buddha, the parties were soothed. They entreated Droṇa to divide the relics into eight equal portions, and so he did, keeping for himself the urn over which he built a shrine[1].

After the event came a messenger of the Mauryas of Pippalivana to ask for a portion of the relics. No portion being left, the Mauryas had to content themselves with the coals, over which they erected a shrine[2].

Thus there were then 8 Stūpas: in Rājagṛha, Vaiśālī, Kapilavastu, Allakappa, Rāmagrāma, Veṭhadīpa, Pāvā, and Kusinārā, besides the shrines erected by Droṇa and the Mauryas.

In the preceding pages the principal facts in the legendary life of the Buddha have been commemorated. A disquisition into the historical or other elements entering into its composition lies beyond the scope of this manual, wherefore we must refer the reader to other works[3].

PART III.

THE LAW OF THE BUDDHA.

1. FUNDAMENTAL PRINCIPLES.

When the Buddha had taken possession of the seat of full enlightenment, he evolved from within two formulas, ever since revealed by him to all beings, and represented as the fundamental truths of his teaching. These formulas are the four Āryasatyāni[4] and the twelvefold Pratītyasamutpāda.

The four Satyāni, i. e. Axioms or Certainties, summarily denoted by the four terms *duḥkha*, suffering, *samudaya*, cause, *nirodha*, suppression, and *pratipad* or *mārga*, path, way, state it as undeniable that there *is* suffering; that suffering necessarily has a cause; that in order to suppress the evil one must know the right way[5].

It is not difficult to see that these four Satyas are nothing else but the four cardinal articles of Indian medical science, applied to the spiritual healing

1 In Divy. 380 the Droṇastūpa was erected by Ajātaśatru. It may be surmised that the term *droṇastūpa* has given birth to the Brahman Droṇa. Burnouf Intr. 372, note, is of another opinion.

2 The partition of the relics is told much in the same manner in the N. version; see Rockhill op. c. Cp. also Beal SBE. XIX, p. 325—334, and Fa Hian Rec. chs. XXVIII and XXIV, with Pl. IX.

3 More especially to Senart's *Légende du Buddha* and Oldenberg's *Buddha; his Life, his Doctrine, his Order*, in which the problem has been treated, if not with uncontrovertible results, at least with considerable skill and great learning.

4 These are taught by all Buddhas; see e. g. Therag. vs. 492.

5 The theme is worked out in the first sermon addressed to the 5 mendicant friars MV. I, 6, 19; Lal. V. 540; and in other passages, e. g. Majjh. N. I, p. 48.

of mankind, exactly as in the Yoga doctrine[1]. This connection of the Āryasatyas with medical science was apparently not unknown to the Buddhists themselves, for in Lal. V. p. 448 we find immediately after the announcement of the discovery of the two formulas the significant words: "*utpanno vaidyarājaḥ pramocakaḥ sarvaduḥkhebhyaḥ, pratiṣṭhāpako nirvāṇasukhe, niṣaṇṇas Tathāgatagarbhe Tathāgatamahādharmarājāsane*". And again p. 458:

> cirāture jīvaloke kleśavyādhiprapīḍite |
> vaidyarāṭ tvaṃ samutpannaḥ sarvavyādhipramocakaḥ ‖

The second formula, the Concatenation of causes and effects, the twelvefold Pratītyasamutpāda or causal production, otherwise termed "the 12 Nidānas (causes)" is intended to lay bare the root of evil, and stands to the 4 Satyas in the same relation as Pathology, (Nidāna or Nidāna-śāstra), to the whole system of medical science. The terms of the series are: *avidyā*, ignorance; *saṃskārās*, impressions; *vijñāna*, clear consciousness; *nāmarūpa*, name-and-form[2]; *ṣaḍāyatana*, the six organs of sense; *sparśa*, contact (of the senses with exterior objects); *vedanā*, feeling; *tṛṣṇā*, desire; *upādāna*, clinging, effort[3]; *bhava*, becoming, beginning of existence; *jāti*, birth, existence; *jarāmaraṇam*, *śokaparidevanaduḥkhadaurmanasyopayāsāḥ*, old age and death, sorrow, lamentation, pain, grief, despondency[4].

It seems probable that the whole series, in which the difference between the *post hoc* and the *propter hoc* is utterly ignored, is, like the corresponding Yoga tenet, stating *avidyā* to be the ultimate cause of *duḥkha*[5], an imitation or adaptation of some ancient cosmogonical myth, poetically describing the creation, and the destruction of the world, i. e. the successive stages in the daily phaenomena, beginning when light emerges out of darkness, the world out of chaos, up to the end of day after its troubles. A similar adaptation is the Pratyaya-sarga of the Sāṅkhya, the very name of which suggests some connection with the Pratītya-samutpāda. The connection, however, is not such as to warrant the assumption of a mutual dependence between the Buddhist and the Sāṅkhya series; we only surmise that both systems derive from a common remote source[6].

When we try to connect the twelvefold formula with cosmogonical notions, we arrive at the following conclusions. *Avidyā*, ignorance, is the

[1] E. g. in Yogasūtra II, 15, Comm.: "yathā cikitsāśāstraṃ caturvyūhaṃ: rogo, rogahetur, ārogyaṃ, bhaiṣajyaṃ iti, evam idam api śāstraṃ caturvyūham eva, tadyathā: saṃsāraḥ, saṃsārahetur, mokṣo, mokṣopāya iti. Tatrah duḥkhabahulaḥ saṃsāro heyah; pradhānapuruṣayoh saṃyogo heyahetuḥ; saṃyogasyātyantikī nivṛttir hānaṃ; hānopāyaḥ samyagdarśanam". Cp. Sarvad. Saṅgr. p. 180. Hence follows that the activity of *buddhi*, which as being an evolution of *pradhāna* belongs to *prakṛti*, ceases at the *nivṛtti* of the union; in other words: the activity of the *Buddha* ceases at Nirvāṇa or Nirvṛti (which looks like an intentional substitution for Nivṛtti).

[2] I. e. all physical and mental phaenomena, the same as *papañca* S. Nip. p. 95, and consequently = *māyā*. In an idealistic system like Buddhism the phaenomena are, of course, no realities. Since every human body consists of an aggregate of physical and mental elements, of the 5 Skandhas, such a being can be designed as *nāmarūpa*.

[3] The definition Majjh. N. I, p. 266 is: *yā vedanāsu nandī, tad upādānaṃ*; as to the 4 Upadānas, see there p. 66; cp. p. 51, and Saṃy. N. II, p. 3.

[4] MV. I, 1; Lal. V. 442 ff. Lotus p. 109; and the references in CHILDERS s. v. *paṭiccasamuppāda*, and Dharma-S. XLII, note.

[5] Yogas. II, 15: "duḥkham eva sarvaṃ vivekinaḥ", on which the Comment: "tad asya mahato duḥkhasamudāyasya *prabhavabījam avidyā*; cp. II, 4: "avidyā kṣetram uttareṣām".

[6] It is not in the Pratyaya-sarga, but in the Sāṅkhya theory of creation that there is a partial parallelism to be discovered between the Buddhist and the Sāṅkhya system; as follows:

state of not-knowing, of sleep. An allusion to this state of man is found in Lal. V. p. 458:

> ciraprasuptam imaṃ lokam tamaḥskandhāvaguṇṭhitam |
> bhavān prajñāpradīpena samarthaḥ pratibodhitum ||

Man at first awaking enters into a state of half-consciousness; his mind is affected by vague impressions (*saṃskāras*) before he has reached the state of clear consciousness. Then the phaenomena appear to him, and the activity of his organs of sense commences. By the contact of the organs with some exterior object (either real or ideal) a certain feeling or sensation is produced. Feeling leads to the wish (*tṛṣṇā*) of getting what seems desirable, and that wish, steadily increasing[1] produces a strong clinging and effort to bring about a state of things differing from the present state. So a new state begins, and immediately after the process of becoming, of transition, the new existence springs to light. That existence, having a beginning, must also have an end, which is ushered in, so to say, by all kinds of misery[2].

The Northern Buddhist know more than one explanation of the process. The next approach to the interpretation just proposed is that prevailing in the Kārmika school[3]. It can be formulated as follows: from false knowledge spring delusive impressions; from these, general notions; from them, particulars; from them, the six seats of the senses; from them, contact; from it, definite sensation; from it, desire; from it, embryonic existence; from it, actual physical existence; from it, all the distinctions of genus and species among animate things; from them, decay and death. According to another theory[4] the series represents the history of human life, in twelve acts; a history beginning *ab ovo* or even arelier, and ending with decay and death. The root of all is Avidyā, i. e. the error of deeming transient things to be permanent; from error spring Saṃskāras, affections, temporary dispositions, as love, hate and infatuation; from them springs Vijñāna, incipient consciousness of the embryo; from this proceeds Nāmarūpam, i. e. the rudimentary body consisting of *nāman*, earth and the other three elements, and *rūpa*, form[5]. Thence proceed the Ṣaḍāyatanas, organs of the senses; when the organs come in conjunction with Name-and-Form, there is Sparśa, contact. Thence follows Vedanā, feeling, sensation; then arises Tṛṣṇā, longing (for renewal of pleasant feeling and desire to shun what is painful). Hence Upādāna, effort, beginning of action; then Bhava, state (of merit or demerit). Then comes Jāti, birth, i. e. the aggregation of the 5 Skandhas. On birth will follow decay, death, etc.

A recent discovery[6] among the frescoes of the caves of Ajaṇṭa has

Avidyā	parall.	Pradhāna
Saṃskāras	„	Buddhi
Vijñāna	„	Ahaṃkāra
Nāmarūpam	„	Tanmātrāṇi
Ṣaḍāyatanam	„	Indriyāṇi.

1 *Upādāna* also means "fuel".

2 For a totally different translation and explanation see Prof. Rhys Davids and Oldenberg in SBE. XI, pp. 75 ff., and the latter's "Buddha" (Engl. transl. p. 226 ff.); Childers in "Life and Essays of Colebroke" II, p. 453; Bigandet I, 93. Cp. also Beal SBE. XIX, 161.

3 Hodgson Ess. p. 79. The Nidānas with exception of the first and last term are called the 10 Karmans, Acts.

4 Mentioned by Govindānanda in the Ṭīkā on Brāhma-Sūtra p. 549.

5 Hodgson l. c.: "thence proceeds an organised and definite, but archetypal body, the seat of that consciousness".

6 By L. A. Waddell, to whose paper "Buddha's Secret from a sixth century Pictorial commentary and Tibetan Tradition" in JRAS of 1894, p. 367 and Buddh. of Tib. 105—121, we refer the reader.

brought to light a picture which pourtrays the Nidānas in concrete form. This picture, supplemented by its Tibetan versions and its explanation by the Lamas, shows unmistakably a diagram of Human Life. This agrees with the theory known to Govindānanda, notwithstanding discrepancies in the rendering of some terms in the Wheel of Life. Whether we may see in it "a complete authentic account of human life from the absolute standpoint of the earliest Buddhist philosophy"[1] does not seem to be beyond all doubt. This much, however, is plain that the purport of the Pratītya-samutpāda is to show how all evil, death &c. ultimately springs from Avidyā. Formally this does not differ from the Yoga axiom: "Avidyā is the germ from which the whole mass of evil proceeds", but the sentiment underlying the phrase is another. For the Yoga philosopher has a craving for permanency, he is a *śāśvatavādin*. Hence all that is impermanent and changeable is to him an evil[2], and therefore he seeks after true knowledge, the right insight that the *puruṣa* is in reality not affected by its union with *prakṛti*, and that it is only *avidyā*, the wrong notion, about that union which is the cause of evil and grief.

The two fundamental formulas, to which may be added the stanza "*Ye dhammā hetuppabhavā*[3], do not presuppose the belief in retribution and rebirth, the Karman theory, nor do they contain anything decidedly opposed to it. The same can not be said of the Buddhist doctrine regarding the Ātman, self, soul, individuality.

A concise and clear exposition of the three principal contending theories regarding Ātman is found in Pugg. P. p. 38[4]. These theories are the *Sassatavāda*, the *Ucchedavāda*, and the doctrine of Buddha. The first holds that the soul is truly existing, both in this life and in the life to come; the second, that the soul is truly existing, but only in this life; the Buddha teaches that soul is not truly existing, neither in this life, nor in the life to come[5].

The categorical and absolute denial of an *ātman* is evidently in conflict with the common Hindu view of *karman*, which is based upon the assumption of the existence of a soul. Therefore the Buddhists could not adopt the theory in their own system without modifications. The shape which the dogma has received under their hands is admirably described by CHILDERS[6]: "When a man dies the khandhas of which he is constituted perish, but by the force of his Kamma a new set of khandhas instantly starts into existence, and a new being appears in another world, who though possessing different khandhas and a different form is in reality identical with the man just passed away, because his Kamma is the same. Kamma then is the link that preserves the

---

1 WADDELL op. c. p. 370. Curious is the interpretation of *bhava*. It is "pictured by a married woman; and the Lamas explain the picture by saying that she is the wife of the individual whose life-history is being traced". Cp. the phrase *taṇhā janeti purisaṃ* Samy. N. I, p. 37. This explains, to a certain extent, how *sañjananī* and *janikā*, Skr. *janikā* (Lal. V. 541) "natural impulse" are nearly synonymous with *taṇhā*, Dh.-Saṅgaṇi 1059, where *bhava*, however is not taken in a realistic or material acceptation, as may be inferred from 1312, where *bhavataṇhā* is explained as "*yo bhavesu bhavacchando*", and *bhavadiṭṭhi* 1313 as "*bhavissati attā ca loko cāti evarūpā diṭṭhi*".

2 The phrase *yad aniccaṃ dukkhaṃ* is Buddhist also, e. g. Saṃy. N. II, p. 244.

3 So above p. 25.

4 Cp. Digh. N. I, pp. 12 ff., 35 ff. and Saṃy. N. III, p. 205.

5 CHILDERS s. v. *ucchedo* has the following remark: "This doctrine was hold in great abhorrence by the Buddhists, being directly antagonistic to the whole spirit and scheme of Buddhism". This is not very clear. If the *ucchedavāda*, admitting the existence of the soul, albeit only for this life, strikes at the root of the transmigration theory, then Buddhism, denying the existence of soul altogether, does so with double force.

6 Dict. s. v. *khandho*.

identity of a being through all the countless changes which it undergoes in its progress through Saṃsára"[1].

Such a theory, it will be admitted, is beyond the reach of human reason, but that is no argument against its appropriateness in the original system of the creed. For Buddhism is professedly no rationalistic system, it being a superhuman (*uttarimanussa*) Law founded upon the decrees of an omniscient and infallible Master, and in such a creed mysteries are admissible. A somewhat greater difficulty arises if we wish to reconcile the maxim *sarvam anityam*, "all is impermanent", with this theory; for if all is impermanent, the Karman can not be productive *ad infinitum*. Yet, even this difficulty can be got rid of, on the assumption that the phrase is only a certain way of speaking to denote that all is changeable except the ideal link connecting the successive stages of being. It is less easy to account for such examples of punishment as are related of Ciñcā and others, who are represented as being swallowed by the earth and going down to hell before the eyes of all present. Does this belong to the mythology of the creed? If so, why should not the Karman theory pertain to the same category?

The more we try to remove the difficulties, the more we are driven to the suspicion that original Buddhism was not exactly that of the canonical books. If we suppose that the teaching of the founder of the Order was free from mythology and the Karman theory, we get a system intelligible, self-consistent and perfectly apt to lead persons possessing a contemplative bent of mind, by means of a dignified and harmless solitary and cenobitic mode of life, to the blissful state of calm beatitude, called Nirvāṇa[2], a state only surpassed by the final Nirvāṇa or Parinirvāṇa, when all suffering is absolutely and for ever at an end[3].

Whatever may be our doubts about the original form of Buddhism, it is certain that the dogma in question made part and parcel of the whole system of Dharma before the great bulk of the canonical books were composed. The hypothesis that in course of time some elements were incorporated into the creed to which originally they were foreign, does not involve the belief in a radical change. In our view Buddhism was from the very beginning *essentially* such as we find it in the Tripiṭaka; a creed aptly characterized[4] in the following words: "As a philosophy, Buddhism thus seems to be an Idealistic Nihilism; an Idealism which, like that of Berkeley, holds that "the fruitful source of all error was the unfounded belief in the reality and existence of the external world"; and that man can perceive nothing but his feelings, and is the cause to himself of these. That all known or knowable objects are relative to a conscious subject, and merely a product of the *ego*, existing through the *ego*, for the *ego*, and in the *ego*[5]. But, unlike Berkeley's Idealism, this recognition of the relativity and limitations of knowledge, and the consequent disappearance of the world as a reality, led directly to Nihilism, by seeming to exclude the knowledge, and by implication the existence, not only of a Creator, but of an absolute Being[6]."

1 For a scholastic exposition of the theory see Mil. P. 40 ff. Cp. Hardy M. of B. 396 ff.

2 I. e. the *upādisesa-* or *sa-upādisesa* Nirvāṇa, the *jīvanmukti* of the Hindus, whereas the final N. is *anupādisesa*; see Childers s. v. The definition of *anupādisesā nibbānadhātu* in Itiv. p. 38 is wrong, and in glaring conflict with the words in the stanza there: *anupādisesā pana samparāyikā yamhi nirujjhanti bhavāni sabbaso*.

3 Cp. Wassilief B. 94.

4 By Waddell, op. c. p. 384.

5 This is Vedānta.

6 Nihilism is tersely expressed in S. Nip. p. 203: "*natthi ajjhattañ ca bahiddhā ca kiñcāti passato*"; cp. p. 194: "*natthīti nissāya tarassu ogham*".

2. THE ELEMENTS OF EXISTENCE. KARMAN. THE ROAD TO DELIVERANCE.

Every organized being consists of Name and Form. The former denotes all mental or internal phenomena; the latter, all physical or external phenomena[1]. *Nāman* generally includes four of the five Skandhas, viz. *vedanā*, feeling; *sañjñā*, notion; *saṃskārās*, mental dispositions, and *vijñāna*, clear consciousness, discrimination. *Rūpa* comprehends the four elements (*mahābhūtāni*): earth, water, fire, air, and every form springing from them[2].

It appears from this enumeration that Nāmarūpa and the 5 Skandhas are coextensive terms. The definition of the mental Skandhas is attended with considerable difficulties, owing to the ambiguousness of most terms, and the loose way in which they are used. Not to go farther than the Pāli texts, we see how *saññā*, notion or first perception, and *vedanā*, feeling, sensation, form each a separate Khandha and at the same time occur as two subdivisions of the Saṃkhāra-kkhandha. This, however unlogical, is not inexplicable, provided we do not assign to Saṃkhāra the meaning of "discrimination", as HARDY has done. The first of the 52 Saṃkhāras is *phassa*, touch, contact, whereas the sentiments as fear, joy, shame &c. are likewise Saṃkhāras; which would be impossible if the term had the meaning assigned to it by HARDY[3]. Saṃkhāras are, in our opinion, passing impressions, mental dispositions, comprising both intellectual affections and sentiments. Hence the first step in the line of Saṃkhāras is *phassa*, contact[4]; the second *vedanā*, feeling; the third *saññā*, notion (e. g. of different colours); *cetanā*, thought, intention; *manasikāra*, attention; *jīvitindriya*, vitality[5]; *cittekaggatā*, concentration of the mind; *vitakka*, consideration; *vicāra*, deliberation; and so on[6].

Viññāna, clear consciousness, has 89 subdivisions, and comprises clear consciousness of what is transmitted by the organs of seeing, hearing, smelling, tasting, touch, and the sixth sense, *manas*; farther the clear consciousness or discrimination of what is good, bad, or indifferent. In the latter case the term denotes spontaneous or instinctive moral discrimination[7].

The N. definition of the four mental Skandhas[8] is, shortly formulated, as follows: *Vijñāna* is clear consciousness of what is going on in our interior. From it in combination with the Rūpaskandha springs *vedanā*, feeling of what is pleasant, painful, &c. *Sañjñā* is the distinct notion of an object, by which

---

1 Cp. Śatapatha-Brāhmaṇa XIV, 11, 4, 3.

2 MV. I, 6, 36. Dh. Saṅg. 1309 adds a fifth, viz. *asaṅkhatā dhātu*. In Saṃy. N. II, p. 3 the four Skandhas are *vedanā*, *saññā*, *phassa*, and *manasikāra*. The usual N. enumeration of the 5 Skandhas is: *rūpa, vedanā, sañjñā, saṃskāra, vijñāna;* see BURNOUF Intr. 511, but Śaṃkara on Brahma-S. II, 2, 18, Dharma-S. XXII, and Sarvad. Saṅg. p. 20 follow a different order, a circumstance connected with the variance in the definitions of the terms. — A scholastic enumeration of the twenty-eight-fold Rūpakkhandha occurs in Vis. M.; see CHILDERS s. v. *rūpam*. — On the 18 Dhātus, principles or properties of primary substances, see Dharma-S. XXV and the references there. How these are connected and how unconnected with each of the 5 Skandhas, see Dhātuk. P. p. 2; cp. p. 51 f.

3 In Vyu. § 104 *sparśa* &c. are simply called *caitasikā dharmās*, mental conditions.

4 Somewhat differently Mil. P. 60 ff.

5 Cp. Dh. Saṅg. 295.

6 Abhidhamma-Saṅgaha, cited by CHILDERS Dict. p. 455 for the whole series; Dh. Saṅg. 338. Minor differences in the terms and in the order may be left unnoticed. The list in Vyu. l. c. contains 94 terms; cp. HARDY M. of B. 404 ff. Dharma-S. distinguishes Cittasamprayuktasaṃskāras, 40 in number, from 12 Cittaviprayuktasaṃskāras. XXX, XXXI.

7 The enumeration of the subdivisions in HARDY M. of B. 419 ff. Cp. the extracts from Vis. M. and Abhidh. Saṅg. with CHILDERS p. 577. The list much shorter Vyu. § 105.

8 Sarvad. Saṅg. p. 20.

we are enabled to recognize the object. *Saṃskāras* are affections, temporary mental or moral dispositions, having their motive in *vedanā;* to them belong the *kleśas* (defiling passions[1]) as love, hatred, &c.; the *upakleśas* (secondary *kleśas*), as pride, conceit &c., piety and impiety[2].

The aggregation of the five Skandhas constitute the *pudgala, puggala,* what we would call the individual, but what in the idealistic system of Buddhism is a being without real individuality. Although the Skandhas constitute the Pudgala, it is explicitly asserted that neither separately nor conjointly they *are* the Pudgala[3].

The cause of the aggregation of the Skandhas, i. e. of birth and rebirth, is Karman. Hence it is said: "It is Name-and-Form which is reborn". We have seen that Nāma-rūpa is coextensive with the 5 Skandhas[4]. The passage through a succession of existences, transmigration, bears the usual name of Saṃsāra.

The Karman is supposed to have no beginning, but it *can* have an end. The means of attaining that end, of destroying the working of Karman is the Eightfold Path, as the Master set forth in his first discourse[5].

According to the stage one has reached in one's course towards Deliverance, Nirvāṇa, there is a fourfold division. Those who are walking in this path of Sanctification in four stages are called, respectively: Śrotaāpanna, Sakṛdāgāmin, Anāgāmin, Arhat (Pāli: Sotāpanna, Sakadāgāmin, Anāgāmin, Arahā), and with a common designation Śrāvaka, Sāvaka, disciple. Each of the stages or path-divisions is subdivided into a higher and a lower degree, the *mārga, magga,* and its *phala,* result, fruition[6].

The Srotaāpanna is he who has entered the first stage (*srotaāpatti, sotāpatti*), the neophyte. He has got rid of the first three bonds of human passion, *saṃyojana*[7]; the doors of the states of punishments, *apāya,* are shut for him.

The Sakṛdāgāmin is so termed because he will once be reborn in the world of men. He is not only free from the first three bonds, but has in addition reduced to a minimum *rāga,* affection, *dveṣa*; P. *dosa,* hatred, and *moha,* infatuation[8].

The Anāgāmin is he who has freed himself from the first five or lower

---

1 Dharma-S. LXVI, note.

2 The number in Dharma-S. LXIX is twentyfour; other sources as Pugg. P. II, 1—9 give only twenty; see Dharma-S. l. c. note.

3 Mil. P. 25 ff.; cp. 61, where the expression *ekacco puggalo* may not unaptly be rendered with "somebody", but in an idealistic, i. e. nihilistic sense.

4 How the process of rebirth is going on, is minutely expounded Mil. P. 43; 72; 77.

5 See above p. 23. The Pali terms are: *sammā-diṭṭhi, s.-saṅkappa, s.-vācā, s.-kammanta, s.-ājīva, s.-vāyāma, s.-sati, s.-samādhi;* in Skr. *samyag-dṛṣṭi, s.-saṅkalpa, s.-vāc, s.-karmānta, s.-ājīva, s.-vyāyāma, s.-smṛti. s.-samādhi.* Definitions Dh. Saṅg. 297—304. Cp. BURNOUF, Intr. 519. The Fivefold Path, *pañcaṅgiko maggo* comprises Nos. 1, 2, 6, 7 and 8 of the eight; Dh. Saṅg. p. 21.

6 See CHILDERS s. vv. *maggo* and *phalaṃ;* cp. BIGANDET I, 153. For the four saints and their characteristics see Vyu. §§ 46, 48; and cp. BEAL Cat. p. 191; cp. MINAYEF Recherches I, 217 ff., where sectarian views also are noticed.

7 Viz. *diṭṭhi* or *sakkāydiṭṭhi,* heresy or the heresy of individuality; *vicikicchā,* scepticism, and *sīlabbataparāmāsa,* observance of superstitious rites. Aṅg. N. II, p. 238; Dh. Saṅg. 1002—1005; Dharma-S. LXVIII. There are several classes of Srotaāpannas; the lowest is he who will be reborn 7 times at most, called *saptakṛdbhavaparama,* P. *sattakkhattuparama,* Vyu. § 46; CHILDERS s. v. *paramo; kulaṃkula,* P. *kolaṃkola,* one who will be reborn 2 or 3 times; Pugg. P. p. 16; Aṅg. N. p. 233; Vyu. l. c. Cp. Dharma-S. CIII, note.

8 Synonymous with Sak. is *Ekabījin,* corrupted in Skr. to *Ekavīcika;* Pugg. P. p. 16; Aṅg. N. I, 233 ff. Vyu. § 46.

(*avarabhāgīya*, P. *orambhāgiya*) bonds[1] and will not be reborn on earth or in a Kāmaloka, but in a Brahmaloka.

The Arhat is he in whom the causes of moral infection[2] are exhausted, the impurities washed away, the Kleśas[3] rejected; who has fulfilled his task, laid down his burden, removed all bonds[4], obtained the four kinds of transcendent faculties[5]. He is no more subject to rebirth[6].

One who, without having entered the first stage, is in possession of those conditions upon which the commencement of sanctification immediately ensues, is called a Gotrabhū[7]. Such a previous stage, which is, so to say, the court-yard of Holiness, is known to the N. Buddhists by the name of Gotrabhūmi[8].

Those who are walking in the four paths in their progress towards final beatitude rank as true Āryas in contradistinction to the *profanum vulgus*, the Pṛthagjanas. Their power far surpasses that of common mortals, which is nothing strange, as the notion that transcendent power is attainable by man is prevalent among Hindu sects; the Yogin more especially is, to vulgar apprehension, a worker of miracles. Further on we shall have occasion to revert to this subject.

The object of the Ārya is to reach Nirvāṇa[9]. It is impossible within a short compass to refer to all the opinions emitted on the subject; it would fill a volume. We will, therefore, limit ourselves to the main points.

In the first place we must distinguish between the secondary Nirvāṇa and the final or absolute one. The former Nirvāṇa, attained by Arhats in this life, is virtually the same as the Jīvanmukti of the Vedāntins. It is specified by the addition of *upādisesa* or *sa-upādisesa* in Pāli, *upadhiśeṣa* with the N. Buddhists[10], i. e. having the residuum of a substratum.

The second or final, absolute Nirvāṇa (*nirūpadhiśeṣa*, P. *anupādisesa*) — in case of the Buddha usually styled Parinirvāṇa — can only be reached after death. By it all suffering ceases, completely and for ever, and in so

---

1 To wit the 3 specified above, with *kāmarāga*, attachment, and *paṭigha*, antipathy; Majjh. N. I, p. 432; Aṅg. N. II, p. 238; somewhat different in Dh. Saṅg. 1460. Cp. Divy. 533; 553; Vyu. § 109. — Five classes of Anāgamins are enumerated Pugg. P. p. 16 f. Vyut. § 46; cp. CHILDERS s. v. *anāgāmī*.

2 *Āsrava*, P. *āsava*. Their number is three: *kāma-*, *bhava-* and *avijjāsava*; or four: the foregoing with addition of heresy; BURNOUF Intr. 823; CHILDERS s. v. *āsavo*.

3 I. e. besetting evil propensities of the mind, 10 in number; enumerated Dh. Saṅg. 1548; with some variations in Lal. V. p. 59 (where we have to read *rāgo* for *rogo*); 348 (r. *rāgo*, and add *mrakṣa*); 349.

4 Not only the lower, but also the higher (*ūrdhvabhāgīya*, P. *uddhambhāgiya*); see CHILDERS s. v. *saṃyojana*; the list in Dh. Saṅg. 1460 shows variations. Cp. Vyu. § 109.

5 *Paṭisambhidā*; more about this term in the sequel.

6 The character and qualities of the four degrees of Saints are fully described in Mil. P. 102 ff. Cp. Vyu. § 46. — The fourfold division of Yogins is: Prāthamakalpika, Madhubhūmika, Prajñājyotis, and Atikrāntabhāvanīya; Yogas. III, 50, Comm.

7 Pugg. P. p. 13; cp. CHILDERS s. v.

8 WASSILIEF B. 239.

9 Synonymous terms are Nirvṛti, Nibbuti; Amṛta, Amata, and others. The terms are known also to other Indian sects, with a different shade of meaning. The usual term in the Yoga is Kaivalya; in the Vedānta, Mukti, Mokṣa; in the Nyāya, Apavarga; in the system of the Śaiva-monks, Duḥkhānta. In Caraka IV, 5 occur as synonymous with "final rest": *śānti*, *amṛta*. *brahman*, *nirvāṇa*.

10 Vyu. § 95; BURNOUF Intr. 590; CHILDERS s. v. *upādiseso*, where the remark that *nirupadhi* is with the S. Buddhists a distinctive epithet of the Arhat, must be coupled with what the same author says s. v. *upadhi*: "the term *nirupadhi* may also be applied to one who has attained anupādisesa-nibbāna, has ceased to exist". Now the N. Buddhists use *nirūpadhi* exactly in the latter sense, and yet they are blamed by the author! On the confusion in Itiv. p. 30 see above p. 50.

far it may be extolled as a blissful state, and as eternal, *amṛta* (*amata*). Does it imply a complete cessation of consciousness? It does, of course, if we draw the logical conclusions from the fundamental principles underlying the creed[1]. But not every one draws logical conclusions, and it would seem that even in the bosom of the Congregation there reigned some uncertainty anent the point in question. This would not be very wonderful. When the brethren repeatedly heard how the Buddha was conscious of all occurrences in his former births, some of them may involuntarily have been led to believe that memory, consciousness survives after death. We may understand how in order to prevent fruitless discussions among the brethren the Buddha is represented to have laid down the rule that the question: "Does the Tathāgata exist after death, or does he not?" is one of those questions that must be set aside as useless and remain unanswered[2].

Practically, Nirvāṇa means a happy death without fear of rebirth. If so, how then can the Buddha be said to have conquered Māra? Because he conquered, not, indeed, physical death, but the abject fear of death. The means of bringing about that result, consists in representing death as something extremely blissful.

3. SPIRITUAL EXERCISES.

The striving for Nirvāṇa requires a good deal of constant spiritual exercise, meditation and contemplation, such as with insignificant variations are practised by all Indian ecstatics.

As a preparatory to soaring into the higher regions of thought, must be considered the *bhāvanā*, cultivation, cherishing of the sentiments of *maitrī*, benevolence, *karuṇā*, compassion, *muditā*, cheerfulness, and *upekṣā*, indifference, equanimity. These four Bhāvanās, identical in name and character with those of all Yogins[3], are otherwise termed *brahmavihāra*, living in the spiritual world, and P. *appamaññā*, Skr. *apramāṇa*[4].

Sometimes a fifth Bhāvanā is added to the four Brahmavihāras, to wit the Aśubhabhāvanā, realisation of the loathsomeness of the body, but in this case *bhāvanā* means conception, realisation; synonymous terms are *asubhasaññā* and *aśubhapratyavekṣā*[5]. There are 10 Aśubhas, notions arising from the contemplation of a dead body; the names in P. are: *uddhumātaka*, bloated; *vinīlaka*, blackish; *vipubbaka*, festering; *vicchiddaka*, fissured from decay; *vikkhāyitaka*, gnawed by animals; *vikkhittaka*, scattered; *hatavikkhittaka*,

---

1 We refer to the exhaustive and masterly article *nibbāna* in CHILDERS Dict. Cp. D'ALWIS, Buddhist Nirvāṇa; FRANKFURTER, Buddhist Nirvāṇa and the Noble Eightfold Path, JRAS of 1880; RHYS DAVIDS B. 14. — For the Mahāyānist the idea of Nirvāṇa is a mere delusion, as we shall see in the sequel.

2 Majjh. N. I, 426 ff.; 484; Saṃy. N. II, p. 222; Mil. P. 145. It is not easy to reconcile, unless by sophisms, this agnosticism with the words spoken by the Tathāgata in Saṃy. N. II, p. 232: „Puggalaṃ passāmi param maraṇā Nirayam upapannam". And how to explain another passage, Saṃy. N. III, p. 109, where the theory that the "khīṇāsavo ucchijjati, na hoti paraṃ maraṇā" is rejected as being heterodox?

3 Definition in Yogas. I, 33.

4 Aṅg. N. II, p. 130; Nip. p. 89; Vyu. § 72; Lal. V. 35; 371; Jāt. Mala XXXII. CHILDERS is right in deriving the P. term from *appamāṇa*, as appears from *mettaṃ cittaṃ bhāvanaṃ appamāṇaṃ* S. Nip. l. c.; *appamāṇasamādhi* = *appamaññā* Aṅg. N. I, p. 236; *appamāṇaṃ cetosamādhiṃ* II, 54; cp. Majjh. N. I, p. 283. We have also *aparimāṇa* S. Nip. p. 26.

5 Majjh. N. I, p. 424; Vyu. § 52, Title; Lal. V. 36; CHILDERS s. v. *asubho*.

injured and scattered; *lohitaka*, bloody; *puḷavaka*, full of worms; *aṭṭhika*, bones[1].

The ten Asubhas, as well as the four Brahmavihāras, belong to the 40 philosophical Operations or Kammaṭṭhānas[2]. These Operations include the tenfold Kasiṇa, a kind of mystic Bhāvanā. The ten objects on which the attention at this operation must be fixed are: earth, water, fire, air, blue, yellow, red, white, light, and ether or space[3]. The same rite is practised by the the N. Buddhists, who term it *kṛtsnāyatana*, object or base of Kṛtsna. The ten modes of operation are given in the following order: *nīla-*, *pīta-*, *lohita-*, *avadāta-*, *pṛthivī-*, *ap-*, *tejas-*, *vāyu-*, *ākāśa-*, and *vijñāna-kṛtsnāyatana*[4].

The 40 Operations further comprise the 10 kinds of *anusmṛti*, P. *anussati*, recollection, constant thinking: on the Buddha, the Dharma, the Saṅgha; morality; liberality (*cāga, tyāga*); the gods; death; the body; the regulation of inspiration and expiration (*ānāpānasmṛti*); and quietude[5].

The exercise of Ānāpānasmṛti consists in fixing the mind intently on one's own breathing, in connection with certain set subjects of reflection; it is a highly valued kind of Samādhi[6].

Four species of Kammaṭṭhāna are termed Āruppa, belonging to the 4 incorporeal Brahmalokas: *Ākāsānañcāyatana*, place of infinity of space; *Viññānānañcāy.*, p. of infinity of clear consciousness; *Ākiñcaññāy.*, p. of nothingness; *Nevasaññānāsaññāy.*, p. of neither-consciousness-nor-unconsciousness; in Skr. Ākāśānantyāyatana, Vijñānānantyāy., Ākiñcanyāy., Naivasañjnā-nāsañjñāyatana[7]. Those who by dint of ecstatic meditation soar into those regions, have reached a very high standpoint, there remaining but one superior: the *Saññāvedayitanirodha*, Skr. *Sañjñāveditanirodha*, cessation of consciousness; the same have arrived at the corresponding exalted states of *vimokṣa*, P. *vimokha*, emancipation, deliverance[8]. There is, of course, not much that is particularly Buddhist in this system. For we know that Ārāḷa Kālāma was proficient in the state of Nothingness, and Udraka Rāmaputra in that of Neither-consciousness-nor-unconsciousness, but they were surpassed by the Buddha, who attained to cessation of consciousness[9].

---

1 Dh. Saṅg. 264. The corresponding terms Vyu. § 52 are: *vinīlaka-*, *vipūyaka-*, *vipaḍumaka-*, *vyādhmātaka-*, *vilohitaka-*, *vikhāditaka-*, *vikṣiptaka-*, *vidagdhaka-*, and *asthi-sañjñā*. This list counts one term less than the P. Asubhas, for a detailed account of which see HARDY E. M. 268.

2 Enumerated from Vis. M. by CHILDERS s. v. They are included in the more extensive series of 108 Dharmalokamukhas in Lal. V. 34 ff.

3 See CHILDERS s. v. *kasino*. In Majjh. N. I, 423 we find the 5 elements, earth, water, fire, air, and ether or space as objects of *pathavīsamā bhāvanā* &c. The 5 elements with Vijñāna constitute the 6 Dhātus; see Dharma-S. LVIII, note. The following bhāvanās l. c. are *metta-*, *karuṇā-*, *muditā-*, *upekkhābhāvanā*; then *asubha*; further *aniccasaññā*; finally *ānāpāna-sati*.

4 Vyu. § 72. The *vijñāna-k.* instead of *āloka-k.* recurs in a Pāli source, Saṅgīti-S.; see CHILDERS l. c. and HARDY E. M. 252 ff. for a more detailed description.

5 Aṅg. N. I, 42. Out of these 10 the first six are given by CHILDERS s. v. *anussati*; likewise in Lal. V. 34; Vyu. § 51; Dharma-S. LIV, note.

6 For the details of this mystic operation we refer to Majjh. N. I, p. 425; S. Vibh. I, p. 70; Vyu. § 53 (where the term is *ānāpānabhāvanāvidhi*); HARDY E. M. 267 ff. Cp. WASSILIEF B. 139.

7 Vyu. §§ 68; 119; BURNOUF Lotus p. 811; HARDY E. M. 261. Cp. Majjh. N. I, p. 455.

8 Majj. N. I, p. 456; cp. p. 296; Vyu. § 70; Dharma-S. LIX; the form Sañjñāvedayita° in Mhv. I, 126. — In some passages we meet with a fourfold *cetovimutti*, mental emancipation; viz. *appamāṇā*. *ākiñcaññā*, *suññatā*, and *animittā c.*; Majjh. N. I, p. 297; Aṅg. N. I, p. 4; in others, five; see CHILDERS s. v. *vimutti*. The *cittavimukti* in the Yoga is threefold; Yogas. II, 27, Comm.

9 Majjh. N. I, p. 165; Lal. V. 295; 306; Buddhac. XII, vss. 63; 83.

It results from the foregoing that the four degrees of Dhyāna, P. Jhāna, abstract meditation, though nominally, excluded from the system of Kammaṭṭhānas, are nothing else but the four lower stages of ecstasy. Since the exercise of Dhyāna is confessedly anterior to Buddhism[1], we content ourselves with producing the following passage from the racy description by CHILDERS[2]. "The priest — concentrates his mind upon a single thought. Gradually his soul becomes filled with a supernatural ecstasy and serenity, while his mind still reasons upon and investigates the subject chosen for contemplation; this is the first Jhána. Still fixing his thoughts upon the same subject, he then frees his mind from reasoning and investigation, while the ecstasy and serenity remain, and this is the second Jhána. Next, his thoughts still fixed as before, he divests himself of ecstasy, and attains the third Jhána, which is a state of tranquil serenity. Lastly, he passes to the fourth Jhána, in which the mind, exalted and purified, is indifferent to all emotions, alike of pleasure and of pain". Each of the first three Dhyānas is subdivided into three degrees, the inferior, the medial and the superior meditation; the attainment of the first Dhyāna gives the power of working miracles, *ṛddhi*, P. *iddhi*. In general the Dhyānas secure access to the sixteen corporeal (*rūpa*) Brahmalokas, the peculiar *loka* being determined by the degree of Dhyāna attained[3]. It is, consequently, plain that the 4 Dhyānas represent a lower stage of ecstatic contemplation than the 4 Āruppas.

Sometimes there is question of 5 Dhyānas (*pañcangikaṃ jhānaṃ*). They differ in no essential point from the 4 Dhyānas, the second stage being separated into two[4].

In connection with Dhyāna we have to speak of Samādhi, properly a state of most intense concentration and absorption[5], but in Buddhist writings a wider term. There are different sets of Samādhi. The 3 Samādhis are Savitakka-savicāra-, Avitakka-vicāramatta-, and Avitakka-avicāra. Three others are Suññata, void, Animitta, groundless, reasonless, and Appaṇihita, without fixed purpose[6], to which correspond 3 states of emancipation[7]. A set of 4 Samādhis is designated by the qualifications of *hānabhāgiya*, leading to rejection; *ṭhitibhāgiya*, l. to firmness; *visesabhāgiya*, l. to distinction, and *nibbedhabhāgiya*, l. to excellence[8].

In Samādhi one distinguishes two degrees, the inferior called Upacāra-samādhi, and the superior, Appanā-S., i. e. initiatory, and penetrating, thoroughly grasping[9].

The original meaning of Samādhi is such that any profound pious meditation can be brought under that head. Hence it is not to be wondered at that the Mahāyānists with their ritualistic propensities invented a series of Samādhis

1 See e. g. Jāt. I, p. 58; Mhv. I, 228; Lal. V. 147; Buddhac. XII, vs. 49. Cp. Yogas. III, 2.

2 Dict. p. 169. Original text e. g. in Majjh. N. I, pp. 21; 117; 455; Lal. V. 147; 439; Mhv. I, 228; Vyu. § 67. Cp. Buddhac. XII, vss. 49 ff.

3 The names of these Lokas in the sequel.

4 In Dh. Saṅg. 83 the degrees are *vitakka*, *vicāra*, *pīti*, *sukha*, and *cittass' ekaggatā*.

5 Mil. P. 38; Yogas. III, 3; Sarvad, S. 164.

6 Aṅg. N. I, p. 299; Mil. P. 337, where the 6 Samādhis are qualified as one of the 7 Ratnas of the Buddha. — Cp. Yogas. I, 17 f.

7 Dhp. vs. 92, and Comm.; CHILDERS Dict. p. 270. The three Vimokṣas or Vimuktis in Vyu. § 73 are: Śūnyatā, Animittaṃ, Apraṇihitaṃ. Cp. Dharma-S. LXXII, note.

8 Vyu. § 55 *Nirvedhabhāgīya*, synonymous with *uṣmagata*, *mūrdhāna*, *kṣānti*, and *laukikāgradharma*. Cp. *uṣmagata* &c. WASSILIEF B. 139; 246; Pāli *usmāgata* = *samaṇateja*, Jāt. V, p. 208; *usmīkata*, highly proficient, brilliant, Majjh. N. I, p. 132.

9 HARDY E. M. 257. The same division applies to the Kammaṭṭhānas.

adorned with more or less sensational names, but with no definite meaning. The number in the Prajñā-Pāramitā is no less than 108[1].

Theoretically there should be as many Samāpattis as Samādhis. For the latter does not differ more from the former than a process going on does from its accomplishment. It is, in fact, expressly stated that there are eight Samāpattis, coinciding with the four inferior kinds of Samādhi, i. e. the four Dhyānas, and with the four Āruppa Kammaṭṭhānas. The ninth, Nirodha-samāpatti, answers to the Saññāvedayitanirodha[2].

Reverting to the Kammaṭṭhānas, we farther come across the *Āhārapaṭikkūlasaññā*, consciousness of the impurity of material food[3]. The last of the list is *Catudhātu-vavatthāna*, determination of the four elements.

Besides the forty Operations occasionally occur some exercises not included in the list, and yet termed Kammaṭṭhānas; e. g. the Suññatā-kammaṭṭhāna, but this is obviously merely another name for Suññato (sic) samādhi[4].

The base or substratum of an idea, and as such the subject for meditation is called *ārammaṇa*, Skr. *ārambaṇa* or, more usually, *ālambana*[5].

In the foregoing we have had occasion to name several ideal worlds, the corporeal and the incorporeal Brahmalokas. These and similar worlds are spoken of in a way as if they constituted parts of the universe. The Buddhists, being idealists, make no marked difference between cosmical facts based on observation[6] and the products of fancy. The one and the other belong to their cosmical system, whereof we will try to give a succinct view.

4. COSMICAL SYSTEM. CLASSIFICATION OF LIVING BEINGS.

The universe consists of innumerable spheres, Cakravālas, each of which has its own earth, sun, moon, heavens and hells[7]. Between those spheres are situated certain hells, termed Lokāntarika. The centre of our earth is occupied by Mount Meru or Sumeru (P. also Sineru), around which are the principal mountains, Kulācalas[8] and beyond these the four continents or Mahā-dvīpas, viz. Uttara-Kuru, the country of the Hyperboreans; Jambudvīpa, India, to the South of the Meru; Apara-Godāna or -Godānīya (P. Apara-Goyāna) to the West; Pūrva-Videha (Pubba-V.) to the East[9].

Each of the spheres consists of three Avacaras, regions, also styled Lokas, worlds, or Dhātus, layers, floors, the lowest being the region of Kāma, sensual pleasure; higher is the region of Rūpa, form, divided into four stages of Dhyāna; the highest is the region of Arūpa, formlessness[10].

The lowest region is the abode of six classes of gods: 1. the four Rulers of the cardinal points; 2. the Thirty-three gods; 3. the Yāmas; 4. the Tuṣitas; 5. the

---

1 Enumerated in Vyu. § 21.

2 Pugg. P. p. 20; Saṃy. N. II, p. 216 (nine Vihārasamāpattis); Vyu. § 68; BURNOUF Lot. 348; 789; WASSILIEF B. 140; 240. Cp. Yogas. I, 42—48.

3 HARDY E. M. 96, from Vis. M.

4 Aṅg. N. I, p. 299.

5 *Ārambaṇa* in Aṣṭas. P. Pāram. *passim*, e. g. p. 138; 269; Vyu. § 21; cp. *anārambaṇa* Chāndogyopaniṣad 2, 9. But *ālambana* Yogas. I, 10; 38; 42, Comm.

6 In an idealistic system where there is no room for absolute reality, as the whole world is a product of imagination; in other words: the world is created by Dhyāna. Cp. HODGSON Ess. 28; BEAL Cat. 124.

7 For details see CHILDERS s. v. *sattaloka*; HARDY M. of B. 1 ff.; Legends 80 ff. BURNOUF Intr. 599 ff.; WADDELL Buddh. of Tib. 77—104.

8 Cp. Dharma-S. CXXV, note.

9 Cp. Vyu. § 154; Lal. V. 170; Divy. 213 ff.

10 Vyu. § 155: *kāma-, rūpa-, arūpya-dhātu*.

Nirmāṇaratis; 6. the Parinirmita-vaśavartins[1]. These six Devalokas constitute with the world of men, of Asuras, of Pretas, the animal kingdom and the hells, the eleven Kāmalokas[2].

The second region, that of Rūpa, or more accurately the Rūpa-brahmaloka — for Rūpaloka in a wider sense includes the Kāmaloka — is divided into sixteen sections, the abodes of as many classes of gods who are free from *kāma*. Beginning from below we have: 1. Brahmapārisajjas; 2. Brahmapurohitas; 3. Mahābrahmas; 4. Parittābhas; 5. Appamāṇābhas; 6. Ābhassaras; 7. Parittasubhas; 8. Appamāṇasubhas; 9. Subhakiṇṇas; 10. Vehapphalas; 11. Asaññasattas; 12. Avihas; 13. Atappas; 14. Sudassas; 15. Sudassins; 16. Akaniṭṭhas[3]. The abodes of 1—3 are attained by those who exercise the three degrees of the first Dhyāna, severally. The next three by proficients in the second Dhyāna; the next three by the adepts in the third Dhyāna; 10 and 11 are assigned to the fourth Dhyāna, and the remaining five to the Anāgāmins[4].

The Northern texts contain nearly the same names. The first group is made up of Brahmakāyikas, Brahmapāriṣadyas, Brahmapurohitas, Mahābrahmas[5]; the second, of Parīttābhas, Apramāṇābhas, and Ābhāsvaras; the third, of Parīttaśubhas, Apramāṇaśubhas, and Śubhakṛtsnas; the fourth, of Anabhrakas, Puṇyaprasavas, and Vṛhatphalas[6]. The last five are Avṛhas, Atapas, Sudṛśas, Sudarśanas, and Akaniṣṭhas[7].

Higher than the Rūpabrahmaloka is the Arūpabr., divided into four degrees which bear the same names as the Āruppa-kammaṭṭhānas[8].

The very lowest of the thirtyone abodes of living beings are the hells or places of punishment (*naraka*, *niraya*). The principal hells are eight in number and known by the names of Sañjīva, Kālasūtra, Saṅghāta, Raurava, Mahāraurava, Tapana, Pratāpana, and the very deepest, Avīci[9]. Apart from these there is the Lokāntarika hell, already mentioned, and many minor hells. In the old system of the N. Buddhists there are besides the eight hot hells just enumerated as many cold hells: Arbuda, Nirarbuda, Aṭaṭa, Hahava, Huhava, Utpala, Padma, and Mahāpadma[10]; in the Pāli canon we meet with the same and a few more: Aṭaṭa, Abbuda, Nirabbuda, Ahaha, Ababa, Kumuda, Uppalaka, Sogandhika, Puṇḍarīka, and Paduma[11]. In later N. works the number of hells is still greater[12].

---

1 Lal. V. 170; Divy. 200; BURNOUF Intr. 212. The gods are longlived, *dīghāyuka*, but not immortal; Aṅg. N. II, 33. The same view is common enough among Hindus; e. g. Yājñavalkya Dharmaś. III, 10; Yogas. II, 5, Comm.

2 Vyu. § 156 only eight; to wit the worlds of 6 kinds of gods, of terrestrial beings, and of inhabitants of the atmosphere (*antarikṣavāsin*).

3 In Majjh. N. I, p. 329 occur the groups 6—10, followed by Abhibhu; cp. there p. 327.

4 CHILDERS s. v. *jhānaṃ*.

5 Thus Vyu. § 157; the second name is wanting in BURNOUF Intr. 212. As there ought to be only three names, it is probable that Brahmakāyikas properly is a comprehensive term for the whole group, as in Pāli; see CHILDERS Dict. p. 486. Cp. Dharma-S. CXXVIII.

6 Lal.V. 171 adds.: Asañjñisattvas, agreeing with P. Asaññasattas; so, too, Dharma-S. l. c.

7 The Atapas wanting in Lal. V. l. c. Vyu. § 161 adds Aghaniṣṭhas(!) and Mahāmaheśvarāyatana.

8 An account of the exact duration of life of the gods residing in the Ākāsānañcāyatana &c. is found Aṅg. N. I, p. 267.

9 A detailed description of these hells occurs e. g. Aṅg. N. I, pp. 141 ff. Mhv. I, 7 ff. Cp. Vyu. § 214.

10 BURNOUF Intr. 201; Vyu. § 215; Divy. 67. Somewhat different Dharma-S. CXXII, where Apapa = P. Ababa.

11 S. Nip. p. 123. These terms also denote certain high numerals.

12 E. g. in Kāraṇḍa-Vyūha. Cp. L. FEER, L'enfer indien, JA 1892 and 1893.

Above the hells is placed the animal kingdom or brute creation. Not unlikely we have to see in this notion the survival of ancient myths, for real animals are living on our planet, the world of men. Higher than the animal kingdom is the abode of Pretas, ghosts, spectres, though these beings are also placed in the Lokāntarika hell[1]. Still higher is the domain of Asuras, demons, among whom ranks foremost Rāhu, the personified eclipse[2]. The hells, together with the next three worlds, constitute the four Apāyalokas[3], places of suffering. Adding to them the state of men, we get the 5 Gatis or states of existence[4].

It is difficult for us to realise in how far such theories were matter of serious belief. This much is certain that in the canonical books, both of the South and the North, we repeatedly hear the Master gravely and in a tone of perfect earnest discoursing on his visits to various heavens &c. A visit to the Brahmaloka is vividly described by him in the Brahmanimantaṇika-Sutta[5]. In another passage he asserts that he had received a visit from Brahma Sahampati[6]. Suchlike declarations are numberless, not to speak of the passages where in the history of the Buddha the gods, especially Brahmā and Indra enter as actors, represented with as much reality as the Tathāgata himself. The Master knows all about the destiny of persons in the life to come, and freely predicts where so and so will be reborn, at the same time expressly — and suspiciously — stating that he does not use his transcendent faculty, as other teachers do, out of greed or in order to deceive the world[7].

What have we to infer from all this? Whatever may have been the conviction and purpose of those who composed the canonical texts, it can hardly be doubted that the majority of the believers, both among the laity and the monks, have, up to this day, put implicit faith in the contents of their sacred books[8].

Besides this system of 31 worlds and their inhabitants, there is another in which living beings are distinguished according to their higher and lower degree of spiritual excellence; a distinction, it must be observed, of a temporary character. For the lowest beings in the scale may by dint of Karman rise to the highest rank, and the most elevated can descend, with the exception of Buddhas, Pratyekabuddhas and Arhats, who are certain of reaching final Nirvāṇa.

According to this classification the highest beings are: 1. the Supreme Buddhas; then follow: 2. Pratyekabuddhas; 3. Arhats; 4. Devas; 5. Brahmas; 6. Gandharvas, celestial musicians; 7. Garuḍas, winged beings flying through the sky like lightning; 8. Nāgas, snake-like beings, resembling clouds; 9. Yakṣas[9];

1 Cp. the tales in the Book of Ghost stories, Petavatthu, and CHILDERS s. v. *peto*.

2 CHILDERS s. v. *asuro* and Vyu., § 171.

3 Lal. V. 236 mentions three Apāyas, without specifying them.

4 Or six, if the Asuranikāya be added; BURNOUF Lot. 309; cp. Dharma-S. LVII, note.

5 Majjh. N. I, p. 326.

6 Aṅg. N. II, p. 20; Majjh. N. I, p. 458.

7 Majjh. N. I, p. 464.

8 On the other hand it cannot be denied that in later Mahāyānist or Tantric works we come across instances of thorough going scepticism. In the Vajramaṇḍa Dhāraṇī the Buddha declares: "The hells, o Mañjuśrī, are a creation of ignorant men who foolishly believe in what does not exist; the hells are a product of their fancy"; BURNOUF Intr. p. 544.

9 This word has in B. writings sometimes a wider and older meaning, viz, that of a being to be worshipped or a powerful spirit; Indra e. g. is called a Yakṣa; even the Buddha is glorified by Upāli as an *āhuneyyo yakkho uttamapuggalo atulo*, Majjh. N. I, p. 386. The term is used synonymously with *devaputta* Saṃy. N. I, p. 54. In a more restricted sense the Yakṣas are the attendants of Kubera as in Hindu mythology; cp. Vyu. § 169.

10. Kumbhāṇḍas, goblins; 11. Asuras, demons; 12. Rākṣasas, giants, monsters; 13. Pretas, ghosts, spectres; 14. the inhabitants of hell[1].

Of all these only the first three will occupy us; the others need no particular notice, the less so, because they belong to Indian mythology in general.

5. ARHATS, PRATYEKABUDDHAS, AND THEIR CHARACTERISTICS.

Arhats are, dogmatically, all those who are walking in the fourth and highest stage of the path leading to Nirvāṇa. They are distinguished by faculties far surpassing those of common mortals. First of all then they possess the four sorts of *paṭisambhidā* — in N. texts *pratisaṃvid* — regarding 1. Artha; 2. Dharma; 3. Nirukti; 4. Pratibhāna. The purport of these terms seems to be: a transcendent faculty in grasping the meaning of a text or subject; in grasping the Law of all things as taught by the Buddha; in exegesis; readiness in expounding and discussing[2].

Besides the four distinctive faculties just named, the Arhat possesses five kinds of transcendent knowledge, Abhijñā (Abhiññā); to wit: Ṛddhi (Iddhi), the power of working miracles[3]. Further the Divine ear by which he is enabled to hear and understand all sounds in the universe[4]; knowledge of the thoughts of others; memory of former existences; and the Divine eye, by which he sees all that is occurring in the world and perceives how beings in different worlds die and are reborn. There is also a sixth Abhijñā, being the transcendent knowledge which causes the destruction of defiling passions[5].

The Arhat is also endowed with eight Vidyās, branches of knowledge, which, however, are nothing else but the six Abhijñas with the addition of *vipassanañāna* and *manomayiddhi*. The latter is properly only one of the 10 Ṛddhis[6].

Vipassanā, Skr. Vipaśyanā and more correctly Vidarśanā, is contemplation and the true insight connected with it. It is often mentioned together with Samatha, Skr. Śamatha, quietude, as an attribute of Arhats. Accordingly it is said that there are two orders of Arhats, the Sukkhavipassaka, the barely contemplative philosopher, and the Samathayānika, he who is devoted to quietude[7].

The power of working miracles requires the aid of the fourfold Padhāna

---

1 The series in Vyu. § 166 is: Devas, Nāgas, Yakṣas, Gandharvas, Asuras, Daityas, Garuḍas, Kinnaras, Mahoragas, and Kumbhāṇḍas. Several names of these beings are recorded § 167—175. Cp. Divy. 148. Lal. V. 184 omits Daityas, but adds Śakra, Brahmā, the Lokapālas, monks, nuns, lay devotees of both sexes.

2 See the dissertation of CHILDERS s. v. *paṭisambhidā*. For *paṭibhāna* cp. Mil. P. 340. Paṭisambhidā, apparently, means speciality, special and distinctive gift. *Pratisaṃvid* is wholly inappropriate as has been pointed out by CHILDERS. Cp. Vyu. § 13; Dharma-S. LI, note.

3 It has 4 subdivisions, *pādas;* see CHILDERS s. v. *iddhipādo;* the passage there adduced is identical with Vyu. § 40.

4 The same faculty belongs to the Yogin; Yogas. III, 40.

5 HARDY E. M. 284; M. of B. 38; BURNOUF Intr. 295; Lot. 820. Cp. CV. VI, 6, 2; Lal. V. 184. Slight variations in Vyu. § 14; the miraculous performances due to Abhijñā are summarized § 15. Cp. Dharma-S. XX, note.

6 CHILDERS s. vv. *vijjā* and *manomayo*. For the 10 sorts of Ṛddhi see HARDY M. of B. 500. Sometimes there is question of 3 kinds of Iddhi-pāṭihāriya, and we know e. g. from Aṅg. N. I, p. 172, that many monks had the power of performing such miracle. Miracles, *pāṭihīra*, on sacred monuments (*cetyia*) of past Arhats, are not rare; Mil. P. 309. There are 3 species of Prātihārya: *ṛddhi-*, *ādeśanā-* and *anuśāsanī-prātihārya;* Dīgh. N. I, pp. 212 ff. Vyu. § 16.

7 CHILDERS s. v. *samatho;* Dhp. p. 425; WASSILIEF B. 141; Lal. V. 146; 218; Mhv. I, 120; Vyu. § 90.

or Sammā-p., right exertion or application[1], consisting: 1. in the restraint of the senses, Saṃvara-p.; 2. in the abandonment of sinful thoughts; 3. in the Bhāvanās; 4. in steady perseverance[2]. — Certain spiritual qualities which the Arhats share with the Bodhisattvas will be noticed in the sequel.

The prominent characteristic of the Arhat is Wisdom, Prajñā. It is by Wisdom that he crosses the ocean of existence; hence he is said to be Prajñāvimukta. His inferior, the Anāgāmin, cannot yet reach that ultimate goal, but becomes a denizen of the Brahmaloka, by means of Samādhi, whilst the Sakṛdāgāmin and Srotaāpanna by virtue of Morality, Śīla, occupy places intermediate between the Brahmaloka and the Apāyas[3].

The Arhat is the Ārya *par excellence*, though all others who are progressing towards Deliverance are entitled to that denomination. In many cases Ārya, Arhat and Śrāvaka are controvertible terms. Primarily Śrāvaka is a hearer, a disciple of Buddha, but it is not seldom used synonymously with Arhat or Ārya[4], and the compound Ariyasāvaka in general denotes a pious believer[5].

In a later period we see the Mahāyānists apply Śrāvaka to denote the primeval Buddhists, but it is with them also a comprehensive term for their opponents, the Hīnayānists, whom we may call Old Buddhists.

The Mahāyānists divide all sons of Buddha into three classes, according to the *yāna*, the vehicle they use, the curriculum they go through: 1. the Yāna of the Śrāvakas, the lowest; 2. that of the Pratyekabuddhas; 3. that of the Bodhisattvas[6]. In connection with the whole tenor of the passage in Saddh. P. where the three Yānas are spoken of, it would seem that by the followers of the Śrāvaka-yāna are meant the Sthaviras or Buddhists of the old orthodoxy; with the second class the solitary contemplative philosophers[7]; with the third, the accomplished teachers and preachers.

Although such a distinction is made, one should know that essentially there is only one Yāna, the Buddhayāna, because ultimately all beings, at one time or another, shall reach the same goal. Therefore the Tathāgata declares that he will lead all beings to final Nirvāṇa, adding: "all beings are my children".[8]

Both with the Mahāyānists and the adherents of the old creed the Arhats are inferior to the Pratyekabuddhas or private Buddhas. Dogmatically the Pratyekabuddha, P. Pacceka-b. is a being who has attained, like a Buddha,

[1] Aṅg. N. II, p. 15; S. Nip. p. 74; cp. Dharma-S. XLV; Lal. V. 37; 218; 327. The form Prahāṇa in N. texts is a decidedly blundering rendering of a Prākṛt term into Skr. This is proved by the fact that the verbal expression corresponding to *samyak-prahāṇa* is *samyak pradadhāti* Vyu. § 39; cp. Lal. V. 499.

[2] Aṅg. N. II, p. 16; Vyu. § 39.

[3] Vis. M. I, p. 22 and p. 26; cp. Vyu. § 26.

[4] Thus *ariyā* Dhp. vs. 22 is explained p. 180 by *Buddha-paccekabuddha-sāvakā*, where *sāvaka* takes the place of Arhat. *Sāvaka-bodhi* is the knowledge possessed by an Arhat, opposed both to supreme Buddha-knowledge and to Pratyeka-buddhi; see CHILDERS s. v. *sāvako*. The same results from Vyu. §§ 46—48.

[5] In Aṅg. N. I, p. 210 the Ariyasāvakas are exhorted to keep the Sabbath in a worthy manner; here the word can only mean a pious believer. So, too, the *gahapati ariyasāvako;* op. c. II, p. 68.

[6] BURNOUF Lot. p. 52; 315. *Yānīkṛta*, P. *yānikata* seems to be synonymous with *bahulīkata* and *bhāvita* (e. g. Saṃy. N. I, p. 114; II, p. 264, MPS. III, 75; Mil. P. 140), and to mean "gone through, studied, steadily exercised", pretty much the same as Skr. *abhyasta*. — For the 3 Yānas see Dharma-S. II, and the references in the note; and WASSILIEF B. 7. BEAL compares the Platonic ὄχημα; Cat. 124.

[7] In such passages like Mhv. I, 301, it is not difficult to recognize a hermit under the disguise of the term Pratyekabuddha.

[8] Lot. p. 89. Cp. Dharma-S. l. c.

by his unaided powers the knowledge necessary to Nirvāṇa, but does not preach it. He is not omniscient, and is in all respects inferior to a supreme Buddha. It is a law of nature that he can not live at the same time with a Buddha[1].

6. BUDDHAS AND THEIR CHARACTERISTICS.

The Buddhas are the highest spiritual beings. So the supreme Buddha has said himself, and repeatedly. Now what kind of being is a Buddha? Before attempting to answer this question, we have to take a survey of his characteristics, external and internal.

Among the external characteristics of a Buddha the most remarkable are the 32 Mahāpuruṣa-lakṣaṇas, which he shares with Cakravartins, Arhats and other eminent persons[2]. The number of secondary characteristics, Anuvyañjana, is 80. The enumeration and description of those primary and secondary marks, which with insignificant variations are equally found in S. and in N. texts, is too long to be here inserted. It will suffice to indicate the chief sources of information[3]. Besides these marks, 216 Māṅgalya-lakṣaṇas or auspicious marks, 108 on each foot, are attributed to the Buddha[4].

It is a remarkable custom of all Buddhas that with their Divine eye they survey the world six times every day[5]. As something peculiar to Gautama Buddha, it is recorded that he measured 12 cubits, or as others have it, 18 cubits in height. This tradition is somehow countenanced by the dimensions of his sacred footstep, Śrīpāda, on the Adam Peak in Ceylon, measuring more than 5 feet in length and 2½ feet in breadth[6].

The mental characteristics of a Buddha are divided into three categories, each of them comprising a certain sum of qualities: I. the 10 Balas or forces, powers; II. the 18 Āveṇika Dharmās or peculiar properties; III. the 4 Vaiśāradyas or points of selfconfidence, of assurance.

The 10 Balas are: 1. the knowledge of what is fit or unfit; 2. of the necessary consequences of Karman; 3. of the right road leading to any end; 4. of the elements; 5. of the different inclination of beings; 6. of the relative powers of the organs; 7. of all degrees of meditations and ecstasy, as well as of their power to purify and fortify the mind; 8. of remembering former births; 10. of removing moral corruption[7]. On account of these powers a Buddha bears the epithet of Daśabala.

Sometimes we read of a set of four, of five, and of seven Balas[8]. These, however, are not peculiar to Buddhas.

---

1 Childers s. v. *pacceko* and the references there. From the epithets *khaḍgaviṣāṇakalpa*, solitary as the rhinoceros, and *vargacārin*, mixing with society, associating himself, Vyu. § 45 (*vaggacārin*, S. Nip. p. 151) we may gather that some Pratyekas are rigid hermits of the wilderness; others more sociable, perhaps living as monks, or at least frequenting villages.

2 Mahāpuruṣa-lakkhaṇaṃ as a branch of science occurs S. Nip. p. 102; cp. Bṛhat-Saṃhitā Chap. LXIX. — It need not be told that Mahāpuruṣa and Puruṣottama are common epithets of Viṣṇu.

3 See Dharma-S. pp. 53—60; and add Mhv. II, 29 ff. and 213 ff.; Alabaster Wheel of the Law 115 ff.

4 Hardy M. of B. 367.

5 Divy. 95.

6 Hardy M. of B. 364 ff. Burnouf Lot. 622.

7 See Dharma-S. LXXVI, with the references, and add Mhv. I, 159, f. where we have to read, instead of Senart's conjecture *manovibhutā: anodhikatā*; i. e. *anavadhikatā*, illimitedness, and *anodhikabalā*, illimited powers, almost as the MSS. have it.

8 Four in Aṅg. N. II, p. 141; seven in Dh. Saṅg. 95—102; three with Childers s. v. *balaṃ*, and cp. Dharma-S. XLVIII, note.

The 18 Āveṇika Dharmas, otherwise termed Buddha-dharmas or qualities of a Buddha, are, shortly stated, the following: 1. the seeing of all things past; 2. of all things future; 3. of all things present; 4. propriety of actions of the body; 5. of speech; 6. of thought; 7. firmness of intention; 8. of memory; 9. of Samādhi; 10. of energy; 11. of emancipation; 12. of wisdom; 13. freedom from ficklenes or wantonness; 14. from noisiness; 15. from confusedness; 16. from hastiness; 17. from heedlessness; 18. from inconsiderateness[1].

The 4 Vaiśāradyas (Vesārajjas) are: 1. the assurance of the Tathāgata that he has attained omniscience; 2. that he has freed himself from sin; 3. that he knows the impediments (*antarāyika-dharma*) to Nirvāṇa; 4. that he has shown the right way to salvation[2].

It is quite in keeping with Indian habits that the qualities and functions of such a sublime being as the Tathāgata are indicated by a host of epithets which more or less assume the character of proper nouns. The most common appellations are Buddha, Jina, Sugata, Tathāgata; decidedly titles are Arhat, Śāstṛ, Bhagavat; many other names are descriptive epithets, as Daśabala, Lokavid, Puruṣadamyasārathi, Sarvajña, Ṣaḍabhijña, Anuttara, Narottama, Devātideva, Trikālajña, Triprātihāryasampanna, Nirbhaya, Niravadya, and the like[3].

Apart from the epithets applying to Buddhas in general, there are special names for the Buddha of the present period; as Sākyasiṃha, Sākyamuni, Sākyapuṅgava, Sākya, Sauddhodani, Ādityabandhu (in contradistinction to Kṛṣṇabandhu, i. e. Māra), Sūryavaṃśa, Siddhārtha, Sarvārthasiddha, Āṅgirasa, Gautama[4].

In the oldest system of historical Buddhism, we have cognizance of, the Buddha of the present period had been preceded by 24 others. Their names are, in Pāli: Dīpaṃkara, Kondañña, Maṅgala, Sumanas, Revata, Sobhita, Anomadassin, Paduma, Nārada, Padumuttara, Sumedha, Sujāta, Piyadassin, Atthadassin, Dhammadassin, Siddhattha, Tissa, Pussa, Vipassin, Sikhin, Vessabhū, Kakusandha, Koṇāgamana, and Kassapa[5]. Each of them has his peculiar Bodhi tree, e. g. Dīpaṃkara the Ficus religiosa, just as Gautama Buddha.

Many of these Tathāgatas are also mentioned in N. writings, but not systematically, and lumped together with others of later invention[6]. The last

---

1 The order slightly different in Vyu. § 9. Cp. Dharma-S. LXXIX, note. *Āveṇika* or *āveṇiya* means "peculiar, exclusively proper"; e. g. Jāt. IV. p. 358.

2 Aṅg. N. II, 9. See further Dharma-S. LXXVII.

3 A remarkable string of epithets is contained in Upāli's hymn Majjh. N. I, p. 386, which would afford matter for a complete Buddhology. Rich also is the list Vyu. § 1, and the enumeration Lal. V. 549—564; very poor in Amara-kośa I, 8, and Divy. 95.

4 Gautama without the addition of Buddha is a rather irreverential term for a believer. It is only by his opponents and unbelievers (who need not be unfriendly, though) that he is called "Śramaṇa Gautama". The most reverential term is Bhagavat, Lord. The rendering of this word with "Blessed One" is hardly right, as is proved by the meaning of the shortened *bhagos* and *bhos*. Bhagavat is essentially the same word as Slavonic *bogatŭ*, rich; Russian *bogačŭ*, a rich man; a meaning naturally passing into that of "a lord". It bears to the shortened Vedic vocative *bhagos* and the still shorter *bhos* nearly the same relation as French Seigneur to Monsieur, and English Sir. Nothing is more common than that words properly meaning *dominus* are applied to ecclesiastical worthies; e. g. Dom, Domine, Kuningas, Rabbi etc.

5 Their history is recorded in Buddhav. and Jāt. Intr. I, p. 3 ff. Properly there are three more Tathāgatas, to wit Taṇhaṃkara, Medhaṃkara, and Saraṇaṃkara, but they are not taken into account, because it was Dīpaṃkara who first predicted the future Buddhaship of Gautama Buddha; Dhp. p. 117, and cp. Mhv. I, 237, ff.

6 See in HODGSON Ess. p. 33 the lists drawn from Lal. V. and other works. Thirty-two Tathāgatas are enumerated Lot. p. 113.

seven Tathāgatas, to wit, Vipaśyin, Śikhin, Viśvabhū, Krakucchanda, Kanakamuni[1], Kāśyapa, and Śākyamuni are common to the North and the South, and are designated in N. texts as the Mānuṣi-buddhas. Sometimes we find that the four last Buddhas, Śākyamuni included, received special worship[2].

Just as there were Tathāgatas in the past, so there will be in future. The Buddha of the next following period is Maitreya, P. Metteya, surnamed Ajita, at present still a Bodhisattva living, it would seem, in the Tuṣita heaven[3].

All Tathāgatas are alike, save in a few points of no importance; they differ e. g. in size, and in duration of life; some are born as Kṣatriyas, others as Brahmans[4]. The Law proclaimed by all Tathāgatas is likewise one and the same, and when it is stated that Gautama Buddha evolved the Law from within himself without the aid of a master, the meaning is that by his intuition he re-discovered the old truths which had been forgotten in the night of dark times[5].

A peculiar sort of Buddhas, wholly anomalous, — for they are eternal and never were Bodhisattvas, — are the five Dhyāni-Buddhas of the Mahāyānists: Vairocana, Akṣobhya, Ratnasambhava, Amitābha, or Amitāyu(s), and Amoghasiddhi. Their female counterparts, Tārās or Śaktis, are: Vajradhātvīśvarī, Locanā, Māmakī, Pāṇḍarā, and Tārā[6].

It is a common opinion among European *savans* that the Buddhas preceding Śākyamuni are mythical, the latter alone being historical. That theory, whether true or false, is entirely opposed to the fixed dogma of *historical* Buddhism. Of course, we may surmise that in original Buddhism the matter stood otherwise. Such a supposition is allowable, provided we do not confound an hypothesis of our own making with the facts of sober history.

Having surveyed the external and internal characteristics of a Buddha, we revert to the question: "What kind of being is a Buddha?" The answer is given by the Lord himself. Once upon a time the Brahman Doṇa, seeing the Lord sitting at the foot of a tree, asked him: "Are you a Deva?" And the Lord answered: "I am not". — "Are you a Gandharva?" — "I am not". — "Are you a Yakṣa?" — "I am not". — "Are you a man?" — "I am not a man". On the Brahman asking what then he might be, the answer was, "Know, o Brahman, that I am a Buddha"[7]. Here the Buddha denies flatly and categorically that he is a man. This dogma has not undergone any change by the later development of the creed in Mahāyānism. In such an authoritative book as the Lotus the anthropomorphism of the Tathāgata has

---

[1] Krakutsanda and Konākamuni in Mhv. I, 2; II, 265; Koṇagamana on a *basrelief* of Bharhut, Pl XXIX; *Koṇakamana* in the edict of Niglīva (BÜHLER, Academy of 27 April 1895). — Cp. Dharma-S. VI and note and the translation of the Sapta-buddha-Stotra in WILSON Works II, 5.

[2] Already in the sculptures of Bharhut and Sanchi; in the time of Fa Hian at Saṅkaśya, Rec. p. 51.

[3] This may be inferred from the story related by Fa Hian, Rec. p. 25; in the Lotus we meet him on the Vulture Peak. His future appearance is predicted by the Lord in Mil. P. 159.

[4] The Buddha of the present period is by birth a Kṣatriya, by genius and conduct a Brahman; Mil. P. 225.

[5] See the discussion Mil. P. 217; cp. 236.

[6] See references at Dharma-S. III and IV, where some variations may be observed. Cp. D. WRIGHT Hist. of Nepāl, Pl. VI; a discussion on the origin and character of the Dhyāni-Buddhas in Versl. Meded. K. Akad. of 1888, p. 38 ff. Cp. also WADDELL Buddh. of Tib. 346—360; WILSON Works II, 11—25.

[7] Aṅg. N. II, p. 38. Cp. such passages as Saṃy. N. I, p. 67: *sadevakassa lokassa Buddho aggo pavuccati;* his title *devātideva;* his power to free the Sun and Moon from Rāhu; op. c. pp. 50; 52.

been reduced to a minimum, and the traits lent to him are not a whit more real than e. g. those of Avalokiteśvara[1]. Consequently, in all periods of the creed the Buddha is only anthropomorphic, not a man. What he may have been in prehistoric Buddhism, must be left to individual taste and fancy; it is no matter of science.

7. BODHISATTVAS AND THEIR QUALITIES.

The sublime place occupied by the Buddha cannot be reached before his having gone through numerous, nay innumerable existences, and having lived in lower and higher states. A being destined to develop into a Buddha is called a Bodhisattva; he is, we may say, a Buddha *potentiâ*, not yet *de facto*. Properly "Bodhisattva" simply means "a sentient or reasonable being", possessing *bodhi*, but this faculty has not yet ripened to *samyak-sambodhi*, perfect sensibleness. He is, in a word, the personification of what the Yogins call *buddhisattva*, potential intelligence, just as the Buddha, the Samyaksambuddha, personifies *buddhi*, the highest product of nature in most Indian systems of philosophy based on cosmogony.

In the evolution of a Bodhisattva — usually called his course, *caryā* — one distinguishes three periods: 1. that of the aspiration (*abhinīhāra*); 2. of the prediction (*vyākaraṇa*) by the Tathāgata of the period that the aspirant once shall become a Buddha; 3. of the tumultuous acclamation (*halāhala*) at the approach of his last birth[2]. Others distinguish four periods: 1. that of the intention (*manas*); 2. of the vow or firm resolution (*praṇidhāna*); 3. of pronouncing that vow (*vākpraṇidhāna*); of the revelation (*vivaraṇa*)[3]. Similarly in N. writings, albeit with some variations: 1. Prakṛticaryā, original course; 2. Praṇidhāna-c., course of the vow or firm resolution; 3. Anuloma-c., course in accordance with the vow taken; 4. Anivartana-c., the course in which no sliding back is possible[4].

The Bodhisattvas, like the Buddhas, are honoured with various epithets, the most common being Mahāsattva[5]. A great number of them are honoured by the Mahāyānists. The most celebrated, apart from Maitreya, who is also known in the South, are Avalokiteśvara or Lokeśvara and Mañjuśrī[6]. It is

1 The Mādhyamikas, reasoning upon the old Buddhist axiom *sarvam śūnyam*, arrive, most logically, at the conclusion that the Buddha himself is as void and nothing as all the rest; BURNOUF Intr. 481; WASSILIEF B. 348; SCHMIDT, Ueber das Mahāyāna, 207. Implicitly this absolute Nihilism is contained in the passage S. Nip. p. 203, already cited; cp. Majjh. N. I, 297; BIGANDET II, 239. In absolute truth, Paramārtha, there is neither *nirodha* nor *bhāva;* Śantideva, Zapiski IV, p. 219. In other words: there is no such thing as Nirvāṇa; it is a mere delusion; the very idea of Nirvāṇa springs from Avidyā; BEAL Cat. 125.

2 This we may infer from Jāt. Intr. p. 47.

3 HARDY M. of B. 88.

4 Mhv. I, 1; 46 ff. The prediction, Vyākaraṇa, of future Buddhahood, takes place in the fourth period; it is repeated by subsequent Buddhas.

5 This we may render with "Noble Being", though it looks as a veiled synonymous term for Bodhisattva. For *mahat* is synonymous with *buddhi* = *bodhi*. Other epithets in Vyu. § 22.

6 Vyu. § 23, where the list opens with *Avalokiteśvara;* in Dharma-S. XII only eight are named, and, strangely, with omission of Avalokiteśvara; see the note on l. c. for synonymous names, and other divisions. Several Bodhisattvas are honoured by Śāntideva in Bodhicary., chiefly Mañjughoṣa; Zapiski IV, pp. 158; 161; 225. On Lokeśvara, al. Matsyendra cp. Versl. Meded. K. Ak. of 1888, pp. 14; 42. See further WADDELL JRAS. of 1894, p. 51; Buddh. of Tib. 356 on Avalokita.

hardly to be doubted that these worthies, like so many other Buddhas and Bodhisattvas, have been canonized after the time of Aśoka.

The being who one day should appear as Gautama Buddha, went through numberless births during incalculable ages before he attained Buddhahood, after receiving the prediction to his future destiny from 24 Buddhas[1]. The prehistory of Sākyamuni, the Buddha of the present Bhadrakalpa, in connection with the predictions of former Tathāgatas, is recorded in S. and in N. Buddhist texts without material discrepancies[2]. Memorable occurrences and great feats (*apadāna*, *avadāna*) in his prehistory, are related in a number of tales called Jātakas and Avadānas. Such stories occasionally occur inserted in other works, but there exist also separate collections of Jātakas and Avadānas, some of them reckoned to belong to the canonical books, others composed or rather retouched by profane authors. The P. Cariyā-Piṭaka contains 35 stories exemplifying as many proofs of Pāramitā furnished by the future Gautama Buddha; a Skr. composition by Ārya Śūra, the Jātaka-Mālā, describes 34 Jātakas or Bodhisattvāvadānas[3]. There is certainly some connection between the number of stories in Sūra's composition and the epithet Catustriṃśajjātakajña of Buddha, although in the absence of a fixed date to be assigned to the origin of the epithet, the cause of the coincidence is not traceable. As to the 35 tales of the Cariyā-Piṭaka, we suspect that the number has something to do with the number of years passed by the Bodhisattva Siddhārtha-Gautama before he attained perfect and complete Enlightenment. However that may be, it is not easy to see how both numbers can be commeasurable with the 10, or, if we reckon the subdivisions, 30 Pāramitās.

The Bodhisattvas are endowed with many eminent moral and intellectual qualities. Their most striking characteristic is compassionateness. They represent, in general, active virtue and highmindedness, in contradistinction to the Arhats, who are inactive. One might mark the difference between the two classes of persons by saying that the Bodhisattvas are compassionate, the Arhats unpassionate or passionless.

The 10 Pāramitās or Pāramīs, perfect virtues, are, in Pāli, the Pāramitās of *dāna*, almsgiving; *sīla*, morality; *nekkhamma*, renunciation of the world; *paññā*, wisdom; *viriya*, energy; *khanti*, forbearance; *sacca*, truthfulness; *adhiṭṭhāna*, resolution; *mettā* or *mettī*, charity; and *upekkhā*, indifference, equanimity; each of them divided into three degrees[4].

Along with their eminent moral virtues the Bodhisattvas possess such intellectual qualities as are conducive to enlightenment, and which are therefore termed Bodhipākṣika dharmas, Bodhipakṣadharmas, P. Bodhipakkhika, °pakkhiya, or Bodhapakkhiya, thirty-seven in number[5]. These qualities are

[1] The exact number is 4 Asaṅkhyeyas and 100000 Kalpas; Saddh. S. p. 1; Bodhi-v. p. 11; less definite Mhv. I, 1: "in innumerable Asaṅkhyeyas, numberless Kalpas."

[2] Jāt. Intr. pp. 4 ff. HARDY M. of B. 89 ff. It should be observed that according to the theory of the Lokottaravādins the primeval Buddha, near whom the future Śakyamuni made his vow to become a Tathāgata, is likewise named Śākyamuni; Mhv. I, 1. This seems to mean that the later Śākyamuni is an Avatāra of the primeval Śākyamuni, i. e. Ādibuddha or Svayambhū; a tenet fully developed in the school of the Aiśvarikas; see HODGSON Ess. 46; 76. Cp. WADDELL Buddh. of Tib. 126; 130; 348.

[3] On similar other collections see S. d'OLDENBURG's paper "On the Buddhist Jātakas", already quoted above p. 7, note; and IWANOWSKI's in Zapiski VII, 289.

[4] CHILDERS Dict. p. 335. Vyu. § 34 has likewise 10 P., but with substitution of Dhyāna, Upāya, Bala, and Jñāna for Mettī, Nekkhamma, and Upekkhā; Praṇidhāna answers to the synonymous Adhiṭṭhana. A list of 10 P. also in Dharma-S. XVIII, but of 6 in XVII; see the notes there, and add Kāraṇḍa-Vy. II, 9; cp. on Kṣānti-, Vīrya-, Dhyāna- and Prajñā-Pāramitā Bodhicary. Chapp. 8—11, in Zapiski IV, pp. 178 ff.

[5] CHILDERS s. v. *bodhapakkhiyo;* Lal. V. 8; 218; Dharma-S. XLIII.

not, as is the case with the Pāramitās, peculiar to the Bodhisattvas, for they belong likewise to the Arhats. They comprize seven categories.

I. The four kinds of Smṛtyupasthāna[1], presentness of memory, thoughtfulness: 1. in regard to the body; 2. to sensations; 3. to rising thoughts; 4. to Dharma.

II. The four kinds of application, right exertion, Sammappadhāna, N. Samyak-prahāṇa, already enumerated.

III. The four parts of miraculous power, Ṛddhipāda, Iddhipāda; as above.

IV. The five Indriyas, mental energies, faculties: faith, energy, memory or thoughtfulness, concentration of mind, and wisdom[2].

V. The five Balas, mental powers, not differing from the Indriyas, unless in intensity[3].

VI. The seven constituents of Bodhi, Bodhyaṅga, Sambodhyaṅga, to wit: memory, investigation (*dharmavicaya*), energy, contentment (*prīti*), calm, concentration of the mind, contemplation (*samādhi*), and indifference or equanimity[4].

VII. The Eightfold Path, Aṣṭāṅgika-mārga of the Āryas; already treated of.

Occasionally we come across other qualifications or faculties of Bodhisattvas, but they do not belong to the system of 37 Bodhipākṣika dharmas, and are partly common to Bodhisattvas and Arhats[5]. To the latter amiable qualities, which should by no means be confined to those saintly persons, may be reckoned the four Saṅgrahavastus (Saṅgahavatthus), elements of friendly treatment; to wit: liberality in almsgiving; affability; officiousness, and cooperation[6].

In N. texts the whole career of a Bodhisattva is divided into ten degrees or stages, Bhūmis, the system of which is amply described in Mahāvastu[7]. The most usual names are Pramuditā, Vimalā, Prabhākarī, Arciṣmatī, Sudurjayā, Abhimukhī, Dūraṅgamā, Acalā, Sādhumatī (or Madhumatī), and Dharmameghā[8].

The prerogatives or immunities of being a Bodhisattva are numerous[9], and proportionate to their duties.

Before leaving this chapter we ought to note that the Bodhisattva births

[1] P. Satipaṭṭhāna, a compound of *sati* and *upaṭṭhāna*, as already observed by CHILDERS; cp. *parimukhaṃ satiṃ upaṭṭhapetvā* Aṅg. N. II, p. 38; *pratimukhaṃ smṛtim upasthāpya* Divy. 20. See further Saṃy. N. I, 180; Lal. V. 218; Dharma-S. XLIV. Synonymous terms are *kāyagatānusmṛti* etc. Lal. V. 36; *kāyagatā sati*, *kāyānupassanā*, etc. belonging to the Kammaṭṭhānas.

[2] Dharma-S. XLVII and the references; Vyu. § 41. The four Indriyas are the same with exception of wisdom; Aṅg. N. II, p. 141.

[3] Dharma-S. XLVIII; Vyu. § 42. The four Balas are the same, except wisdom; Aṅg. N. l. c.

[4] Dharma-S. XLIX and note; Vyu. § 43; Majjh. N. I, p. 61; Mil. P. 83. Sometimes only 6 Sambojjhaṅgas are mentioned, memory being excluded; Aṅg. I, p. 53; herewith cp. the Yogaṅgas of the Yoga. — As to the rendering of Samadhi cp. the synonymy of Samādhāna and Dhyāna in Bodhicary., Zapiski IV, p. 208.

[5] To the Bodhisattvas are ascribed 10 Vaśitās, mights; Vyu. § 27; Dharma-S. LXXIV.

[6] The P. terms are: *dāna*, *peyyavajja* or *piyavacana*, *atthacariyā*, and *samānattatā*, Aṅg. N. II, p. 32; in Dharma-S. XIX: *dāna*, *priyavacana*, *arthacaryā*, and *samānārthatā*; so, too, in Lal. 39; 183; 218; but *priyavākya* and *arthakriyā*. Slightly different in Mhv. I, 3: *dāna*, *tathārthacaryā*, *priyavādya*, and *samānasukhaduḥkhatā*, i. e. taking part in another's joy and sorrow. — The addition of the words "appertaining to kings" in CHILDERS p. 447 is a mistake, as is evident from Aṅg. N. l. c. and Divy. 95.

[7] I, 76 ff. The names are: Durāroha, Baddhamāna, Puṣpamaṇḍitā, Rucirā, Cittavistarā, Rūpavatī, Durjayā, Janmanideśa, Yauvarājya- and Abhiṣeka-bhūmi.

[8] For references see Dharma.S. LXIV; cp. Daśabhūmīśvara in JRAS. of 1875, p. 4, — A list of 13 Bhūmis occurs Dharma-S. LXV.

[9] Enumerated Jāt. Intr., vss. 252—258.

of Śākyamuni are frequently called his Avatāras, at least with the N. Buddhists. In the creed of the N. Church, or of some sects, it is admitted that those Avatāras had occurred not only in former times, but that the Buddha retained his power of Avatāra, of appearing on earth as a Bodhisattva, even after his complete Nirvāṇa. Such an Avatāra of Śākyamuni was the prince Kuṇāla, the virtuous son of Aśoka[1]. If we remember that in the Lotus Śākyamuni declares his Nirvāṇa to be only a feint for the benefit of mankind, we cannot refrain from supposing that the masters of the Mahāyāna had no belief in an historical Nirvāṇa[2]. In fact, we have seen that with them the very idea of Nirvāṇa is a delusion.

8. MORALS.

The moral code of the Brahmanist Indians has professedly its roots in the Veda, tradition, the custom observed by good men, and one's own conscience[3]. Buddhist morality is dogmatically founded on, and referrible to the Buddha, for we read: "*Bhagavaṃmūlakā no dhammā Bhagavaṃnettikā Bhagavaṃpatisaraṇā*"[4]. Yet it does not necessarily follow from this dogma that the Buddha was supposed to have invented the whole of morality. On the contrary, the Master himself repeatedly extols the morals and virtues of the ancient Ṛṣis. "The Dharma", says he, "is the ensign of the Ṛṣis"[5]. The exemplary life and the great feats of generosity, self-sacrifice &c. of the Bodhisattvas might be adduced as an implicit evidence of what the Buddhists themselves believed about the moral faculties of mankind in prebuddhist times. But more significant is the explicit statement by the Master that the Brahmans of yore were distinguished by the highest moral qualities[6]. Even the fact that the true, the genuine Brahman is not seldom represented as the noblest of creatures, in contradistinction to those who are merely Brahmans by birth, Bhovādins, or as the unbelievers call them, Brahmabandhus, would have been impossible if the type had wholly failed in common life.

In spite of the fore-mentioned dogma, Buddhism has wisely adopted many articles of morality and pious customs flowing from the sources of the Brahmanist code. When the Master commands that the pious Buddhist householder, *gahapati ariyasāvaka*, ought to perform the five Balis: to the family, the guests, the Pitaras, the king, and the gods[7], it is manifest that he draws from the Smṛti; and when he appeals to conscience, *ātman*, notoriously a non-entity in Buddhism[8], he authorized a view thoroughly at variance with the fundamental maxims of the creed.

---

1 This is distinctly stated by Kṣemendra in Avad. Kalp. Nr. 59; an older redaction of this charming tale occurs, as is well-known, in Divy. 403 ff.

2 SBE. XXI, p. 307, ff. — It is a fact that the half pantheistic, half theistic views of the Mahāyānists were condemned by their opponents; Wassilief B. 263.

3 Manu II, 6.

4 Majjh. N. I, p. 310.

5 Aṅg. N. II, p. 51. An exemplary Ṛṣi was the hermit Asita Devala, notwithstanding his following heterodox rules (*bāhiraka mārga*); S. Nip. pp. 128 ff. Cp. Mhv. II, 30, where the text, after due correction, runs thus: "ṛṣipravrajyām pravrajito mūlaphalapattrabhakṣo uñchavṛttiḥ." He had exercised the 4 Dhyānas and had realized the 5 Abhijñās.

6 Brāhmaṇika-dhamma-S. in S. Nip. p. 50. The statement is the more remarkable because the same Sutta otherwise is a piece of wholesale and unscrupulous, silly slander; cp. Hardy Legends 42 ff. Though the Brahmans themselves are often calumniated, their gifts to the monks are always welcome and highly praised; Itiv. p. 111. Praise of the true Brahman, S. Nip. p. 116.

7 Aṅg. N. II, p. 68.

8 Aṅg. N. I, p. 149: "Attā te, purisa, jānāti saccaṃ vā yadi vā musā." The addition

The other sources, the *smṛti-śīle tadvidām* and the *ācāraḥ sādhūnām* of Manu, have not been lost sight of by the Buddhists. To these categories belong the duties qualified as *paṇḍitapaññatta* and *sappurisapaññatta*, and consisting in almsgiving, in *ahiṃsā*, and in supporting father and mother[1].

It is hardly accidental that almost all passages where moral duties are enjoined are either wholly or partly in metrical form, and this circumstance in combination with the fact of those passages containing so much that is contrary to the fundamental articles of the creed, leads us to the inference that the sect originally had no moral code at all, except the prohibitious and duties prescribed to the members of the Order, which only partly coincide with the laws of society in general.

If we wish to form a just estimate of the character of Buddhist morals, such as laid down in the final redaction of the canonical books, we must bear in mind: 1. that the prescriptions were intended to supply the wants both of the ecclesiastics and of the laity; 2. that the Arhats are, to a certain extent, above common morality. The Sage, *muni*, has no attachment, does nothing what is pleasant nor what is unpleasant[2]. Those who are wise abandon their children[3]. A man who leaves his poor wife, the mother of his child, in order to become a monk, and obstinately refuses to take care of her and the child, is held up to the admiration of the world as having done something very grand. Still at other times we read that one's wife is the best friend, and that a wife is the most excellent of goods, though repeatedly women are described as horribly wicked creatures with hardly any exception[4]. Such inconsistencies are endless.

There is no formal discrepancy between the two great branches of the Church as regards their moral code; but as a rule it may be said that with the N. Buddhists moral activity comes much more into the foreground than with their brethren in the South. Not the Arhat, who has shaken off all human feeling, but the generous, self-sacrificing, active Bodhisattva[5] is the ideal of the Mahāyānists, and this attractive side of the creed has, more perhaps than anything else, contributed to their wide conquests, whereas S. Buddhism has not been able to make converts except where the soil had been prepared by Hinduism and Mahāyānism[6].

All moral laws, either in India or elsewhere, may roughly be brought under two heads: 1. prescriptions the infringement of which is followed by penalty; 2. injunctions the fulfilment of which is meritorious and somehow meeting with its reward. The former commandments are everywhere the strongest, because they are absolutely necessary for the maintenance of society. Therefore they are expressed in the form of prohibitions, as only forbidden acts are liable to punishment. The usual Indian term for this category of obligations is *yama*, the second being known by the name of *niyamas*, i. e. obligations only binding for certain classes of persons, or under certain circumstances, though meritorious for all. The principle underlying the

---

of *sakkhi*, O witness! proves that the whole metrical passage, clumsily joined to the prose, has been taken from some Dharmaśāstra; the lines occur in a slightly different redaction in Manu VIII, 84 ff.

1 Aṅg. N. I, p. 151.

2 S. Nip. p. 153: "Sabbattha munī anissito na piyaṃ kubbati no pi appiyaṃ."

3 Therag. vs. 302.

4 Ud. I, 8; Saṃy. N. I, pp. 37; 43; Aṅg. N. II, p. 80; Mil. P. p. 205.

5 In the picture of the Supreme Buddha the traits of the Arhat and the Bodhisattva have been blended into an harmonious whole. In Vedānta phraseology, one might say, he combines the traits of the neuter *brahman* and the masculine *brahmán*.

6 Cp. TAW SEIN KO in Ind. Ant. XXII, 165; Tār. 262.

division of the commandments into two categories is visible also in the Buddhist Decalogue, the Daśaśīla, otherwise termed the ten Śikṣāpadas (Sikkhāpadas), precepts of training. The ten Śīlas are all of them binding on the members of the Order; the first five on lay devotees[1]. These forbid: 1. the destruction of life; 2. theft; 3. unchastity; 4. lying; 5. the use of intoxicating liquors; the other five prohibit: 6. eating at forbidden hours; 7. attending worldly amusements; 8. the use of unguents and ornaments; 9. the use of a large or ornamented couch; 10. the receiving of money.

The prohibitions 1—5 are couched in the same terms for all persons, but there is some difference in the application. Thus chastity, *brahmacarya*, means in the case of monks and nuns absolute abstinence from sexual intercourse, just as in the case of Brahmacārins; for lay devotees it means refraining from adultery[2]. Theft is, in common life, taking anything that has not been given, but a monk commits a thievish act even if he smells at a flower[3].

If persons appertaining to the laity keep besides the first five precepts the three next following, at least on Sabbathdays, it is a highly meritorious act for which heaven will be their reward[4].

The moral obligations of those who have renounced the world extend beyond the Daśaśīla. In their morality three degrees are distinguished, the inferior, the middling, and the superior degree. The first two degrees are coextensive with the Daśaśīla in its strictest interpretation; the third consists in refraining from pagan sacrifices, prognostications, astrology and such-like professions[5]. No one, unless unacquainted with Brahmanic literature, will fail to perceive that this superior morality is nothing else but the rule of life of the Dvija in the fourth Āśrama, when he is a Yati or Mukta. It is difficult to explain why, and at what time all such minute prescriptions were deemed necessary for Sramaṇas, as their vow of embracing a spiritual life would seem to be sufficient. The only plausible explanation is that all those superfluous details were bodily or with some modifications[6] taken from Dharmasūtras and Dharmaśāstras, in which they were appropriate, because Brahmans and other Dvijas are not obliged by any vow to observe the rules specified.

Buddhism deserves credit for its having discountenanced the coarser forms of superstitious rites, and degrading ascetic observances[7].

The sons of Śākya have as a rule respected the moral feelings and

1 See Childers s. v. *sīlaṃ*, and his references. Cp. Yogas. II, 30; 32.

2 The five precepts for the laity are more amply expounded S. Nip. p. 69.

3 Samy. N. I, p, 204; Jāt. III, 308.

4 A sabbath thus observed is termed *aṭṭhaṅgiko uposatho;* S. Nip. p. 70; Aṅg. N. I, p. 215; in the Gāthās ascribed to the Buddha we find the phrase: "Etam hi aṭṭhaṅgikam āhūposathaṃ, Buddhena dukkhantaguṇaṃ pakāsitam". It is curious to hear the Master speaking in the 3d person.

5 An elaborate exposition of all this is given in Sāmaññaphala-S. and Subha-S. of the Dīgh. N. Cp. Burnouf Lot. 463 ff. Even the practice of medicine is forbidden to a Buddhist; S. Nip. p. 172. Sacrifices are totally discredited p. 190; but Aṅg. N. II, p. 43 only bloody sacrifices; it is added that unbloody sacrifices (*nirārambha yañña*) are approved by the Masters, and agreeable to the gods; p. 44.

6 The metrical parts betray here and there their unbuddhistic origin; cp. above p. 69, note.

7 E. g. the *śīlavrataparāmarśa*, P. *sīlabbataparāmāsa*, the abuse of moral vows or observances; Vyu. § 104; Majjh. N. I, p. 433; Aṅg. N. I, 242; Dh. Saṅg. 1005. Not all Śīlavratas are condemned, as appears from S. Nip. p. 196; Dhp. vs. 271; Bodhi-v. p. 76; only some (Mhv. I, 292), of the bad and foolish sort, like the *govrata*, Lal. V. 259; *govratin*, *govatika* is an ascetic who feeds upon grass like a cow; Majjh. N. I, p. 387; MBhārata V, 3359; *kukkuravatika* is one who lives like a dog, a cynic; Majjh. N. l. c.

social customs of their heterodox country-men and contemporaries[1]. Far from being indifferent to public opinion, they anxiously avoided giving offence. Repeatedly we read how people are scandalized by the behaviour of some monks; how the question whether such a behaviour is or is not lawful is brought before the Master, and how his decision is always conform to public opinion[2]. In all such cases the Buddha is simply the echo of the public voice. This deference for the opinion of the world, *lokādhipateya*, P. *lokādhipateyya*, goes so far that the Congregation, for aught we know, never straightforwardly attacks the family and matrimony. Therefore we cannot wonder if we meet in the canonical books with a detailed exposition of the various duties which children and parents, man and wife, master and servant, friends, ecclesiastics and lay men have to observe towards each other. A treatise in which the Buddha teaches a young layman the duties that were generally acknowledged in the Indian Smṛtis, is the Sigālovāda, known in a S. and a N. redaction[3]. Of moral lessons in poetical form there is no lack. Collections containing beautiful maxims, partly universally Indian in character, partly more specifically Buddhist, are the Dhammapada, the Maṅgala-Sutta, and the Udānavarga[4].

As a whole the moral teaching of the Church bears witness to a certain breadth of view, not superior, indeed, to what is professed by individuals of other persuasions in India, but certainly to the usual catechism of other Indian creeds, which are moreover mixed up with offensive superstitions. A striking example that exclusiveness in matters of trifling importance cannot be laid to the charge of Buddhism is the answer given by the Lord to Devadatta, when the latter urged him to command that the monks should during their whole life abstain from fish and meat[5]. We know that the Tathāgata declined the demand.

Highly characteristic, too, is the discourse between the Buddha and the Licchavi Duke Sīha, at Vaiśālī. On that occasion the Master declares that in a certain manner he teaches the value of action (*kiriyavāda*), and in another respect the value of non-action (*akiriyavāda*); that in a certain sense he teaches annihilation (*ucchedavāda*), &c. Whereupon the terms used are subjected to a process of twisting and distortion to such an extent that all definiteness is lost[6].

---

1 Exceptions as the attack directed against the caste system in Assalāyana-S. are comparatively rare. The Vajrasūci with its contents stolen from Śaṅkara deserves notice only as a literary curiosity.

2 Instances occur *passim* in the Vinaya; see e. g. MV. V; CV. III. Cp. Yājñav. I, 156.

3 Text in GRIMBLOT'S "Sept Suttas Palis"; transl. by CHILDERS in the Contemporary Review of 1876. The N. text is only partially known from a Chinese version; BEAL Trip. 112. — A detailed account of the duties of laics occurs in MINAYEF Recherches I, 163—174, with copious references.

4 The Maṅgala-S. ed. and transl. by CHILDERS in JRAS. IV, 2 (New s.); Udānavarga transl. from Tibetan by ROCKHILL. The Dhp. belongs properly to the Theravāda sect, as we may infer from Jātaka-M. p. 98, l. 24. It is intended chiefly for members of the Order.

5 The eating of fish and meat is allowed if it is pure in three respects, to wit: if one has not seen, nor heard, nor suspected (that it has been procured for the purpose); MV. VI, 31, 14; CV. VII, 3, 15; Majjh. N I, 368 ff. From the express prohibition of eating the flesh of men, elephants, horses, dogs, snakes, lions, tigers, bears, hyenas, we must infer that the flesh of other animals was no forbidden food; MV. VI, 23.

6 MV. VI, 31; cp. I, 38; Tib. Leb. 268. The Buddha is both a Kiriyavādin and an Akiriyavādin, Aṅg. N. I, p. 62; Saṃ. N. I, p. 38: *kammaṃ tassa (sattassa) parāyaṇaṃ* is no contradiction. He does not teach *sabbam atthi*, nor *sabbam natthi;* Saṃy. N. II, p. 76; he declares to proclaim nothing else but what the *loke paṇḍitās* teach; III, p. 138.

In the same discourse there is a trait of liberal-mindedness which should not be left unnoticed. When the Licchavi Duke, who was an adherent of the Jain sect, had become a convert to Buddhism, the Master administered to him the following charitable counsel: "For a long time, Sīha, your house has been a place of refreshment for the Nirgranthas. Therefore you should deem it proper that alms shall be given to them when they come to you".

It does not follow that the sons of Śākya much liked the Jains, nor that they were latitudinarians in matters of doctrine. On the contrary, heresy, *mithyādṛṣṭi*, is considered by them, like by many other religious communities, a most damnable sin, to be punished by the torments of hell[1]. Whether erroneous views outside the community were considered all equally wicked, is questionable. At any rate some heterodox sects were more abhorred than others; the gymnosophists of the Ājīvaka sect e. g. had the reputation of being most impious. On a certain occasion the Buddha is asked by a wandering mendicant of the Vatsa clan whether any Ājīvaka after death can become a denizen of heaven, not to speak of Deliverance. The answer is: "In the 91 Kalpas, Vātsya, I have remembrance of, I do not remember of any Ājīvaka having become a denizen of heaven, except one, and he was one who acknowledged the effect of Karman (*kammavādin*) and the value of actions (*kiriyavādin*)"[2].

It is difficult to characterize the peculiarity of the Buddhist code of worldly morality, and that for two reasons. Firstly, because its articles do not differ from the standard recognized in India; secondly, because the spirit penetrating the prescriptions is different according to the divisions of the Church. Buddhism properly being a monastic institution, and the laity but accessory, it is natural that social customs and obligations were tolerated, after some pruning, if they were not in flagrant conflict with the dogma of the Church. Current moral tales were collected and received into the canon, after some remodelling and by transforming such tales into Jātakas and Avadānas[3]. By this contrivance the stories have acquired a strongly pious tinge, which is less accentuated or wholly wanting in the corresponding tales in the Mahā-Bhārata, Pañcatantra, Bṛhat-kathā, &c.

The second difficulty arises if we try to reproduce the different shades of moral sentiment we discover, on comparing the S. Buddhists with their brethren in the North, and further the Hīnayānists with the Mahāyānists. Hīnayānism has gradually been ousted by its opponents, and it may be said without exaggeration that the Buddhism of medieval India bears the stamp of the Mahāyāna. Now it cannot be denied that charity and mercifulness are more predominant or at least more highly extolled in Mahāyānist texts than in other books, and so it is not to be wondered at that those virtues or sentiments have been looked upon as distinctive of Buddhism, even by Brahmanical authors, like Bāṇa. The ideal of the Mahāyānists, however lofty, is unhappily marred by the fact that to exemplify their own charity and mercifulness they begin with abjudicating those virtues to all other creeds[4].

---

[1] Aṅg. N. II, p. 227.

[2] Majjh. N. I, p. 483. — The doctrine of the Ājīvakas — according to their opponents — is: *natthi kammaṃ, natthi kiriyaṃ, natthi viriyaṃ;* Aṅg. N. I, p. 248; cp. Dīgh. N. I, p. 53.

[3] The circumstance that the Jātakas refer the occurrences to the times of the King Brahmadatta of Benares, shows that the home of these tales is the country near Benares, and not Magadha, where Buddhism arose.

[4] WASSILIEF B. 124.

Even towards their brethren of the Hīnayāna their feelings were far from charitable[1].

As a whole the Buddhists have shown themselves to be less exclusive and more liberal-minded than the adherents of other Indian religions inasmuch as in propagating their faith they did not attempt to hinduize their converts. By acting upon so sound a principle they have elevated their creed to the rank of a universal religion.

PART IV.

THE CONGREGATION. MODES OF WORSHIP.

1. INDIAN MONACHISM. DISCIPLINARY AND ASCETIC RULES.

In many countries and at various times there were men who dissatified with the condition of society around them, or disappointed in their dearest expectations, fled the bustle, troubles, deceptive pleasures and wickedness of the world in order to seek in solitude or in the company of sympathizers quietude and peace of mind. Nowhere the conditions are so favourable for the development of anachoret and monastic life as in India. Climate, institutions, the contemplative bent of the national mind, all tended to facilitate the growth of a persuasion that the highest aims of human life and real felicity cannot be obtained but by seclusion from the busy world, by undisturbed pious exercises, and by a certain amount of mortification.

The time-honoured Indian institution of the four Āśramas contained all the germs of monachism; more than that, it afforded the example of a saintly mode of life. To begin with the Brahmacārin, he is obliged during the whole course of his study to observe absolute chastity; must refrain from intoxicating drink; take care not to hurt any living being; avoid the use of perfumes, unguents and finery; hold himself aloof from dancing, singing and other mundane amusements; show good breeding in all his manners; be clad in a deer hide and a red, reddish yellow or yellow robe. Moreover he has daily to beg his food[2]. These and similar obligations recur in the disciplinary code of the Buddhists and other mendicant Orders.

A Brahmacārin may, if he choose, remain a student for life at his teacher's, or after the teacher's death with the family of the latter, which, however, according to some authorities, is not necessary[3]. Such a Brahmacārin for life does essentially not differ from the Bhikṣu in a more restricted sense, otherwise called Yati, Mukta, Sannyāsin, Parivrājaka, i. e. the Ārya who has entered the fourth Āśrama. The rules of conduct for a Bhikṣu or Sannyāsin[4] have, up to minute details, served as the model for ordained monks of various sects.

We can understand that Brahmacārins for life, thirsting after true know-

[1] Huen Thsang qualifies them as "heretics" and accuses them of complotting against his life; Voy. I, 246.

[2] See e. g. Āpastamba I, 1; Gautama II; Manu II.

[3] Āpast. II, 9, 21, 6; 8; Gautama III, 3, 7; Manu II, 247.

[4] Āpast. II, 9, 21, 9—17; Gautama III; Manu VI, 41—86.

ledge, followed the lessons and guidance of some renowned teacher; that even Bhikṣus did the same; and it is highly probable that persons of that type constituted the nucleus of distinct sects, which after the death of the revered master, or already during his life time developed into congregations with their disciplinary regulations, into monastic Orders with distinctive outward characteristics.

Although the epoch of the rise of Buddhism cannot be determined with certainty, we know that in the days of Aśoka the Congregation, Saṅgha, was a well-organized body in possession of canonical books. Hence we infer that it had already existed for a considerable space of time, as well as the rival Orders of the Nirgranthas and Ājīvakas. Considering that the oldest books of the Buddhist canon incessantly speak of the Nirgranthaṣ and Ājīvakas, and of the frequent bickerings between them and the sons of Śākya, we have no reason to doubt that the three Orders were founded almost simultaneously. Nor need we be sceptical when we read that the custom of regularly keeping the Sabbath, Uposatha or Posatha[1] and of preaching on those days was introduced in imitation of other sects[2]. This is not the only instance. In general it may be said that the whole organization of the Saṅgha and a good deal of the rules for monks and nuns, — if we may trust the canonical writings, — were introduced by imitation or by accident. The Master is less a legislator than an upholder of the law; he invents few new ordinations, he only ratifies the public opinion, and decides in highest instance when there have arisen questions among the brethren. The dogmatical fables, invented to account for the introduction or ratification of this or that rule, have no historical value, of course, but they certainly reflect the theory prevalent in the Congregation, and that theory could not but have its root in experience[3]. Some of those stories are based upon a misunderstanding or distortion of the plain text of the rules, so that there can be no doubt about their having been invented considerably later than the disciplinary rules to which they refer[4].

The disciplinary and penal code of the Saṅgha, undoubtedly one of the oldest, if not the very oldest part of the canonical compositions, barring some additional articles, is the Pātimokkha, Skr. Prātimokṣa[5]. This fundamental code of discipline is common to all Buddhists, in different redactions, which, however, agree in all essential points. The Pāli version is unquestionably the oldest and, accordingly, the shortest. The Pātim. for monks contains 227

---

[1] In would-be Skr. Poṣadha, an impossible form, because the *o* for *ava*, being secondary, never could produce the change of the dental into the Mūrdhanya, which moreover had disappeared from the Prākṛt. — *Posatha* occurs Jāt. IV, 342; cp. DMG. 48, 63.

[2] MV. II, I.

[3] A great part of the disciplinary rules of the Order are represented as being due to the incessant misbehaviour of six monks, who, like the six Tīrthikas, always enter in company and are equally irrepressible. Instances occur *passim* in S. Vibh.

[4] E. g. Pātim. Pācittiya 43; S. Vibh. II, p. 94.

[5] About the meaning of this title there is some doubt. In SBE. XIII, p. XXVIII it is asserted that *pātimokkha* means "Disburdening, Getting free." Unhappily *paṭimuñcati, pratimuñcati* is not *pamuñcati*, and denotes exactly the reverse, viz. "to put on, fasten, bind." It never has another meaning in Pali, nor in older Sanskrit. If we compare the phrase *pātimokkhasaṃvarasaṃvuta* Aṅg. N. II, p. 14, where the word cannot but denote "a covering accoutrement, a protecting armour", with the standing explanation *yo taṃ pāti, rakkhati* (Childers p. 363; Minayef Prātim. S. I), though erroneous in accessories, we conclude that Prātimokṣa was taken in the sense of cuirass, or rather "something serving as a (spiritual) cuirass." Cp. the term *kavaca*, used in a later period by Buddhists in a similar acceptation, and *dharmakañcuka;* the Bodhisattva is *sannāhasusannaddhavarmitakavacita*, Lal. V. 217.

articles all in all; the Chinese version of the Dharmagupta sect numbers 250, the Tibetan 253, that of the Mahāvyutpatti 259[1].

It has been ordered by the Lord that the Prātimokṣa is to be recited twice a month, on the Sabbath of the 15th (or 14th) of the halfmonth, in an assembly of at least four monks[2]. At the end of each section the reciter asks whether any of the brethren present has transgressed one of the articles. If so, the transgression must be openly confessed; if not, the recital proceeds. It is usual that the monks confess their sins to each other before the ceremony. Thus the disciplinary code is at the same time a formulary of confession.

Quite distinct from the Prātimokṣa in origin and purport is the summary of ascetic rules known as the Dhūtāṅgas, the complete observance of which is only possible for monks who, like the brahmanical Vānaprasthas or Vaikhānasas, lead the life of hermits in the woods. The number of the Dhūtāṅgas or Dhūtaguṇas is 13 in the South, 12 in the North[3]. We will treat of them severally in the order followed by the Pāli sources.

I. Pāṃsukūlika, scil. *aṅga*[4], is the rule that the dress is made of rags taken from a dust or refuse heap. This rule is not observed by all monks, no more than several of the following practices. So far as we can judge, there always were in the Saṅgha cenobites and hermits, Āraṇyakabhikṣus, the latter more rigid and partizans of an austere mode of life, Dhūtaguṇavādins or Dhutavādas, as whose head in the times of the Buddha is considered Kāśyapa, P. Kassapa the Great[5]. This predilection for a solitary life is strongly expressed in many poetical songs, as if inspired by the fresh air of the woods[6].

II. Traicīvarika, P. tecīvarika is the precept enjoining the possession of no more than three robes at a time. This rule is binding on all the brethren, abstraction made of occasional exceptions.

III. Paiṇḍapātika, P. piṇḍapātika is the rule to live on food obtained by begging from door to door. Those who are strict observers of the rule make no use of food distributed by tickets (*salāka-bhatta*), of food given to the Convent (*saṅgha-bhatta*), of invitations for dinner. The last is contrary to the custom of the Buddha and his attendants, who regularly receive and accept invitations.

IV. Sapadāna-cārikā, explained to mean a proceeding from door to door in due order when begging[7].

---

1 Translations of the whole Pātim. have been published by MINAYEF (in Russian), and by Proff. RHYS DAVIDS and OLDENBERG in SBE. XIII; of the part for monks by DICKSON in JRAS. VIII (New s.), and of the Chinese version by BEAL, Cat. pp. 204 ff.; of the Tibetan version of the Naiḥsargika section by HUTH.

2 MV. II, 4, 2.

3 HARDY E. M. 9, 73, 97 ff. 120; BEAL Cat. 256; for other references see Dharma-S. LXIII, note. On the 28 merits of the Dhutaṅgas see Mil. P. 351. Synonymous or nearly so with Dhutaṅga is *saṃlekha*, austere observance, Vyu. § 245; *sallekha*, Pugg. P. p. 69; Majjh. N. I, 42; MV. VII, 3.

4 This and the following terms, when masculine, denote the persons observing the rule; Pugg. P. p. 69; in Dharma-S. the masc. refers to *guṇa*.

5 Dīpav. IV, 3; V, 7; Saṃy. N. II, 156; Divy. 61; 395. The sect which is said to observe more rigidly than any other the Dhutaṅgas, are the Kassapiyas, Kāśyapīyas. — *Dhutavādin* in a less technical sense occurs Jāt. I, 130.

6 Marked instances are the Khaggavisāṇa-S. (Nr. 3 and Nr. 12 of S. Nip.); Therag. vss. 518—526. The rigorists have much in common with the Pratyekabuddhas; cp. above p. 61, note.

7 The Skr. form is *sāvadānam*, an adverb (as in P.) qualifying the manner of begging of an ascetic; it occurs e. g. Mhv. I, 301; Vyu. § 263, but it is not expressly included in the list of Dhutaṅgas. In Vis. M. (cp. CHILDERS s. v.) *sapadāna* is interpreted by *a-avakhaṇḍana*, and *dāna* "cutting" with *ava-khaṇḍana;* but *dāna* = *khaṇḍana*,

V. Aikāsanika, ekāsanika, the rule of eating at one sitting[1].

VI. Pattapiṇḍika, an article wanting in the N. enumeration, and enjoining "eating from one vessel only".

VII. Khalupaścādbhaktika, P. khalupacchābhattika, the prohibition of taking a meal after it has become improper to do so; this has been interpreted as partaking of food already refused and superfluous[2].

VIII. Āraṇyaka, P. Āraññaka, living as a hermit in the woods.

IX. Vṛkṣamūlika, P. rukkhamūlika, residing at the foot of a tree.

X. Ābhyāvakāśika, P. abbhokāsika, living in an unsheltered place[3].

XI. Śmāśānika, P. Sosānika, living in or near a cemetery.

XII. Yāthāsaṇstarika, P. yathāsanthatika, said to be "taking any seat that may be provided"; evidently wrong, for *saṃstara* is what is spread; *santhata*, spread. The nuns are forbidden to observe this, a prohibition which would have no sense if the term had the meaning assigned to it. The word denotes "spreading a night-couch where one happens to be"[4].

XIII. Naiṣadyika, P. nesajjika, enjoining a sitting posture while sleeping[5].

The articles IV and VI are absent from the N. list, which on the other hand has a special Nāmatika (aṅga), the use of felt for clothing[6].

In theory it is meritorious, but not obligatory for all monks to observe all of the Aṅgas. The articles VIII—XI do not apply to nuns, XI—XIII are expressly forbidden to them; Śrāmaṇeras and Śrāmaṇerīs are excluded from the observance of II, for the simple reason that they are not yet members of the Order. Lay devotees are allowed to keep the rules V and VI, but none of the others.

The 12 articles of the N. list are more logically arranged than the 13 Dhutaṅgas in Pāli; it is plain that the first six are rules for all members of the Saṅgha, whereas the last six are intended for the Āraññakabhikkhus[7].

2. ADMISSION TO THE SAṄGHA. NOVICES. ORDINATION.

Persons desiring to renounce the world and embrace the life of a monk or nun, may be admitted without any distinction of rank or caste, with a few necessary restrictions; e. g. murderers, robbers, persons with contagious diseases, slaves, soldiers and the like are excluded. The act of admission is termed Pravrajyā, P. Pabbajjā, properly denoting in general "leaving the world, adopting the ascetic life." The ordination properly so called is the Upasampadā, by which one becomes a monk or nun with all the privileges belonging to the Order. The Upasampadā may be conferred on all who have previously been admitted to the Pravrajyā, except those who have

---

whereas *avakhaṇḍana* (*apakhaṇḍana*) = *apadāna*. The rule is superfluous, being included in the foregoing.

1 Cp. *ekāsanabhojana* Majjh. N. I, 437. The form Aikāsanika occurs Aṣṭas. P. Param. 387.

2 For the scholastic interpretations we refer to CHILDERS D. p. 310.

3 In Brahmanist works *abhrāvakāśika*, Rām. I, 43, 14; Manu VI, 23. It is quite possible that the P. term answers to this word, as has been suggested by OLDENBERG; Dharma-S. p. 49.

4 Cp. Aṣṭas. P. Param. 387. Analogous words are *yātratatraśaya* and *yatrāstamitaśāyin* in Brahmanistic Literature.

5 Cp. Therag vs. 904; 1120. — Vyu. § 49 has the form Naiṣadika.

6 In CV. X, 10 the wearing of *namataka* is forbidden to the nuns; the use of felt for a covering is allowed; V, 11; 19.

7 Some prescripts of the most nugatory character for this class of persons are found CV. VIII, 6.

committed heinous crimes, eunuchs, hermaphrodites and the like[1]. As to nuns, there are 24 blemishes disqualifying them for the Upasampadā[2]. For the admission of Śrāmaṇeras, i. e. young novices, or rather seminarists, is required the consent of their parents and an age of full seven years.

The broad distinction between the first admission, Pravrajyā, and the Ordination, Upasampadā, is clear enough, but if we descend into the details, the matter becomes embarassing. It would seem that at the rise of Buddhism the two terms denoted nothing else but what they originally mean, the former: "leaving one's home to become an ascetic"; the latter: "accession" to the Order. It appears from Scripture that the Buddha, after converting the Five mendicant friars, further Yaśas and other young men, gathered around him sixty Disciples, who in a very short space of time passed through the four stages, and asked the Master for the Pravrajyā and the Upasampadā simultaneously, whereupon the Lord received them[3]. After a while the Disciples who had been sent abroad to propagate the Law, returned with persons who wished to receive Pravrajyā and Upasampadā from the Master himself. This circumstance led the Buddha to the consideration that it would be well if henceforth the monks were permitted to confer themselves Pravrajyā and Upasampadā on candidates. He accordingly gives to the monks that permission, and adds: "Let him (who has to receive P. and U.) first have his hair and beard cut off; let him put on the Kāsāyas, adjust his upper robe so as to cover one shoulder, bow down before the feet of the monks, and sit down squatting; then let him raise his joined hands and utter: I take refuge in the Buddha, in the Law, in the Congregation". Thrice. "I ratify, o monks, the P. and U. with this threefold formula"[4]. Afterwards, however, this regulation was cancelled, in so far as he ordered not to confer the Upasampadā, unless by a ceremony in which a formal motion (*ñatti*) is followed by three questions[5]. Even in this amended form the Upasampadā is nothing else but the solemn consecration of the Pravrajyā, as the story l. c. shows[6]. Cases of persons receiving simultaneously P. and U. are not rare; even in the days of Aśoka the lay devotee Bhaṇḍuka received P. and U. in the same moment, and Arhatship to boot[7]. As twenty years is the lowest age at which a man is qualified for U., it follows that a boy who has become a Śrāmaṇera at eight, will have to wait 12 years before he can receive Upasampadā[8]. It seems questionable whether in the beginning of the spread of

[1] The circumstances disqualifying persons for admission and ordination are minutely expounded MV. I, 39—76; cp. HARDY E. M. 17 ff. Vyu. § 271. Not a few of these disqualifications are merely theoretical; e. g. eunuchs and hermaphrodites are excluded from the Upasampada, as if these physical disabilities were unknown at the Pravrajyā. More than absurd is the exclusion of Snakes; MV. I, 63.

[2] CV. X, 17; Vyu. § 271.

[3] Jāt. Intr. p. 82; MV. I, 6; 7. Cp. above p. 24.

[4] MV. I, 12. An extended form of the Triśaraṇa-gamana is: "Buddhaṃ śaraṇaṃ gacchāmi dvipadānām agryam; Dharmaṃ s. g. virāgāṇām agryam; Saṅgham s. g. gaṇānām agryam." Vyu. § 267.

[5] Ñatthicatuttha; MV. I, 28; Skr. jñapticaturtha-(karmopasampanna) Vyu. § 270. In border countries the conferring of U. is allowed in a chapter of four monks, besides the Vinayadhara; MV. I, 10, 12.

[6] It results from MV. I, 76 that the U. need not be preceded by a formal Prav. For the Senior who confers the U. asks the canditate: "Are you a human being?" etc. Such a question is always foolish, but excessively so if the candidate has already been examined before.

[7] Dīpav. XII, 62 f.

[8] CHILDERS D. p. 532; cp. p. 305, where the Sāmaṇera is compared with "a deacon". A deacon of 8 years is something strikingly original. HARDY E. M. 45 has much better understood the character of a Sāmaṇera.

Buddhism children were admitted, notwithstanding the tale of Rāhula's *Pabbajanā*[1]. However that may be, the Śrāmaṇeras are no more Bhikṣus than the Brahmacārins, their model, are. They are Śramaṇoddeśas, Śramaṇoddeśakas, P. Samanuddesas, i. e. aspirants for the state of monk, persons destined to become monks, in a word, seminarists[2]. One of their duties is to learn the ten Śikṣāpadas[3].

Converts from other, heterodox sects, who desire to receive P. and U., are subjected to the same formalities, and have moreover to pass a probation time, Parivāsa. Only two classes of persons, viz the Jaṭilas, fire-worshippers with matted hair, and the Sākyas, received Upasampadā — there is no question of Pravrajyā — without a probation time being imposed, the former because they believed in the retribution of moral actions, and the latter because the Master wished to grant a privilege to his kinsmen[4].

The passages and testimonies adduced seem to warrant the conclusion that the real Ordination or Consecration takes place by the Upasampadā, whereas the Pravrajyā is the act by which the candidate formally declares his intention to take the vows. The regulations prescribed in Scripture have been collerted in the manual for various Kammavācās, Skr. Karmavācanās, ecclesiastical resolutions[5].

In a chapter of at least 10 monks — under certain circumstances only 5, as already remarked above — the candidate, after having provided himself with the requisite alms bowl and robes, and chosen his spiritual leader or tutor, Upajjhāya, is examined by the president of the chapter[6] concerning his eventual disabilities, his name and the name of his spiritual tutor. These things being ascertained, the candidate requests to be ordained, whereupon the president formally proposes to the chapter to assent to this request, twice repeated. If the assembly by their silence give the consent, the president exhorts the newly ordained brother to stick to the four Necessaries[7], and to avoid during his whole life the four capital sins. All things above the Necessaries, though not absolutely forbidden, are to be considered superfluities.

It would be difficult to point out a single case in Buddhist writings, sacred or profane, that the sons of Sākya kept to the four Necessaries, except the hermits. As to the four capital sins, which we shall meet again under

---

1 The more so because, MV. I, 50, the Lord expressly forbids to confer the Pravrajyā on a boy under 15 years of age. In Tibet a Śrāmaṇera can receive a socalled 2d consecration in his sixteenth year; in China it is not unusual that at the same age the ceremony of hair-shaving is performed; the Cūḷakanta-maṅgala in Siam is a rite performed in the 9th, 11th, 13th, or 15th year. All these customs may be called "pagan accrescences"; KÖPPEN Rel. des B. II, 265; HARDY E. M. 18; GERINI, Chūḷākantamaṅgala, 2; 29.

2 S. Vibh. II, p. 139; the femin. is Śramaṇoddeśikā, Div. 160.

3 MV. I, 56. The rule now followed in Ceylon (HARDY E. M. 23) is exactly the counterpart of the Brahmanic Upanayana.

4 MV. I, 38.

5 The manual has been published under the title Kammavākyaṃ, syn. with Kammavācaṃ, by SPIEGEL, with Latin transl.; partly by DICKSON with English transl. in JRAS. VII, 1 ff. (New s.). Cp. BOWDEN in JRAS. of 1893; HARDY E. M. 44; BIGANDET II, 272; MV. I, 28; 30; 76; 77. A "collection of Kammavācās" in FRANKFURTER's Handb. pp. 142—150. Cp. also the Kalyāṇī Inscription of A. D. 1476, text and transl. by TAW SEIN KO, Ind. Ant. XXII.

6 Wrongly called Upajjhāya in BIGANDET l. c., contrary to MV. I, 76; cp. 25.

7 The 4 Nissayas (MV. I, 30; 77) are: *piṇḍiyālopabhojana*, living on a pittance of begged food; *paṃsukūlacīvara*, rags from a dustheap; *rukkhamūlasenāsana*, lodging at the foot of a tree; *pūtamuttabhesajja*, cow urine as medicine. The corresponding Skr. terms of the Niśrayas are: *pāṃsukūla; piṇḍapāta: vṛkṣamūla*, and *pūtimuktabheṣajya*, an unsuccesful attempt at rendering *pūtimutta* into Skr. Vyu. § 266.

another head, the vow of the ordained monk to abstain from all sexual intercourse as long as his life lasts, is contrary to the theory that one may, under circumstances, leave the Order[1].

The ordination of nuns is performed almost in the same manner as that of monks. She who proposes the candidate is titled the Pavattinī[2].

Regarding the Upasampadā ceremony in the old N. Church we possess few accounts, but sufficient to show that it was, essentially, the same as in the South. In course of time some modifications have been introduced which we must leave unnoticed[3].

3. CLOTHING AND EQUIPMENT. LODGING. FOOD AND MEDICAMENTS.

The complete, distinctive dress of the monks consists of three pieces, Tricīvara, P. Ticīvara; to wit: P. Antaravāsaka, Uttarāsaṅga, and Saṅghāṭī[4]. Another name for the habit after the colour, is Kāṣāya, P. Kāsāya, Kāsāva, tawny, reddish yellow. In the South the usual colour is yellow[5]; in India, at least in the Middle Ages, it was reddish.

The description of the garments, as well as the identification of sundry other names, is attended with some difficulty. The Antaravāsaka is a lower garment, something like a petticoat, hanging low down, and bound to the loins with a girdle, *kāyabandhana*[6]. As synonymous is given Nivāsana, but the description of this garment by Huen Thsang is somewhat different[7]. The Uttarāsaṅga is the garment covering the breast and shoulders, and reaching somewhat below the knees. Something like it is the Saṅkakṣikā, according to Huen Thsang, but the P. Saṅkacchikā occurs elsewhere as another garment, and not belonging to the official dress[8]. Whether the Paṭinivāsana, Skr. Pratinivāsana, may be identified with the Uttarāsaṅga is a matter of doubt[9]. Saṅghāṭī, properly meaning "a doublet" may have had a similar history as this English word. Once we meet the expression "the (two) Saṅghāṭis folded together" to denote a third garment after Nivāsana and Pratinivāsana[10]. We infer that the Saṅghāṭī, a kind of cloak, is so called because it is folded and composite[11].

---

1 HARDY E. M. 46.

2 CV. X, 17.

3 For Pravrajyā and Upasampadā in Tibet, see WADDELL, Buddh. of Tib. 178; 185; cp. HODGSON Ess. 139; 145.

4 MV. I, 76; VIII, 13; 15; 20; 23; CV. X, 17. In Skr. the same, only Antaravāsaka; Vyu. § 272.

5 The red Kāṣāya was not wholly unknown; see e. g. Therag. vs. 965.

6 BIGANDET II, 274. This agrees with the "ample plaited petticoat, named Śam-t'abs" in Tibetan; WADDELL op. c. 201.

7 According to Voy. II, 3 the three robes are Saṅghāṭi, Uttarāsaṅga and Saṅkakṣis, but p. 69 Saṅghāṭi, Saṅkakṣikā and Nivāsana! The exact shape of the Nivāsana MV. I, 25 cannot be determined.

8 CV. X, 17. The Saṅkakṣikā is likewise distinguished from the three Cīvaras; also Vyu. l. c., where also a Pratisaṅkakṣikā is mentioned.

9 MV. I, 25; CV. VIII, 11; 12; Vyu. l. c.

10 MV. l. c. Cp. the expression *pāṇḍudukūlaṃ saṅghaṭ[ṭ]īkṛtya sīvayati sma* Lal. V. 334. In the same work p. 231 the Saṅghāṭī is not reckoned as a Cīvara: *saṅghāṭī-piṇḍa-pātra-cīvaradhāraṇena sthitam.*

11 LEGGE, following EITEL, defines the S. as the "double or composite robe, reaching from the shoulders to the knees, and fastened round the waist"; Rec. p. 39, note. WADDELL op. c. 200 says the S. is "the Lower patched robe, and fastened by a girdle at the waist."

It is a peculiarity of the official habit that robes should be made out of patches imitating the ricefields of Magadha[1].

Raiments occasionally used by monks and nuns are the Varṣāśāṭī, P. Vassikasāṭikā, rain-cloak; and the Snātraśāṭaka, P. Udakasāṭikā[2].

It is meritorious for the laity to provide members of the Order with clothing. A great distribution of robes to the local Saṅgha is held immediately after the Pravāraṇā, at the close of the rainy season. The ceremony of that distribution, elliptically called Kaṭhina[3], is common to both divisions of the Church.

The use of foot covering is, in most cases, for the monks a luxury, and in the South almost unknown. In Scripture various descriptions of possible and impossible shoes are expressly forbidden; sandals and plain slippers not absolutely so[4]. Umbrellas are a superfluous article, except in particular cases. The use of fans, and of a plain sort of chowries, is allowed[5].

Besides the three robes the monk's equipment, Pariṣkāra, P. Parikkhāra, consists of an alms bowl or pot, *pātra*, P. *patta;* a girdle; a razor, *vāsi;* a needle, *sūci*, and a water-strainer, *parisrāvaṇa*, P. *parissāvana*[6]. The pot is sometimes carried in a kind of net or purse, *thavikā*, perhaps only by hermits[7]. The razor serves for shaving the hair and the beard. As a rule the brethren shave one another once a fortnight.

In the North the ascetics are in the habit of carrying as a distinctive a staff, *khakkhara*. The walking stick of an ascetic is also known in the South, under the name of *kattara*[8].

According to universal Indian custom they use tooth sticks, *dantakāṣṭha*, P. *dantakaṭṭha* or *dantapoṇa*[9].

Another article, the rosary, now so common in all Buddhist communities, does not date from very old times. Whether it was invented in India, is an open question. It is certainly not of Buddhist origin.

On the residence of the monks the sacred tradition affords much, apparently trustworthy, information. We are told that the Retreat during the rainy season, the Vassavāsa or Vassa, Skr. Vārṣika, was instituted in imitation of the same institution with the heterodox sects[10]. During that time the monks are forbidden to travel, and have to arrange for themselves places to live in. There are two periods for entering upon Vassa, Vassūpanāyikā[11], a longer and a shorter one, the former beginning at full moon of Āṣāḍha; the

1 Ānanda was the first who skilfully contrived to put together such a robe; MV. VIII, 12. The number of patches varies according to the difference of sects; WASSILIEF B. 267.

2 Vyu. l. c.; MV. VIII, 15; 20; 23; CV. II, 1; X, 17.

3 Kaṭhina, hard, denotes "raw cotton." The regulations regarding Kaṭhina are minutely set forth MV. VII, 1, and explained in SBE. XIII, 18; XVII, 148 ff. WASSILIEF B. 85; 88; BEAL Cat. 216. Among the N. writings there is a Kaṭhināvadāna, HODGSON Ess, 19. The spreading out of the raw cotton is termed Kaṭhināstaraṇa, P. Kaṭhinatthāra; Vyu. § 266.

4 More details in MV. 2—8. Cp. BIGANDET II, 286; HODGSON Ess. 19.

5 CV. V, 22; 23. Commonly the leaves of the Tāla palm are used as fans. Hence the name of Talapoins given to the monks in Transgangetic India; YULE-BURNELL, Glossary s. v.

6 See CHILDERS s. v. *parikkhāra* and his references. Many more Parikkhāras are enumerated JPTS. of 1887, p. 27.

7 CV. VIII, 6; Jāt. Intr. p. 55. The Māgadhī-Prākṛt form is *thaïyā*, Skr. *sthagikā*

8 Vyu. § 273; Voy. II, 33. For *(kattara)yaṭṭhi*, *°daṇḍa* see CHILDERS s. v. MV. V, 6; CV. IV, 4; V, 132.

9 CV. X, 31; Voy. II, 55, note.

10 MV. III, 1.

11 Skr. Varṣopanāyikā, Divy. 18; 489; Vyu. § 266.

latter one month later; both ending with the full moon of Kārttika[1]. With the N. Buddhists the usual period of Retreat was three months, from the first of Śrāvaṇa to the first of Kārttika[2].

It is not clear where in the first times of the Order the brethren, apart from the hermits, had their abodes, either during the Retreat or during the other part of the year. It was not necessary that a great number of them lived in the same place, for the half-monthly recital of the Prātimokṣa did not require an assembly of more than four persons. Now-a-days it is customary in Ceylon that the monks during the Retreat leave their monasteries and live in temporary huts. But how to reconcile this with the following statement of Buddhaghoṣa[3], "They are to look after their Vihāra, to provide food and water for themselves, to fulfil all due ceremonies, such as paying reverence to sacred shrines, etc., and to say loudly once, or twice, or thrice: "I enter upon Vassa *in this Vihāra* for these three months?" And besides, the avowed object of the institution is to keep the monks from roaming about. Therefore we arrive at the conclusion that the tenor of the regulation comes to this: during the rains the monks *must* stay in a monastery or any other fixed abode; in other seasons they *may* do so.

In the beginning, as the tale goes, the monks had no fixed abodes, *śayanāsana*, P. *senāsana*. They dwelt in the woods, at the foot of a tree, on a hill, in a grotto, in a mountain cave, a cemetery, a forest, the open air, on a heap of straw. Now a rich merchant of Rājagṛha wished to erect dwellings for the reverends, and the Lord Buddha gave his assent saying: "I allow you, O monks, abodes (*layana, lena*) of five kinds[4]: Vihāras, Aḍḍhayogas[5], towers (Prāsādas, Pāsādas), stone houses with a flat roof (Harmyas, Hammiyas) and crypts". On hearing from the monks that the Lord had given his assent, the merchant had in one day finished 60 dwelling places. The Lord gave thanks to him by the same stanzas as were uttered by him on accepting the gift of the Jetavana; a circumstance which points to some confusion in the tradition[6].

The very absurdity of the story is interesting, because we may gather from it that edifices as above specified were in possession of the Saṅgha when the MV. and CV. were composed.

The term Vihāra does not only denote a monastery, but frequently a temple, a striking instance of which is afforded by a passage in Huen Thsang's Travels, and it is quite so, too, in Ceylon, where the word is more generally applied to the place where worship is conducted, whilst the dwelling of a monk is called a Paṇṇasālā[7]. The most unambiguous, if not the most common term for a monastery is Saṅghārāma. Undoubtedly every great monastery had a Vihāra or temple annexed to it. We know this with certainty of Nālandā, and Sārnāth near Benares[8].

---

1 MV. III, 2; the translators (SBE. XIII, 300) add in a note: "Very probably this double period stands in connection with the double period prescribed in the Brāhmaṇas and Sūtras for most of the Vedic festivals."

2 So at least in the 7th century of our era. Voy. II, 492.

3 Cited SBE. XIII, l. c.

4 MV. I, 30; III, 5; CV. VI, 2.

5 Explained by Buddhaghoṣa (SBE. XIII, 171) by "suvaṇṇavaṅgagehā", i. e. a house of gold and tin? CHILDERS s. v. gives "shaped like a garuḍa bird", which points to a reading *suvaṇṇa-* (or *supaṇṇa*)- *vihaṅga*. Suvarṇa for Suparṇa is not unknown to some N. texts.

6 CV. VI, 9; MV. I, 30; III, 5.

7 Voy. II, 221; HARDY E. M. 129; description of a Vihāra, 200.

8 Voy. II, 355.

The crypt or cave, *guhā*, above alluded to, must be a room wholly or partly excavated in a rock. The oldest crypts known are those of Barābar and Nāgārjuni in Bihār[1], which were given by Aśoka and his grandson Daśaratha to the Ājīvikas, those inveterate opponents of the Saṅgha.

The house where the chapter assembles for celebrating the Uposatha is called in general Uposathāgāra, in Siṃhalese: Poega. A famous Uposatha hall in Ceylon was the Lohapāsāda or Brazen Tower. — The cells in a monastery are termed in Pāli *pariveṇa*[2]. Occasionally we read of *kuṭis*, huts or sheds, inhabited by ascetics.

A matter of considerable interest is the institution of Parishes, *sīmā*. Like so many other regulations of the Church, the institution is due to the irrepressible Six monks[3] who were as indefatigable evil-doers as the six Tīrthikas. After the Lord had ratified the recitation of the Prātimokṣa once every half-month, the Six recited it every one before his own companions. The Master, being informed of it, ordered that the Uposatha should be attended by the whole community. Now the question arose: "how far does the whole community extend?" This was settled by a prescription that it should extend as far as one place of living. Now at that time Kappina[4] the Great dwelt near Rājagṛha. Plunged in meditation, he felt a doubt: "Shall I go to the Uposatha service or shall I not go?" The Lord understanding the thoughts of Kappina, left the Gṛdhrakūṭa and instantly appeared before the eyes of Kappina. Having taken the seat presented to him, the Master asked Kappina, whether he had not felt the doubt just mentioned. On receiving an affirmative answer, the Lord proceeded: "If ye Brahmans do not honour, regard, revere the Uposatha, who then will do it? Attend the Uposatha, Brahman! do not neglect to go[5]." Kappina promised to do so, and the Lord appeared again on the Gṛdhrakūṭa[6]. Still the monks remained in uncertainty as to the question: "How far does a place of living extend?" Therefore the Buddha prescribed to mark out the boundaries of a parish, *sīmā*, in this way: first, the marks are to be mentioned, such as a mountain, a stone, a forest, a tree, a road, an ant hill, a river, a water-sheet. This being done, a competent monk has to bring forward a motion that the Saṅgha may decree to fix by such marks the boundary of a parish for common residence and common celebration of the Uposatha[7]. Some abuses partly occasioned by the crossness of the Six were successively remedied.

Reverting to the monasteries, we observe that the most reliable and detailed accounts about the actual state of the Saṅghārāmas in the Middle Ages, both in India and in Ceylon, are due to the Chinese pilgrims. It appears

---

1 Cunningham Corp. Inscr. I, 30; Ind. Ant. XX, 361 ff.

2 Hence *anupariveṇiyaṃ*, in their successive cells; MV. II, 8.

3 *Chabbaggiya*, in Skr. *Ṣaḍvargika*, *Ṣaḍvargīya;* Divy. 329; 396; 489; Vyu. § 281. Their names § 282 are: Aśvaka, Punarvasu, Nanda, Upananda, Chanda, and Udāyin. In P. sources Assaji and Punabbasu(ka) are directly named as belonging to the group, but it appears from MV. and CV. *passim* that Nanda, Upananda, Channa and Udāyin were obstinate sinners and quite worthy to be reckoned among the company. Assaji is likewise one of the Five, but in Vyu. l. c. (cp. § 47) Aśvajit and Aśvaka are different persons.

4 In N. writings Kapphiṇa, Kaṣpiṇa, Kaphina, etc. See SBE. XX, 2; 198.

5 An unequivocal acknowledgment of the precedence of Brahmans in spiritual matters, and of their giving in general a good example.

6 According to the Mahāyānists Śakyamuni is properly always residing on the Gṛdhrakūṭa, and it is only an illusion when men imagine they have seen him in other places; SBE. XXI, 307 ff. Other Indian sects say: the Ātman is *kūṭastha*.

7 MV. II, 5—9. Cp. the fixing of boundaries of a parish (*sīmaṃ sammannati*) as related Dīpav. XIV, 26; Mahāv. pp. 108 ff. Cp. also Manu VIII, 246.

that the Āvāsikas[1], resident monks, those staying at their own monastery, had a life free from care owing to the liberality of the kings and pious laymen. "The regular business of the monks is to perform acts of meritorious virtue, and to recite their Sūtras and to sit wrapt in meditation. When stranger monks arrive, the old residents meet and receive them, carry for them their clothes and alms-bowl, give them water to wash their feet, oil with which to anoint them, and the liquid food permitted out of the regular hours. When (the stranger) has enjoyed a very brief rest, they further ask the number of years that he has been a monk, after which he receives a sleeping apartment with its appurtenances, according to his regular order, and everything is done for him which the rules prescribe[2]." All this harmonizes with the rules how stranger monks, Āgantukas, should be received, as laid down in the P. Vinaya[3], which contains likewise minute rules for departing monks, Gamikas, for monks when going their begging round, Piṇḍacārikas, and for those living in the woods, Āraññakas[4].

It is a matter of course that the conduct of the necessary business in a monastery is almost wholly entrusted to such brethren as are thought fit for the office and in due form appointed by the Saṅgha[5]. An important office is that of the apportioner of food, Bhattuddesaka, Skr. Bhaktoddeśaka. In the days of the Buddha this office was held by Dabba, who at the same time was the regulator of the lodgings, Senāsanapaññāpaka, Śayanāsanavārika[6]. Other charges said to have been instituted by the Master are: the keeper of stores, Bhaṇḍāgārika, Bhāṇḍagopaka; the recipient of robes, Cīvarapaṭiggāhaka, Cīvaragopaka; the distributor of robes, Cīvarabhājaka; of rice gruel, Yāgubhājaka, Yavāgūcāraka; of fruits, Phalabhājaka, Phalacāraka; of hard food, Khajjakabhājaka, Khādyakacāraka; of trifles, Appamattakavissajjaka[7]; of voting tickets, Salākāgāhāpaka; the keeper of rain-cloaks and bathing-clothes, Sāṭiyagāhāpaka or Varṣāśāṭīgopaka; the keeper of alms-bowls, Pattagāhāpaka; the superintendent of the gardeners, Ārāmikapesaka; of the Śrāmaṇeras, Sāmaṇerapesaka[8]. Some other offices the character of which is but partially inferrible from the names occur in N. sources; e. g. the Pānīyavārika, who has charge of drinkable water; the Bhājanavārika, who has charge of the vessels. Less clear is the meaning of Upadhivāra or Upadhivārika, probably an intendant or steward[9]. The Pariṣaṇḍāvārika may be the guardian of the grove around the monastery[10], and the Muṇḍaśayanāsanavārika the person who has to take care of the lodgings temporarily not in use.

Now and then we read of certain offices for which no formal appointment by the Saṅgha seems to be required. Such an office is that of Navakarmika, P. Navakammika, the overseer of a new building, architect, who is designated on the demand of some lay devotee who wishes to erect a building

1 Naivāsika is the term Vyu. § 270.

2 Fa Hian, Rec. pp. 43, f.

3 Minutely described CV. VIII, 2. In Vyu. § 270 an Āgantuka differs from an Āgāmika; not unlikely the former is a stranger, a visiting monk; the latter one who returns after a longer or shorter absence; but cp. Divy. 50.

4 CV. VIII, 3; 5; 6.

5 Names of functionaries in CV. IV, 4; VI, 21; Vyu. § 274.

6 Dabba Mallaputta was a remarkable man; he realized Arhatship when he was seven years old and had to endure much vexation at the hands of the brethren; for his history see the passages referred to by ED. MÜLLER JPTS. of 1888, p. 41.

7 Perhaps the same as the *bhāṇḍabhājaka* Vyu. l. c.

8 Vyu. l. c. has only *preṣaka*.

9 Decidedly not "an attendant", as appears from Divy. 542; cp. 50; 54; 237.

10 For *pariṣaṇḍā* cp. Divy. 344.

for the Congregation[1]. The function of a proxy or agent, Veyāvaccakara[2], may be held by an inmate of the monastery (*ārāmika*) or a layman[3].

In ancient times no distinction in rank was made between the monks, except such a one as is connected with age and superior knowledge. There were, of course, Seniores, Sthaviras, P. Theras, and Juniores, Dahras, Daharas; Upādhyāyas, P. Upajjhāyas or Upajjhas, i. e. tutors, and Sārdhavihārins, P. Saddhivihārins or Saddhivihārikas, fellows[4]; Ācāryas, P. Acariyas, professors, and Antevāsins, apprentices; but there is no question of anything like hierarchy. This state of things has continued in Ceylon, where, indeed, each monastery has its Mahā-Nāyaka, prior, but he is no more than *primus inter pares*. This was not exactly the case in India during the Middle Ages, at least in the Mahāyānist establishments. For shortness sake we refer the reader to Huen Thsang[5].

The prescriptions in the canonical writings concerning food are framed in such a manner that both the rigorous hermits and the more temperate cenobites may be satisfied. Art. 39, Tit. 5 of the Prātimokṣa says: "If a monk, unless he be sick, shall request for his use, or shall partake of delicacies, to wit: ghee, butter, oil, honey, sugar, fish, meat, milk, curds — it is a Pācittiya sin." This prohibition is not in accordance with the permission to eat fish and meat[6] with the restriction that it should be pure in three respects: unheard, unseen, unsuspected. The restriction being utterly futile, since it is impossible not to suspect how meat and fish are provided by butchers and fishers, the antinomy remains in full force[7]. Yet the origin of such an incongruity, like of so many other antinomies, is not far to seek. It has been the constant study of the Congregation to imitate the morals and customs of fashionable people; they ardently desired to pass for Āryas and therefore made an excessive use of the very word. They began with taking for their models the Brahmans and the Brahman ascetics, though in course of time they did not scruple to spread the most unworthy lies about a class of men of whom intelligent foreigners like the Greeks speak with admiration. Now the use of fish and meat was allowed to Brahmans under certain restrictions[8], but the ascetic had to refrain from meat and honey[9]. The Indians acknowledge that the decreasing use of animal food and complete abstinence is a peculiarity of the Kaliyuga; with other words: a sign of degeneration[10]. We may safely assume that the Buddhists followed the prevailing custom of the times, and that in other countries they have done the same[11].

The spiritual sons and daughters of Śākyamust earn their living by their own exertion, i. e. they must beg their food, like the Brahmacārins, but with this difference that they are not allowed, as the latter are, to ask for alms by

---

1 CV. I, 18; VI, 5; Vyu. 270. Occasionally nuns are Navakammikas; S. Vibh. II, p. 211.

2 Wrongly rendered into would-be Skr. with Vaiyāvṛtyakara, Vyu. § 270; Divy. 52. It should be Vaiyāpṛtyakara.

3 S. Vibh. I, 221. Cp. SBE. XIII, p. 23 for another interpretation.

4 Vyu. § 281; Sārdhaṃvihārin in Divy. 18; 299.

5 Voy. I, 143; II, 78. The title of Karmadāna for the underdirector is probably a mistake. The word itself occurs Vyu. § 281, but not as a title. For the titles of Vihārasvāmin and Mahāvihārasvāmin see Fleet, Corp. Inscr. III, 279; 272.

6 MV. VI, 31; CV. VIII, 3. Cp. above p. 71.

7 The Buddha himself is represented as eating the pork expressly prepared for him by Cunda, and thus proved *ipso facto* that he was no Buddhist.

8 Gautama XVIII, 27—38; Āpastamba I, 5, 17, 29 ff. Manu V, 27.

9 Āpastamba II, 9, 22, 2; Manu VI, 14; a single exception in Gautama III, 31.

10 Cp. Manu V, 22.

11 Bigandet II, 294; Hardy E. M. 92.

words[1]. The son of Śākya must be calm and dignified in his deportment[2], after the model traced in a beautiful passage in the history of the Bodhisattva[3]. The traits of the Bhikṣus of ancient India continue partially visible in the Siṃhalese monks of the present day[4].

The use of ghee, butter, oil, honey and sugar is permitted to the members of the Order in time of sickness, by way of medicament[5]. Rules for preparing various kinds of medicaments, as well as medical and surgical operations, are prescribed in the Vinaya[6], so that we get some notion of the condition of medical science in the period when that part of the canon was composed.

4. THE PRĀTIMOKṢA. DISCIPLINARY MEASURES.

The Prātimokṣa is divided into eight Titles or heads, each of them containing a greater or smaller number of articles.

The first Title treats of the Pārājikā dhammā[7], case involving expulsion from the Congregation. It contains in all redactions four articles on the most heinous of offences, to wit: breach of the vote of chastity; theft; taking life; falsely laying claim to superhuman (*uttarimanussa*) gifts[8].

The second Title has thirteen articles bearing on offences involving suspension and a temporary exclusion. The term is in Pāli Saṅghādisesa, in Skr. Saṅghāvaśeṣa[9]. The agreement between the various redactions is pretty close[10].

The third Title treats in two articles of Undetermined cases, Aniyatā dhammā[11].

The fourth Title, headed Nissaggiyā Pācittiyā dhammā, on offences requiring expiation by forfeiture, numbers thirty articles, somewhat differently arranged in the various redactions, but otherwise nearly identical[12].

---

1 Mil. P. 230.

2 Deportment is termed *īryā*, P. *iriyā;* the four ways of deportment, *īryāpatha*, *iriyāpatha* are: walking, standing, sitting, lying down; BURNOUF Lot. 296; Intr. 168.

3 Lal. V. 230; Mhv. II, 157.

4 HARDY E. N. 309; 312.

5 MV. VI, 1. Medical requisites are termed *gilānapaccaya*, Skr. *glānapratyayabhaiṣajya*, Vyu. § 239. The four requisites (*paccaya*), are *cīvara*, *piṇḍapāta*, *senāsana* and *bhesajja;* consequently virtually the same as the four Niśrayas, with the only difference that the Nissayas are intended for hermits, the Paccayas for monks in general. Sometimes *pariṣkāra* is used as a third synonymous term, e. g. Divy. 143. — For the five sorts of oil see S. Vibh. II, p. 88.

6 MV. VI, 1—15; 17—21.

7 Skr. Parājikā dharmāḥ, Vyu. § 256. The true etymology of *pārājika*, adopted by CHILDERS, is due to the sagacity of BURNOUF. The word is a regular Taddhita derivative of a lost substantive *parāja* or something like it, connected with a verb *parā* + *ajati*, to drive away, whence p. p. p. *parājita*. The derivation from *parā-jayati*, proposed in SBE. XIII, 3, and intended as an improvement upon BURNOUF's, is grammatically impossible.

8 The offences in Vyu. § 257 are: Abrahmacarya, Adattadāna, Vadha, Uttaramanuṣyadharmapralāpa.

9 Vyu. l. c. 7; WASSILIEF B. 82. The Chinese transcription Saṇ-ka-hi-shisha (BEAL Cat. 210) points to a third form nearly allied to Saṅghādisesa. Neither a Skr. Saṅghāvaśeṣa nor Saṅghatiśeṣa, i. e remnant of the Saṅgha, renders a satisfactory meaning. Equally unsatisfactory are the lucubrations of CHILDERS s. v.

10 The offences specified Vyu. § 258; S. Vibh. I, 110—186. Cp. BEAL l. c.

11 Vyu. § 259: Dvāv aniyatau.

12 For Pācittiya, which answers to Skr. Prāyaścittika, the N. Buddhists have *pāyattika*, an imaginary word, further corrupted by scribes or editors to *pāpattika*, *pāpantika*. For Nissaggiya the same blunderers give Naisargika; it ought to be Naiḥsargika, Naissargika. For the names of the offences severally see Vyu. § 260; cp. S. Vibh. I, 195—266; BEAL op. c. 215; HUTH op. c.

The fifth Title, on matters requiring expiation, Pācittiyā dhammā, comprises ninety-two articles in the P. redaction, whereas the Chinese version and the Vyutpatti number ninety. The contents are highly interesting, as affording a glimpse of some ancient customs among the members of the Order. Here we can only refer the reader to the text itself and the translations[1].

In the sixth Title are treated the Pāṭidesaniyā dhammā, four kinds of offences which require a simple confession to be expiated[2].

The seventh Title is a miscellaneous collection of rules of good breeding and deportment, called Sekhiyā dhammā, or Sikṣā. The number of the rules is 75 in P., 100 in the Chinese version, 106 in Vyutpatti[3]. The greater number in the Chin. version is caused by the addition of 25 articles, from 60—85, relating to decorous deportment in regard to sacred buildings.

The eighth and last Title contains seven rules for settling legal questions or cases, Adhikaraṇasamathā dhammā. The rules are only indicated by technical terms for kinds of sentences pronounced. The terms are: 1. Sammukhāvinaya, application of the disciplinary rule (to the person) in presence; Sativinaya, application of the discipline in case of full consciousness (of the accused); Amūḷhavinaya, the same in the case of one not being insane; Paṭiññāya, sentencing one who confesses (being guilty); Yebhuyyasikā, sentencing by majority of votes; Tassapāpiyyasikā, proceeding against the obstinate; Tiṇavatthāraka, covering over as by grass[4].

The Prātimokṣa for nuns is *mutatis mutandis* a copy from that for the male members of the Saṅgha. The number of Titles is equal, but the arrangement of the articles differs considerably without any obvious reason. Many regulations, just as in the Prātimokṣa for monks, have their origin in the incessant delicts of Six nuns, who are lewd, and commit other delicts, apparently without lasting damage to their spiritual character and monastic saintliness.

In order to enforce the prescriptions of a Code, no community can do without a system of coercion for well defined cases. The means of coercion at the disposal of the Saṅgha are not harsh, but quite sufficient. The severest punishment is expulsion from the community. This measure is enacted against those who are guilty of a Pārājika sin. In one case we read that an aspirant for the Order, a Samaṇuddesaka, is expelled, *nāsita*[5].

A slightly less severe proceeding is the formal banishment, Pabbājaniyakamma, enacted against monks who have committed such a Saṅghādisesa

---

1 The offences are specified Vyu. § 261.

2 In Vyu. § 262 the four Pratideśanīyāni are: Bhikṣuṇīpiṇḍakagrahaṇa, Paṅktivaiṣamyavādānivāritabhukti, Kulaśikṣābhaṅgapravṛtti, and Vanavicayagata, terms which would be difficult to understand without the more elaborate text of the Code.

3 Vyu. § 263. The 150 Sikkhāpadāni spoken of in Aṅg. A. I, pp. 230 ff. cannot be identified with the Sekhiya rules, though it may be that the Sikkhāpadas of little and minor importance mentioned CV. XI, 1 refer to them. The long-winded verbiage is obviously intended to leave the matter in obscurity.

4 Notwithstanding the anecdotes invented after date in CV. IV, 1—14 the real purport of most of the terms cannot be made out. The terms Vyu. § 264 are: Sammukhavinaya, Smṛtivinaya, Amūḍhavinaya, Yadbhūyasikīya (printed text: Yadbhūyaḥīsīkīya), Tatsvabhavaiṣīya (?), Tṛṇastāraka, Pratijñākāraka. The Chin. interpretation is wholly different or mistranslated, BEAL op. c. 238. On comparing CV. I, 2 and 18 we perceive that in case of Sammukhāvinaya the defendant is *codetabba;* in case of Sativinaya *sāretabba;* in case of Amūḷhavinaya *avaggena* (= *amūḷhena*) *āpattim āropetabba;* which does not agree with the anecdotes, but better with grammar.; Sativinaya e. g. is "discipline, chastising, correction by reminding one of his duty."

5 S. Vibh. II, 139. Cp. Vyu. § 265 *nāśanīya.*

delict as specified in Prātimokṣa, Title II, Art. 13[1]. The banishment is not perpetual, but can be repealed, provided the delinquent show repentance[2].

It is not easy to make out the difference between banishment and removal, Nissāraṇā, if there be a real difference[3]. The removal usually consists in a Parivāsa, a period of living apart, of probation for five or ten days. Should one during that period sin again, one must begin the term anew[4]. Another sort of penance attached to the commission of a Saṅghādisesa sin is the Mānatta, consisting in the offender being placed for six days under restraint. The offender himself should duly ask in the full chapter for such a penance after confessing his sin. If he conceals his sin he is subjected to a Parivāsa of one day or longer[5].

Against a monk unwilling to acknowledge his fault an act of suspension or temporary excommunication, Ukkhepaniya-kamma, Utkṣepanīya, has to be carried out; the restoration after his having become repentant is termed Osāraṇā[6].

Other measures of maintaining discipline are the act of warning, Tajjaniya, Tarjanīya; that of putting under tutelage, Nissaya[7], and that of making amends (to the laity) Paṭisāraṇiya[8].

The rehabilitation, Abbhāna, of one who has undergone Parivāsa or Mānatta, is an important official act which requires an assembly of more than twenty members of the Saṅgha[9].

A very exceptional punishment seems to be the Brahmadaṇḍa, which from other sources we know to have been the curse inflicted by a Brahman. Shortly before his Parinirvāṇa the Lord enjoined to Ānanda to impose the Brahmadaṇḍa on the monk Chanda. Ānanda had evidently never heard of such a punishment, for he asked: "But what sort of penalty is the Brahmadaṇḍa?" whereupon he received in answer: "Let Channa say whatever he likes, the brethren should neither speak to him, nor exhort him, nor admonish him"[10]. This penalty, manifestly consisting in declaring a person socially dead, was afterwards inflicted, with the happy result that Channa felt remorse, mended his ways and ere-long attained Arhatship.

One of the means of discipline is confession. In theory all sins must be confessed at the recital of the Prātimokṣa, but as this ceremony takes

---

1 S. Vibh. I, 179 ff. = CV. I, 13. Other cases in 14. The term in Vyu. l. c. is Pravāsanīya.

2 CV. I, 16.

3 MV. IV, 4. X, 6.

4 A Parivāsa is also prescribed for followers of heterodox sects who desire admittance to the Saṅgha. The three other kinds of Par. incurred by committing a Saṅghādisesa sin are described MV. I, 38; cp. CV. II. III. The throwing back to the beginning of the disciplinary term is called Mūlaya paṭikassaṇā, e. g. CV. I, 9; Mūlāpakarṣa, Vyu. § 265.

5 CV. III, 1. The would-be Skr. equivalent in Vyu. l. c. is Mānāpya, pointing to a Prākṛt original answering to a Skr. *mānātmya*. The word is obscure; in Pali it is commented by *mānanabhāva*.

6 CV. I, 25; 27. MV. I, 79.

7 CV. I, 9. 11.

8 CV. I, 18—26. The term Vyu. l. c. is Pratisaṃharaṇīya. The origin of the P. word is debateable. CHILDERS is decidedly mistaken in deriving the word from *smar*. In SBE. XVII, 364 it has been connected with *sāraṇīya*, which is unquestionably = Skr. *sāṃrañjanīya*, but this is no decisive proof in case of Paṭisāraṇiya: 1. because we should then expect Pratisaṃrañjanīya in Buddh. Skr., and not Pratisaṃharaṇīya; 2. because in Aṅg. N. II, p. 148 *sappaṭisaraṇa* means "retrievable, restorable, reparable"; *appaṭisaraṇa* "irreparable"; Skr. *pratisārayati* is "to put things right again."

9 MV. IX, 4. CV. III, 2. 5. Different and erroneous is the term Ābarhaṇa, Vyu. l. c.

10 MPS. VI, 4; CV. XI, 12. 15.

place only twice a month, and an immediate confession is required, it is deemed sufficient that the sinner makes his confession to an elder brother. So at least is the practice now-a-days in Ceylon and Burma[1].

5. OBJECTS OF WORSHIP. RELICS.

The highest objects of worship for the Buddhist are the Three Jewels, Triratna or Ratnatraya: the Buddha, the Dharma, and the Saṅgha[2].

Besides the Three Ratnas, to which the highest honour is paid, there are other, more material objects of worship, viz. relics of holy persons and monuments erected to their memory by the piety of a grateful posterity. All such objects are Dhātus, distinguished into three classes: Sārīrika, corporeal relics; Uddesika, memorials, and Pāribhogika or Paribhoga-dhātus, objects having served the use of the Buddha, sacred spots, holy trees, and the like[3].

One would expect that Dhātus, on account of their very nature, acquire their sacred character after the demise of the person to be commemorated, not before. The theory, in fact, seems to be in accordance with this view, it being doubtful whether the few exceptions date from olden times[4]. If we may trust a time-honoured tradition, the oldest corporeal relics are the hairs which the Buddha gave to the merchants Trapuṣa and Bhallika after their conversion[5]. That tradition, albeit perhaps apocryphal, is common to the N. and S. and therefore old. In course of time it went on assuming greater proportions, and in the 7th century it was believed that the pious merchants had received from the Lord not only some hairs and nails, but his bowl, stick and three garments.

The Siṃhalese could claim to the possession of hair relics almost as old as those of the two merchants. It was the handful of hair bestowed by the Jina on Sumanas, the chief of gods, who deposited the relic in a golden casket and enshrined it in a Stūpa of sapphire[6]. In N. India many cities, Kanauj, Oudh, Kauśāmbī, Mathurā, &c. could boast of possessing hairs and nails of the Tathāgata with Stūpas erected over the relics[7]. The relics in Kanauj were far-famed for their miraculous properties.

The chief corporeal relics are those which are properly called Śarīras, i. e. the remains of a corpse after cremation. We have seen how eight Droṇas of relics were divided among the faithful, and it behoves us only to add that one tooth is worshipped in heaven, one in Gāndhāra, one in Kaliṅga, and one more by the Nāgas[8]. The eye-tooth relic which came to the capital of Kaliṅga, Kaliṅganagarī, now-a-days Kaliṅgapatam, but in Buddhistic writings

[1] HARDY E. M. 145; BIGANDET II, 284.

[2] See the hymn ed. by CHILDERS JRAS. IV, 318 (New. s.); FRANKFURTER Handb. 85; and cp. Mhv. I, 290 ff.

[3] The definition of Uddesika with HARDY E. M. 216 "things which have been erected" does not agree with Jāt. IV, 228 = Bodhiv. p. 59, where we read that an Uddesika Dhātu is "immaterial, merely existing mentally", *avatthukaṃ manamattakena;* yet it is a *cetiya*.

[4] Jāt. and Bodhiv. l. c. An exception is made with the Bodhi tree, which is said to be considered a Caitya both during the life time of the Buddhas (*sic*) and after their demise.

[5] Jāt. Intr. 81, but the older text MV. I, 4, is silent as to those relics, as well as Lal. V. 500 ff. It is only in the commentary that the bestowal of the hair relic is made mention of; see MINAYEF Recherches I, 160.

[6] Mahāv. p. 4.

[7] Voy. II, 210; 216; 265; 268; 277; 287; 406.

[8] MPS. VI, vss. 63 ff. Cp. above p. 46.

usually named Dantapura, has had an eventful history, commemorated in the Daladāvaṃsa[1]. In the 4th century of our era the holy object was brought to Ceylon, and deposited in the city of Anurādhapura, where a century afterwards it was seen by Fa Hian[2].

The history of the eye-tooth in Gāndhāra is extremely confuse. Fa Hian mentions a tooth relic enshrined in a Stūpa at Nagara. Two centuries after it had disappeared, as we are informed by Huen Thsang[3]. This pilgrim, when visiting Kanauj, saw in that city a tooth relic no less remarkable for its extraordinary qualities than for its almost miraculous history[4]. Many other places were in the happy possession of Buddha-teeth, as Bamian, Navavihāra near Balkh, Kapiśa[5].

Few countries were so rich in relics as the region of Nagara, South of the Kabul river. In the city of Hidda there was a Stūpa which contained the projecting skull bone of the Tathāgata, the so-called Uṣṇīṣa. Two other sanctuaries of the same places possessed other pieces of the Uṣṇīṣa, and the eye-balls of the Buddha[6].

The S. Buddhists were no less favoured with relics than their brethren in the North. Besides the famous tooth relic Ceylon could show a collar bone of the Jina, which the Thera Sarabhū had taken away from the funeral pile and brought to the island[7]. In a Stūpa at Ruanwelli, the ancient Hemavālī, was deposited, among other treasures, a whole Droṇa of bone relics of Gautama Buddha. The right collar-bone had been brought to the island in the days of Aśoka, by the Śrāmaṇera Sumana, who had received it from Indra in heaven[8].

Bone relics of the more ancient Tathāgatas are rare. We only find that all the bones of Kāśyapa Buddha were deposited under a Stūpa at Śrāvastī[9]. Much more numerous are remants of the Disciples and other Saints. Near Vaiśālī Fa Hian saw a Stūpa raised over one half of Ānanda's body, the other half having remained as a relic in Magadha[10]. The city of Mathurā possessed Stūpas erected in honour of Śāriputra, Maudgalyāyana, Pūrṇa-Maitrāyaṇīputra, Upāli, Ānanda and Rāhula, with their relics. The nails and beard of the patriarch Upagupta, as famous with the N. Buddhists as unknown to the South, were honoured in the same city. Moreover there was a Stūpa erected over the relics of Mañjuśrī and other Bodhisattvas[11]. A Stūpa in a wood of the Konkan contained the remains of Śrutavimśati-koṭi[12]. The entire body of Kāśyapa the Great rests in a deep chasm of the hill named Kukkuṭapāda[13].

---

1 Composed about 310 A. D. and translated into Pāli ± 1200 A. D. under the title of Dāṭhāvaṃsa.

2 Rec. p. 104. The shrine for the relic, the Daladā Māligāva, is described in SMITHER Archit. Remains.

3 Rec. p. 38; Voy. II, 97.

4 Voy. I, 248.

5 Voy. I, 65; 70; 374; II, 53.

6 Rec. Chap. XIII; Voy. I, 77; II, 102.

7 Mahāv. p. 4. The older chronicle does not mention this relic.

8 Dīpav. XV, 15; XVII, 10; Mahāv. pp. 110; 115.

9 Voy. I, 126; Rec. 63.

10 Rec. 72; 76. Cp. Tār. p. 9.

11 Voy. II, 208; I, 104. Since Bodhisattvas from their very nature must be supposed to be still alive, we ought properly not to speak of "relics".

12 Voy. III, 148. The name is wrong and should be Śroṇakoṭīviṃśa; Vyu. § 47; Tib. L. 283; Pāli: Sonakolivisa, whose history is told MV. V, I, in the main agreeing with Voy. III, 67.

13 Rec. 93, where some inaccuracies committed by LEGGE need not be pointed out. Cp. Voy. III, 7.

If we keep to the threefold division of relics, we must comprise under the head of Paribhoga-dhātus all objects having served the use of Buddhas and Saints, be it a garment, a bowl, a stick, or a tree, a shrine, &c. Such objects are no less worshipped than the bone relics, and like the latter, possessed with miraculous power. It is difficult to determine in what period those holy remains commenced to be religiously venerated, but there is no doubt that long before the beginning of the Middle Ages that worship was already fully developed both in the North and in the South.

When Fa Hian was on his pilgrimage, he saw near Nagara Buddha's staff, made of sandalwood and 16 or 17 cubits long, from which circumstance we may deduce that the size of Gautama Buddha was more than gigantic[1]. Not far from that place there was a shrine in which the pilgrim saw Buddha's Saṅghāṭi; his countryman Huen Thsang found there both the Saṅghāṭi and the Kāṣāya[2].

The alms-bowl of the Tathāgata was at the time of Fa Hian kept in Peshawer. This miraculous relic, to which the common people were in the habit of making their offerings, was seen and has been described by the pilgrim. Two centuries later it was in the possession of the king of Persia[3]. Tradition says that the bowl originally was kept in Vaiśālī, and according to a prophecy heard by Fa Hian in Ceylon, the relic would in the following centuries travel to Tokharistān, Khotan, Karachar, China, Ceylon, India, and finally to the heaven of the Tuṣita-gods[4].

The Simhalese chronicle Dīpavaṃsa mentions several Paribhoga relics, as the drinking vessel of the Buddha Kakusandha, the girdle of Koṇāgamana, the bathing cloth of Kassapa, and that of Gautama; the latter's girdle was preserved in the Kāyabandhana-Cetiya[5].

In S. India, at Koṅkaṇapura, there was in the 7th century a Vihāra which possessed the head-dress worn by Siddhārtha when a boy. It was on Sabbath-days exhibited to the believers who honoured it with offerings of flowers[6]. The Chinese pilgrim to whom we owe this information, saw in Bamian the iron pot and the mantle of the patriarch Śāṇavāsika. The mantle was made from hemp, *śāṇa*, and had a reddish colour. During 1500 births the garment had been born with Śāṇavāsika, and it would remain in existence until the Law of the Buddha would be extinguished. And, in fact, at the time of the pilgrim's visit the habit showed traces of wear and tear[7].

Relics of a non-descript kind, albeit not the less remarkable, because so eminently characteristic, are the shadow relics. In many places believers were shown some cavern where the Buddha or Bodhisattva had left his shadow; e. g. near Kauśāmbī, Gayā, Nagara. Huen Thsang did not succeed in his endeavours to see the shadow relic near Kauśāmbī, though the cavern itself still existed[8]. He was more fortunate at Gayā, where he saw the relic formerly already admired and described by his country-man Fa Hian as "the

---

1 Rec. p. 39. This agrees pretty much with the S. tradition; see above p. 62.
2 Rec. l. c.; Voy. II, 103.
3 Rec. 35; Voy. I, 106.
4 Rec. 109.
5 Dīpav. XV, 51; XVII, 9; Mahāv. p. 105.
6 Voy. III, 147.
7 Voy. I, 49. The relic is a produce of etymology, *Śāṇa-vāsin* meaning "having a hemp garment." By the aid of the P. form Sāṇavāsasambhūta we understand why the habit was born *with* the Saint, for the compound can be interpreted as "sprung into existence conjointly with a garment of hemp." Another form in P. is Sāṇavāsi Sambhuto; Dīpav. IV, 50; V, 22. Cp. Tib. L. 308.
8 Voy. II, 286.

shadow of Buddha, rather more than three feet in length, which is still bright at the present day[1]." Still more renowned was the shadow relic near Nagara. In a cavern inhabited by the Nāga Gopāla the Buddha had left his shadow immediately on his reaching extinction[2]. At the entrance of the cavern there were visible two square stones with the Tathāgata's footprints marked by the Wheel.

We shall revert to such footprints and other holy remains after a brief survey of the sacred buildings and images, which require a separate treatment.

6. SANCTUARIES OF DIFFERENT KINDS. STŪPAS. TEMPLES. IMAGES.

The monuments of Buddhist sacred architectural and sculptural art have been the object of unwearied research, and deservedly so, because they constitute a most interesting part of Indian archaeology. In a compendious book like this we can only touch upon that interesting subject in so far as it is more directly connected with worship, for the rest referring the reader to a selection of standard works and important papers, happily not rare, bearing on the matter[3].

The most general name for a sanctuary is Caitya, P. Cetiya, a term not only applying to buildings, but to sacred trees, memorial stones, holy spots, images, religious inscriptions. Hence all edifices having the character of a sacred monument are Caityas, but not all Caityas are edifices.

Among the buildings of a sacred nature the most prominent are the Vihāra and the Stūpa. Vihāra, as we have had occasion to remark, designates both a monastery or abode of the living Buddha and a sanctuary with images, though the latter acceptation is hardly admissible for the olden times. The distinction between a Caitya and a Vihāra, such as it is made by the Nepalese, would, at first sight, seem somewhat arbitrary. They call a sanctuary of Ādibuddha or of the Dhyāni-Buddhas, which has the form of a heap of rice, a Caitya, but the temples of Sākya and the other of the 7 Mānuṣi-Buddhas, as well as those of other Saints, Vihāras[4]. From the detailed description of the Nepalese Caityas it is perfectly clear that those domes or mounds of brickwork are real Stūpas[5].

The Stūpa, P. Thūpa is often in a loose way identified with the Dagob, P. Dhātugabbha, Skr. Dhātugarbha, or shorter: Garbha. Strictly speaking the

---

1 Rec. 88. According to Voy. II, 458 it was the Bodhisattva who left his shadow.

2 Rec. 39; Voy. I, 81; II, 99.

3 Such works and papers are: CUNNINGHAM, Bhilsa Topes; Stūpa of Bharhut; Mahābodhi; Archaeological Survey; — FERGUSSON, History of Indian Architecture; Description of the Amaravati Tope (JRAS. 1868); Age of the Indian Caves and Temples (Ind. Ant. 1872); Tree and Serpent Worship. — BURGESS, Buddhist Stūpas of Amarāvatī and Jaggayyapeta; Arch. Surv. of S. India, Nr. 3; of W. India Nr. 9. — FERGUSSON and BURGESS, Cave temples of India; — RAJENDRA-LALA MITRA, Buddhagayā. — LEITNER, Graeco-Buddhist Sculptures (Ind. Ant. 1873). — V. SMITH, Graeco-Roman influence on the Civilisation of Ancient India. — SMITHER, Architectural Remains, Anurādhapura. — REA, South Indian Buddhist Antiquities. — A comprehensive account of Buddhist Archaeology is found in Prof. GRÜNWEDEL's "Buddhistische Kunst in Indien (1893)"; cp. FOUCHER, L'Art bouddhique dans l'Inde d'après un livre récent (Rev. Hist. Rel. 1895).

4 HODGSON Ess. 49; 52. The idea underlying the distinction is, in our view, this: Vihāra is the abode of Buddhas when living or supposed to be alive or present; Caitya, al. Stūpa, the abode of a Buddha merely living in the memory of men; it is a memorial.

5 HODGSON, l. c.; 30; WRIGHT, Hist. of N. 16; Pl. IV; IX; X.

Dagob is only a part of the Stūpa, being the shrine in which the holy relic is deposited, the *arca* of the sanctuary. Now as most Stūpas are erected over relics, they may be called Dagobs. Still not all Stūpas contain relics[1].

It is more than probable, and, indeed, almost universally admitted that Stūpas originally are grave-mounds of illustrious persons. What we read of the commands of the Tathāgata to Ānanda, and of the solemnities after the cremation, in connection with what we know from non-Buddhist sources[2], leaves no doubt regarding the primitive character of this kind of sanctuary. Even the outward shape of the Stūpa shows its affinity to the grave-mound; the dome answers to the *tumulus*, the railing to the fencing or circle of stones, the top or *palus* to the stake or column on the grave[3].

The Stūpas, such as we see them represented in the sculptures of Sānchi and Bharhut[4] show a square or circular base, either with or without a railing (*sūcaka, sūcī*). On the base is placed a dome surmounted by a graduated inverted pyramid which is connected with the dome by a short neck, *gala*, to use the Nepalese term. The whole is surmounted by an umbrella, or by two umbrellas one above the other. The umbrellas are hung with garlands and flags.

The Dagob in the cave temple of Kārli is of the same type. It is a dome slightly stilted on a circular drum, and surmounted by a head-piece similar to an inverted pyramid, on which are still visible the remains of a wooden umbrella.

The Stūpas in Ceylon, as well as the oldest Caityas in Nepāl are of the same description. A few Siṇhalese Dagobs have a dome shaped like a bell[5], but the most approved form is that of a water-bubble surmounted by three umbrellas, one of the gods, the second of men, the third of final Deliverance or Nothingness[6].

It is known that the Buddhists themselves attach a symbolical meaning to the Stūpa or parts of it. The two, three, five, seven, nine, and thirteen umbrellas, and the gradations of the inverted pyramid suggest divisions of the universe[7]. Both the N. Buddhists and their brethren in the S. see in certain Stūpas symbolical representations of Mount Meru. Considering that the Prāsādas or towers show a multiplicity of stair-like divisions, e. g. the Mahal Prasāda at Pollanarua in Ceylon, we venture to surmise that the more composite type of Stūpas, as at Mengyun in Burma[8] and at Boro-Budur in Java with their graduated terraces owe their development to a blending of the characteristics of the Dagob and the Prāsāda.

In the days when the Chinese pilgrims visited India, the country abounded with Dagobs and other Stūpas of which now the ruins alone are left, if they have not entirely disappeared. It is noteworthy that Huen Thsang more

1 Many Stūpas were erected merely as monuments on the spot where some memorable event had occurred. Near Benares stood a Stūpa on the spot where the Buddha preached his first sermon; not far from it another Stūpa commemorative of 500 Pratyekas who there entered Nirvāṇa; Voy. II; 355.

2 MBhārata I, 150, 13; COLEBROOKE Ess. p. 108, Ep. Ind. II, 313.

3 Ṛgveda X, 13: Sthūṇā.

4 CUNNINGHAM, Bhilsa Topes Pl. III; XIII; Bharhut Pl. XIII; XXXI.

5 See LEEMANS Boro-Boudour p. 391, and the references there.

6 Mahāv. pp. 175; 190; 193.

7 The great cosmical Stūpa produced by the miraculous power of Śakyamuni in Lot. Chap. XI is marked by a series of umbrellas rising upwards to the heaven of the gods of the four quarters.

8 SLADEN, On the Senbyun Pagoda at Mengun, in JRAS. IV, 408 ff. (New s.). Cp. the Universe and the Meru represented in WADDELL Buddh. of Tib. 79.

than once records the ruined state of monasteries and shrines which two centuries before showed no traces of decay[1]. The great Stūpa of Peshawer, which on account of its height, more than 400 cubits, must have been a Stūpa of the more composite type, had already thrice been damaged by fire before the pilgrim visited the country[2].

The foundation of the great Stūpa at Peshawer dates from the reign of Kaniṣka. The Tope of Mānikiāla[3] may belong to the same period. Older, if tradition may be trusted, were two Stūpas erected on a hallowed spot near Puṣkalāvatī, ascribed to Aśoka. Decidedly apocryphal is the story that two other Stūpas of precious stones had been founded by the gods Brahmā and Indra. Huen Thsang saw only the ruins of those wonderful buildings[4]. As little credit deserves the fiction, common to both divisions of the Church, that Aśoka built 84000 Stūpas or Vihāras all over India[5]. The pilgrims add that the king did so after he had opened seven of the eight Stūpas which had been reared after the Lord's Parinirvāṇa. The only Stūpa not opened by him was that of Rāmagrāma, where a pious posterity had erected several Stūpas and monasteries when the pilgrims visited the place[6].

The memorial edifices and the Vihāra at Sārnāth near Benares, still entire in the 7th century, are now in ruins[7]. It is not a little curious that the temple at that place, annexed to the ruined tower, is at present in the possession of the Jains.

Stūpas were dedicated not only to persons, but sometimes to the sacred books. In Mathurā there were such buildings reared in honour of Śāriputra, Maudgalyāyana and Ānanda; others dedicated to the Abhidharma, the Vinaya, and the Sūtras[8].

At Kapilavastu stood a few Stūpas on memorable spots, as well as some monasteries, but the region is described by Fa Hian as "a great scene of empty desolation." The place shown to Huen Thsang as the site of Kapilavastu was as dreary as two centuries before[9].

In Magadha Stūpas were not wanting in the Middle Ages, though that original home of Buddhism was comparatively richer in monasteries, and especially in legends[10].

The most renowned and oldest Thūpa in Ceylon is the Mahāthūpa, dating from the time of Duṭṭha-Gāmani. It was built over Buddha's footprint at the N. of Anurādhapura, and had, according to Fa Hian, a height of 300 cubits. By the side of this tope, the foundation whereof is represented in the chronicles as a most important event[11], stood the splendid monastery

---

1 E. g. in Gāndhāra; Voy. I, 84; II, 105. Cp. Rec. 34.

2 Voy, III, 112.

3 WILSON Ariana Antiqua 55; cp. Arch. Surv. XIV, 1 ff. The ruins have been identified with the Stūpa of Siṃhapura mentioned in Voy. I, 164.

4 Voy. II, 120.

5 Dīpav. VI, 96; Mahāv. p. 185; Rec. 69; 78; Voy. II, 325 ff. 417; 420; Tār. 36. Cp. Divy. 379; 402; the King's motive for opening the mounds was to distribute the relis; there is no question of "destroying", as the Chinese seem to have understood.

6 Rec. 70; Voy. II, 334.

7 Rec. 94; Voy. II, 355 ff.

8 Rec. 44 ff. Slightly different is the account in Voy. II, 209, affirming that the relics of Śāriputra, Upāli and Pūrṇa-Maitrāyaṇīputra were preserved in Stūpas, these three Disciples being honoured by the students of the Abhidharma, the Vinaya and the Sūtras, severally.

9 Rec. 64 ff. Voy. II, 309.

10 Rec. 80 ff. Voy, II, 417 ff.

11 Rec. 102; Dīpav. XIX, 2—10; Mahāv. p. 172; Saddh. S. p. 47. Cp. KNIGHTON in JASB. XVI, 222.

of Abhayagiri, so famous in the ecclesiastical history of the island. Other Thūpas in Ceylon which have retained something of their ancient grandeur are the Thūpārāma and the Thūpa at the Jetavana monastery[1]. To the east of Abhayagiri, on the Cetiya hill, identified with Mihintale, was constructed the Silāthūpa[2]. It is a matter of course that Ceylon abounded with Vihāras and Prāsādas, some of which appear to have been remarkable, but judging from the remains, Siṃhalese architecture never reached the development the art shows in India and in other countries where Buddhism was introduced by the Mahāyānists, as in Camboja and Java.

Passing to Buddhist iconography, we commence with repeating the often made remark that images of the Buddha are wholly absent from the older sculptures at Sānchi and Bharhut. Even in cases where the presence of the Lord must be presupposed, it is indicated by symbols, footprints, a wheel, a seat or altar above which an umbrella with garlands. A scene on the sculptures of Bharhut represents Ajātaśatru kneeling before the footprints of the Lord whereas the inscription distinctly says: "Ajātaśatru pays his homage to the Lord"[3]. There are many other instances which go far to prove that images of the Buddha and their being worshipped date from a period posterior to Aśoka[4].

There is no lack of legends anent the origin of Buddha images, but it would be difficult to discover in those tales, which are wholly discordant, something like an historical nucleus[5]. Nothing definite results from those legends, except the fact that images of the Tathāgata were venerated by the faithful at the time of the tales being invented. If the dates found on the numerous inscriptions added to representations of Buddha and Mahāvīra at Mathurā[6] refer to the Śaka era, which is probable, the custom of honouring the founder of the creed by images must have been common in the first century of our era. As to the model which has served for the Buddha type, it is not safe to speak with overmuch confidence. One of the oldest Buddha images bears the inscription: *Bhagavato Pitāmahasya*. Now Pitāmaha is a well-known epithet of Brahmā, whose lotus-seat, Padmāsana, has become a common feature of the sitting Tathāgata[7]. Yet it is by no means necessary to assume that only one type has been taken for a model; the less so because the influence of the Greeks on Buddhist art is unmistakable. That influence, which has preeminently left its mark on the sculptures of the kingdom of Gāndhāra, is supposed to have lasted from the beginning of our era or thereabouts downward to the 4th century.

The Buddha type on the Gāndhāra sculptures is more Greek than Indian, and has therefore not been able to gain the upper-hand. The Indian type, the common one both in the N. and in the S., though in its best

1 Hardy E. M. 220; Knighton, op. c. Pl. II and III. A full description of the remains of those Thūpas with accompanying Plates is found in Smither, op. c.

2 Dīpav. XIX, 3; cp. Rec. 107.

3 Pl. XVI; cp. Cunningham's text p. 114.

4 Fergusson in JRAS. VIII, 42 (New s.). Cp. Waddell op. c. 13.

5 In the tale of Divy. 545 ff. the name Rudrāyaṇa is a corruption of Udayana. At Śrāvastī Fa Hian was told that it was Prasenajit of Kosala who had caused the image to be carved in sandal wood; Rec. 57. In Voy. II, 284 the same story is told of Udayana, but in another passage, p. 296, a similar image is ordered by Prasenajit. The Siṃhalese say that an image of Gautama was caused to be made by the King of Kosala, consequently Prasenajit; Hardy E. M. 199.

6 Cunningham Arch. Surv. III, 30—37.

7 Cunningham op. c. III, Pl. XVIII; and cp. the description of Buddha-statues in Bṛhat-Saṃhitā LVIII, 44; Hemādri, Cintāmaṇi II, 1, 119; 1037.

specimens far from inartistic, betrays the care of the artists to indicate the canonical Lakṣaṇas of a Mahāpuruṣa[1].

All the evidence collected tends to leave the impression that the beginnings of the worship of Buddha images fall somewhere in the first century B. C. or later, and it is quite certain that A. D. 400 the fables about the first representations of the Lord were accepted as time-hallowed truths. The pious Chinese travellers repeatedly describe or mention statues and other images. Fa Hian saw in Sāṅkāśya a standing Buddha, 10 cubits in height, and so did Huen Thsang[2]. The latter had occasion to admire at Peshawer, not far from the great Stūpa of Kaniṣka, a statue of the Tathāgata in white stone, 18 feet high. The statue was miraculous; at night-time it was in the habit of leaving its place and of walking around the Stūpa. The numerous images in the smaller shrines were richly adorned and of highly finished workmanship; they had the marvellous quality of emitting musical sounds and exquisite scents[3]. In the Deer-park near Benares the Vihāra was adorned with a brass statue of the Tathāgata turning the Wheel of the Law[4].

Images of the Buddha in a recumbent posture, representing his entering final Extinction, are more than once made mention of. At Bamian there was a colossal image of that discription, measuring about 1000 feet[5]. Another representation of the Nirvāṇa was seen by Huen Thsang on the hallowed spot between the Sāl trees near Kuśanagara[6].

Painted images of the Tathāgata, certainly far from rare in the Middle Ages, are but occasionally mentioned. A highly artificial and wonder-working specimen at Peshawer was exhibited to Huen Thsang, who gives a circumstantial description of the picture and the legend connected with it[7]. Not far from the great Stūpa where this picture excited the admiration of the pilgrim, he saw two images, one 4, the other 6 feet in height, representing the Buddha sitting cross-legged under the Bodhi tree.

The Tathāgatas who preceded Sākyamuni were not totally forgotten by the pious believers. In several places the statue of Sākya was accompanied by the images of his three or six last predecessors[8]. In still greater veneration than those past Buddhas was held both in the N. and in the S. the Bodhisattva Maitreya, the future Saviour. Perhaps the most remarkable of his images was the huge statue of gold-coloured wood, 90 cubits high, in a valley near the ancient capital of Udyāna. The Bodhisattva has not yet appeared on earth, and so the artificer who wished to make his portrait was taken up to the Tuṣita heaven through the Ṛddhi of the Arhat Madhyāntika. After observing the height, complexion and appearance of Maitreya, the artificer returned to the earth and made the likeness of the Bodhisattva in wood. "The kings of the countries vie with one another in presenting offerings to it[9]."

The veneration of the N. Buddhists for the Bodhisattvas Avalokiteśvara and Mañjuśrī was not inferior to the honour they paid to Maitreya. We

[1] See the remarks on both types by Prof. GRÜNWEDEL, op. c. 80; 120 ff.; 133.
[2] Rec. 50; Voy. II, 238. Cp. CUNNINGHAM op. c. XI, 22 ff.
[3] Voy. II, 111.
[4] Voy. II, 355.
[5] Voy. II, 38.
[6] Voy. II, 334. Fa Hian, who likewise visited the spot, makes no mention of the image; Rec. 70.
[7] Voy. I, 110.
[8] Voy. I, 84; 133; 205; FLEET, Corp. Inscr. III, 262.
[9] Rec. 25; Voy. II, 149. Visits to the Tuṣitas to see Maitreya occurred even in later times; a signal instance is the visit paid by Guṇaprabha, who lived in the 7th century.

know from the records of Fa Hian that in his time the Mahāyānists in Mathurā were in the habit of presenting offerings to the Prajñā-Pāramitā, to Mañjuśrī and to Avalokiteśvara[1]. Two centuries afterwards the number of statues of Avalokiteśvara was immense. In Kapiśa, in Udyāna, in Kashmir, at Kanauj, at Gayā, at the Kapota monastery in Mahārāṣṭra, we meet with the miraculous statues of this most popular and helpful Bodhisattva[2]. The monstrosity of representing Avalokiteśvara with a plurality of faces, a circumstance connected with his surname of Samantamukha, is nowhere mentioned by the Chinese pilgrim, and may be an outgrowth of a later period.[3].

Mañjuśrī was honoured, as we have seen, in Mathurā, where — *mirabile dictu* — his relics were preserved in a Dagob, but no mention is made of statues. Now-a-days he is often represented with four hands; the image of Mañjuśrī erected by Ādityavarman in Java in Śaka 1265 is free from any deformity[4].

Since the introduction of the Dhyāni-Buddhas into the Pantheon of the N. Buddhists, these personifications have received their due share of reverence; pictorial and other images of them, of their Tārās and their sons are extremely common, in Nepāl, Tibet and Mongolia. The faces and shapes of the Dhyāni-Buddhas show the usual Buddha type; their lotus-seats are marked by the variety of their Vāhanas: lions, elephants, horses, Haṃsas, and Garuḍas being the supporters of Vairocana, Akṣobhya, Ratnasambhava, Amitābha, and Amoghasiddhi, severally. Further the five are marked by the different position of the hand, *mudrā,* and, when paint or colours are used, by differences in colour. The Tārās have the same colour as the Buddhas to whom they belong; likewise the Bodhisattvas, their sons. These are represented in a standing posture[5].

7. BODHI TREES. THE THRONE OF ENLIGHTENMENT. SACRED FOOTPRINTS AND SPOTS. THE WHEEL.

The holy tree of Wisdom, which plays an important part in all mythologies, is a real Caitya. Systematically it is classed as a Paribhoga Caitya, but originally such trees are, of course, Uddeśaka[6]. The reverence paid by the Buddhists to the Bodhi trees goes doubtless back to ancient times; it is decidedly older than the custom of setting up images, and very likely the dogmatically transformed survival of a primitive heathen religion.

The sculptures of Bharhut show us the Bodhis of six out of the seven last Buddhas, to wit, those of Vipassi, Kassapa, Koṇagamana, Kakusandha, Vessabhū, and Śākyamuni[7]. Śākyamuni's holy fig-tree with the seat of Enlightenment, the Bodhimaṇḍa, at the foot, is more than once figured in the *bas-reliefs.* The most elaborate representation shows two umbrellas over the tree with streamers between the boughs. Two winged figures holding

---

1 Rec. 46; 112.

2 Voy. I, 88; 141; 172; II, 45; 141; 182; 249; III, 151.

3 Eleven heads, 100 thousand hands etc. are the attributes of A. in Kāraṇḍa-Vyūha; Burnouf Intr. 225. Cp. Arch. Surv. of W. India, Nr. 9, Pl. XXIV; Waddell op. c. 15; 357; JRAS., 1894, 51 ff. where twenty-two forms are described.

4 Cp. the picture in Waddell op. c. 12.

5 Hodgson Ess. 40; Wright, Hist. of Nepal Pl. VI; cp. Burnouf Intr. 116; Waddell, op. c. 349; cp. 335; Leemans Boro-Boudour 448.

6 *Uddeśa-* or *uddeśaka-vṛkṣa-* and *uddeśya-pādapa.* Cp. Minayef Recherches I, 175.

7 Pl. XXIX and XXX. The trees of these Buddhas are specified in Buddhav. 106; 127; 122; 118; 114; 131 (quoted Intr. Jāt.).

garlands occupy the two upper corners, and under them are seen two male figures, considerably taller than the former, and in a standing posture, but without reaching the ground. The attitude of both marks their astonishment. The trunk of the tree is encircled by columns, and at the foot we perceive a seat before which two persons of common stature are kneeling with the clasped hands stretched out. Behind one of them is standing a female figure, and behind the other a Nāga king with crossed arms[1]. The Bodhimaṇḍa resembles a square stone altar. One of the *bas-reliefs* shows four seats, those of the four last Buddhas[2].

The original seat of Śākyamuni under the Pipal at Gayā, where all past Buddhas have reached perfect Enlightenment, and all future Buddhas will reach, is called by Huen Thsang Vajrāsana, Diamond seat. It was in his time protected by brickwork; at present the sanctuary consists of steps round a Pipal standing on a terrace raised 30 feet above the ground[3]. The Bodhimaṇḍa, or Narasiṃhāsana, is held to be the centre of the earth[4]. The southern branch of the original tree Bodhi was brought to Ceylon, it is said, by the Therī Saṅghamittā, daughter to Aśoka, and planted in the Mahāmeghavana. Eight shoots produced in a most miraculous manner were transferred to different places in the island, and from these again sprung thirty-two trees[5]. The history and prehistory of the Bodhi tree forms the subject of a work with literary pretensions, the Mahābodhivamsa[6].

We discover in the sculptures of Bharhut fewer delineations of footprints than of Bodhis; still there are some instances. On the *bas-relief* representing Ajātaśatru's homage to the Lord are visible two footprints marked by a wheel, and symbolically indicating the presence of the Lord. It is generally known that out of the numerous footprints, which the Tathāgata has left on earth there is none so famous as the Śrīpāda on the Sumana or Adam Peak[7]. Tradition avers that when the Jina came to Ceylon he planted one foot at the South of Anurādhapura, and the other on the top of a mountain, the two being 15 Yojanas apart. Such was the account already current when Fa Ḥian visited the island[8]. This most celebrated Srīpāda, regarded by the Sivaites as the footstep of Śiva, and by the Mohammedans as Adam's, whilst the Buddhists claim it as the impressions of the Lord's foot, is described as a superficial hollow more than 5 feet long and 2½ feet wide.

Still more gigantic was the footprint left by the four last Buddhas in the

1 Pl. XXX; cp. CUNNINGHAM's text p. 114. The two tall figures must be gods, for their feet do not touch the earth. It appears from the description of the Mahāthūpa (Mahāv. pp. 172 ff.) that the image of Buddha sitting on the Bodhimaṇḍa was flanked by Brahmā and Indra; hence we infer that the two figures represent those two gods. — On the manner of whorshipping the Bodhi see MINAYEF Recherches I, 175.

2 Pl. XXXI; text p. 112. Cp. Voy. II, 106; FLEET, Corp. Inscr. III, 262.

3 Voy. II, 458; cp. I, 139. RĀJENDRA LĀL MITRA, Buddha Gayā p. 92; the Vajrāsana Pl. XLIII. Cp. PINCOTT in Trans. 9th Cong. of Or. I, 245—251.

4 Lal. V. 475; *sabbabuddhānaṃ puthavīnābhi-mahābodhimaṇḍo*, Bodhiv. p. 79 = Jāt. IV, p. 232; it is the seat of "all Buddhas." — A N. addition to the confession of faith, as mentioned by MINAYEF Recherches I, 177, runs thus: *aham amukanāmā, imāṃ velām upādāya yāvad ā bodhimaṇḍaniṣadanāt;* i. e. until attaining full Enlightenment, becoming a Buddha.

5 Dīpav. XVII, 20; Mahāv. XVIII; XIX; Bodhiv. 153 ff. S. Vibh. I, pp. 335 ff. Cp. DICKSON JRAS. VIII, 62 (New s.)

6 See STRONG in his Intr. VIII, ff. A part of this work is simply a repetition of the Kāliṅgabodhi-Jātaka, Nr. 479. We learn from both sources that during the life-time of the Buddha a ripe fruit of the Bodhi tree was planted at Śrāvastī by Ānanda; hence it was called "Ānandabodhi."

7 This curiosity has often been described; see BURNOUF Lot. 622 and the authors there quoted; cp. HARDY M. of B. 212. Tār. 264 calls the sacred footprint Śrīpadukā.

8 Rec. 102; Mahāv. p. 7. A Śivapada is mentioned by BARTH, Inscr. Camb. I, 33.

Deer-park. Huen Thsang, who saw that footprint with his own eyes, records that the length of the footstep was 500 feet with a depth of 7 feet[1]. Very small in comparison were the prints of the Lord's feet which the same traveller saw in the neighbourhood of Pāṭaliputra. They measured 1 foot 8 inches in length, and 6 inches in width. But the fact becomes somehow intelligible when we read that these footprints were left by the Buddha in the moment that he was about to be extinguished[2].

Sacred footsteps were seen in various other places, e. g. in Udyāna on a large stone on the N. bank of the Swat. It possessed the striking peculiarity that it was long or short according to the ideas of the beholder[3].

The Nepalese call drawings of the feet of Buddha and Mañjuśrī *pādukā*. The feet of Buddha are marked with some tree-like figures, those of Mañjuśrī with a half-closed eye, evidently the moon[4].

The origin and history of the Śrīpādas are as yet wrapt in darkness, but we have sufficient data to warrant the inference that their worship is connected with the strides, *vikrama*, of Puruṣottama, Viṣṇu. The sacredness of the places where such marks are seen is, from a Buddhist standpoint, not justified, the truly hallowed spots being those where, according to the Scriptures, the Tathāgata abode when walking on earth. Such spots were preeminently the four places of pilgrimage as indicated by the Lord himself to Ānanda, and further the scenes of his blessed career in Magadha and adjacent countries. An interesting description of the hallowed spots near Gayā is given by Fa Hian, whose sober but perfectly reliable account is completed by the more pompous narrative of Huen Thsang[5].

Almost as rich as Gayā in sacred spots and legends from ancient times was Benares. There people were able to indicate the place where the Bodhisattva who once would become Śākyamuni received the prediction of his future Buddhahood. There, too, was the spot where Maitreya received the same prediction from the Buddha of the present period[6]. It is not easy to understand how Maitreya, who has not yet descended on earth, can have received that prediction in the Deerpark. The difficulty increases when we learn from the same source that Śākyamuni was seated on the Gṛdhrakūṭa, when he announced to the monks that in an age to come[7] would appear the future Buddha Maitreya, having a body shining as gold and shedding a bright lustre. Has our Chinese authority confounded two traditions?[8] Or are we in the presence of a mystery, not to say of a mystification?

Apart from the four canonical places of pilgrimage, several other localities where the Teacher had sojourned were dear to the mind of the believer[9]. The authority of Scripture was not always required to seal the sacredness of some spot; in case of need tradition stepped in and gave its sanction. Thus the Siṃhalese would show a spot where the Jina of yore had sat in the shadow of a Rājāyatana tree; the tree and the seat were worshipped as Paribhoga Cetiyas[10].

1 Voy. I, 133; II, 358.
2 Voy. I, 138.
3 Rec. 29; Voy. I, 86.
4 Wright op. c. Pl. VII.
5 Rec. 87—90; Voy. II, 455 ff.
6 Voy. II, 356 ff.
7 When men will have a lifetime of eighty-thousand years.
8 A similar contradiction in case of Maitreya occurs in Lot. I, 94 and p. 186.
9 A list of papers on newly discovered or identified holy spots is given by Barth Bull. Rel. de l'Inde of 1883—1884, p. 6.
10 Dīpav. II, 50.

The Wheel of the Law, Dharmacakra, rather a symbol than a relic, is nevertheless an object of worship. One of the sculptures of Bharhut represents the Lord's Dhammacakka adorned with a strip of cloth, under an umbrella in a shrine. On each side is standing a male person with crossed arms. The lower part of the scene shows a king in a chariot with four horses. From the inscription we learn that it is Prasenajit, King of Kosala. On another plate the Wheel is placed upon a high column[1]. Similar specimens have been discovered at Sānchi, Gayā, Śrāvastī.

The Wheel symbol is only in so far Buddhistic as it is linked with the preaching of the Law. Originally, as the very term denotes, it appertains to the Cakravartin. Other symbols as the Svastika, Śrīvatsa, Nandyāvarta, Vajra, Vardhamāna, Triśūla &c. are in no respect peculiar to the Buddhists and may here be past in silence[2].

8. HOLIDAYS. FESTIVALS. QUINQUENNIAL ASSEMBLY. ANNUAL CONGRESS.

We have seen that the keeping of Uposatha on the 8th and 14th (or 15th) of each half-month is an institution which Buddhism borrowed from other sects. The idea of imitating that custom is ascribed not to the head of the Saṅgha, but to the worldly sovereign; in other words: the keeping of the Uposatha is a concession made by the Tathāgata to public opinion; it is one of the numberless concessions by the brotherhood to the religious and moral feelings of the nation.

The weekly Uposatha is a day of celebration for the monks and the laity. Two of the four holidays in the month are by the former devoted to the ceremony of reciting the Prātimokṣa. An occasional holiday, only for monks, is the Sāmaggi-Uposatha, Reconciliation holiday, which is held when a quarrel among the fraternity has been made up[3].

The four holidays or Sabbaths are kept in Ceylon, Burma and Nepāl on the days of the new-moon, of the full-moon and on the 8th of each Pakṣa; in Tibet on the 14th, 15th, 29th and 30th of the month[4]. This difference is perhaps caused by some ambiguity in the sacred texts. In the Pāli Vinaya the ambiguity, real or apparent, has been removed by an additional elucidation[5], but the wording of the fifth Pillar edict of Aśoka[6] is far from clear, and admits of being interpreted as prescribing a holiday on the 14th and 15th of the Pakṣa. The holidays prescribed by Manu[7] agree with those kept in Ceylon, but Āpastamba lays down the rule that at the new-moon two holidays should be observed, whereas Gautama allows, without absolutely prescribing, two of such holidays[8].

The Uposatha is a day of rest; it is not proper to trade or do any

[1] Pl. XIII; XXXI; XXXIV; text p. 110.

[2] The subject has been treated by BURNOUF Lot. 625 ff.; SYKES JRAS. VI, 454 ff.; SENART Essai, 345 ff.; WADDELL op. c. 387 ff.

[3] CHILDERS p. 335, b. Several times mention is made of an extra holiday termed *pāṭihārikā*, *paṭihāriya* (v. l. *pārihārika*) *-pakkha*, e. g. S. Nip. p. 70; Aṅg. N. I, p. 144; Therg. 31, on the character whereof see MINAYEF Recherches I, 166, and cp. CHILDERS p. 618.

[4] According to KÖPPEN, Rel. d. B. II, 139; 307; cp. WADDELL op. c. 501.

[5] MV. II, 4.

[6] Corp. Inscr. I, Delhi Edict V.

[7] IV, 113; cp. 128, and Yājñavalkya I, 146.

[8] Āpast. I, 3, 9, 28; cp. BÜHLER's note SBE. II, 36. Gautama XVI, 36.

business; hunting and fishing are forbidden[1]; schools and courts of justice are shut. It is also from ancient times a fasting day[2]. The laity must celebrate the day with clean garments and with clean minds, and it is meritorious in them to keep the eight precepts[3].

Preaching and hearing the sermon is a common feature of each Uposatha celebration. The reading, Bhāṇa, of some chapter of the P. Scriptures, Bhāṇavāra, was in former times exclusively done by monks, but now-a-days it occurs in Ceylon that laymen go from house to house to read tracts in the vernacular[4]. In Nepāl, where the Order has ceased to exist, all preachers, the so-called Vajrācāryas, are laics and married men.

The regular period for preaching is the rainy season. This custom or institution, dating from the very beginnings of Buddhism, is common to both divisions of the Church. In ancient India the ritual year was divided into three four-monthly periods. The three terms were celebrated with sacrifices on the full-moonday of Phālguna, of Āṣāḍha, and of Kārttika; or otherwise one month later, in Caitra, in Srāvaṇa, and in Mārgaśīrṣa. These three sacrificial festivals inaugurated summer, rainy season, and winter. The Buddhists have retained this ritual division, and equally celebrate the terms, but, of course, not with sacrificial acts[5]. In the Siṃhalese calendar summer begins at the full-moon of Phālguna, the rainy season at the full-moon of Āṣāḍha, and winter at the full-moon of Kārttika[6].

The entrance upon the Retreat during the rains[7] is fixed either on the day of the full-moon of Āṣāḍha, or one month after. In Ceylon the Vassa is limited to three months. The solemn termination, Pravāraṇā, Pavāraṇā, is inaugurated by an act of the Saṅgha in an assembly of the chapter of at least five members[8].

The Pravāraṇā is held on two successive days, the 14th and 15th of the bright half-month, on which Uposatha is kept. It is a festival and an occasion for giving presents to the monks, for inviting them to dinner, and for processions[9].

Immediately after the Pravāraṇā there follows a distribution of robes which the believers offer to the fraternity. The raw cotton cloth, Kaṭhina, collected by the givers cannot be received except by a chapter of at least five persons. When the chapter has decided which of the brethren stand most in need of a garment, the assembled monks, assisted by the laity, make the cloth into a robe, and dye it yellow; the whole of which process must be concluded in twenty-four hours[10].

In addition to the Varṣopanāyikā and Pravāraṇā there are some other days which the Buddhists are in the habit of celebrating. Thus the Siṃhalese keep a festival in the beginning of spring in commemoration, as they say,

[1] Cp. Delhi Pillar V.

[2] Cp. Satapatha-Brāhmaṇa IX, 5, 1, 6.

[3] More detailed in HARDY E. M. 237 ff. and BOWDEN, The Uposatha and Upasampadā Ceremonies (JRAS. of 1893, 159).

[4] A full and lively description of a Bhāṇa reading is given by HARDY E. M. 232.

[5] Likewise in the Pillar Edict V, where moreover the full-moon day of Pauṣa is mentioned as a great holiday. Cp. Apast. I, 3, 10, 2; Manu IV, 97; Ep. Ind. II, 261 ff.

[6] DICKSON JRAS. VIII, 127 (New s.). Cp. Voy. II, 63.

[7] Cp. above p. 80, f.

[8] The regulations are minutely described MV. IV.

[9] Fa Hian speaks of the solemnity as it was observed at Mathurā; Rec. 45, where the phrase "a month after the rest" yields no sound meaning. It should be "the month", for evidently the Cīvaramāsa, the month succeeding the period of Retreat, is intended.

[10] HARDY E. M. 121. Cp. above p. 80.

of Māra's destruction. This festival, called Awaruda in Ceylon, is likewise known to the Siamese by the name of Sonkran, i. e. Skr. Saṅkrānti. Both the name and the legendary account of the origin of the solemnity are a sufficient proof that it is the Hindu vernal feast of Holāka or Kāmadahana[1].

The Vaiśākhapūjā on the day of the full-moon in Vaiśākha, which is celebrated in Siam and formerly was so in Ceylon[2], coincides with the date of Buddha's birth. The date of the Nirvāṇa was, in the days of Huen Thsang, celebrated at Gayā with a great festival[3].

Fa Hian speaks of a grand festival in Ceylon "in the middle of the third month", when the tooth relic was exhibited[4]. Not unlikely the date intended is that of the full-moon day in Vaiśākha, for this was the official date of the Lord's Nirvāṇa as well as of his birth and his attaining Buddhahood.

In the palmy days of Buddhism in India the quinquennial assembly, Pañcavārṣika or Pañcavarṣapariṣad, otherwise termed Mahāmokṣapariṣad, was a grand solemnity and festival. From the description of it in the Divyāvadāna and other sources[5] we may gather that it was something like a Pravāraṇā, a distribution of presents on a large scale, and an occasion for an extraordinary display of liberality to the Saṅgha[6]. The celebrated King Harṣa of Kanauj, surnamed Śīlāditya, had the custom of regularly convoking such an assembly[7].

PART V.

OUTLINES OF ECCLESIASTICAL HISTORY.

1. FIRST GENERAL COUNCIL.

The first century of the history of the Buddhist community is marked by two events which are separated by an interval of 100 years, no more nor less[8]. Those events are the first and the second Council, Saṅgīti, the account of which makes part of the canonical books, and, with unimportant discrepancies, is common to all sects.

The narrative of the first Council, as given in the Pāli canon[9], is in short as follows. After the demise of the Master a certain Subhadda, who had become a member of the Order in his old age[10], said to his fellows: "Do

1 DAVY, Account of the interior of Ceylon p. 169; PALLEGOIX, Description du royaume de Siam I, 249. Something like it in Tibet; WADDELL op. c. 505.

2 Dīpav. XXI, 28; XXII, 60; Mahāv. pp. 212; 222. PALLEGOIX l. c. For the same festival with the Vaiṣṇavas see Pañcarātra II, 7, 38; for the Sattra from the 5th of Vaiśākha till after the full-moon, Kātyāyana Śrautra-S. XXIV, 7, 1.

3 Voy. II, 462; cp. 335. It is not plain which of the two dates, the 8th day after the full-moon of Kārttika, or the last of Vaiśākha.

4 Rec. 105.

5 Divy. 405; cp. 242; 398; 403; 419; 429; Rec. 22; Voy. I, 374; 392; II, 38.

6 The quinquennial tour of inspection, Anusaṃyāna, by the Dharma-mahāmātras, ordered by Aśoka (Rock Edict III), bears a different character; there is no question of an assembly. P. *anusaṃyāti*, to go for inspecting, to visit, occurs e. g. S. Vibh. I, p. 43; Aṅg. N. I, p. 68.

7 Voy. I, 113; II, 252.

8 Except in some N. accounts which give 110 years; WASSILIEF B. 225.

9 CV. XI; Dīpav. IV. V. Buddhaghoṣa in S. Vibh. I, 285 ff. Bodhiv. 85 ff. Cp. OLDENBERG Intr. to MV. XXVI, ff.

10 Apparently another than Subhadda "the last disciple whom the Lord himself converted", MPS. V, 69. Cp. Tib. L. 293; Voy. II, 339.

not grieve, do not lament! We are happily rid of the Great Śramaṇa. We used to be annoyed by being told: "This beseems you, this beseems you not." But now we shall be able to do what we like, and what we do not like, we shall not have to do." In order to obviate the dangerous effects of such unbeseeming utterances, Kāśyapa the Great, whom the Master had designed as his successor[1], made the proposal that the brethren should assemble to rehearse the Lord's precepts. The proposal was adopted, and Kāśyapa was now entreated to select 500 Arhats. This being done, it was decided that Rājagṛha should be the place of assembly. During a seven month's session in the Sattapaṇṇa or Sattapaṇṇi Cave of the Vebhāra Hill near Rājagṛha the Vinaya was fixed with the assistance of Upāli, the Dhamma with Ānanda's.

It has been remarked by OLDENBERG[2] that "what we have here before us is not history, but pure invention, and, moreover, an invention of no very ancient date. Apart from internal reasons that might be adduced to prove this, we are able to prove it by comparing an older text which is older than this story." That text is the Mahā-Parinibbāna-Sutta, where, indeed, the story of the irreverent conduct of Subhadda equally occurs, but in such a way that it cannot have been the motive for Kāśyapa's proposal to convoke a Council.

Now the motive alleged in the CV. is not only absent from the Sutta, but likewise from the Dīpavaṃsa. Hence the argument for the great antiquity of that Sutta falls to the ground, for the Dīpav. cannot be made older than the CV. But this remark in no wise invalidates the conclusion that the dogmatical story of the first Council, as told in CV., is comparatively young. No wonder that we find nothing of that alleged motive with the N. sects. In the Mahāvastu[3] Kāśyapa is induced to have the precepts collected because he wished to prevent that people might say: "The Sākya-sons kept the precepts only as long the Master was alive, and they forsake them after his demise." This very motive, and almost in the same words, really recurs in the CV., but on occasion of the discussion during the Council regarding the observation of the small and minor precepts[4]. The place where the Council was held, is, in the same work, the Cave Saptaparṇa, a resort of Ṛṣis, on the North of the Vaihāra hill[5]. Other N. accounts we here dismiss, referring the reader to the somewhat troubled sources[6].

All available accounts of the Council at Rājagṛha agree in this that the Vinaya and Dharma were rehearsed. Some add the Abhidharma, but this is not mentioned in CV. nor in Dīpavaṃsa[7]. There is a general agreement

---

1 On a certain occasion Kāśyapa had offered his Saṅghāṭi to the Buddha; Samy. N. II, p. 221; Tib. L. 304.

2 Introd. MV. p. XXVII.

3 I, 69.

4 CV. XI, 9: "Sace mayaṃ khuddānukhuddakāni sikkhāpadāni samūhanissāma, bhavissanti vattāro: dhūmakālikaṃ Samaṇena Gotamena sāvakānaṃ sikkhāpadam paññattaṃ." Cp. Mhv. l. c.

> Tīrthikā ca bahidhānugatāśca
> kuryur apratima śāsanadoṣaṃ |
> dhūmakālikam iti Śramaṇasya;
> etad eva ca tu rakṣaṇīyaṃ no ||

5 Read with the MSS. *Saptaparṇa Ṛṣilenaguhāyām*, and in the following line *Vaihāra*. Cp. Rec. 85 of Fa Hian, who had very dim notions of the Council, for he fancied that Sāriputra and Maudgalyāyana had been present at the assembly, though it is generally known that both died before the Master.

6 Tib. L. 305; ROCKHILL op. c. 148 ff. Voy. I, 156; III, 32. Cp. also MINAYEF Recherches I, 28.

7 ROCKHILL op. c. 160; Tib. L. 307; Voy. I, 158. The collection of the Abhidharma, or Mātṛkās, is ascribed to Kāśyapa. The phrase *Piṭakaṃ tīṇi saṅgītiṃ akaṃsu* CV. p. 293 proves nothing, it only occurring in the *résumé*.

also as to the parts played by Upāli and Ānanda in the proceedings. But on comparing the different accounts we easily perceive that other Disciples, too, were contributors to the whole of the collection. We read that Kāśyapa was the chief "propounder" of the Dhutavāda precepts, whilst Ānanda was the first of those learned (in the Suttas or Dhamma), and Upāli in the Vinaya[1]. If we are asked how much we have to believe of the canonical accounts of the first Council, we are in good conscience bound to acknowledge that the only really historical fact is this that the Council of the Sthaviras at Rājagṛha is recognized by all Buddhists. It is by no means incredible that the Disciples after the death of the founder of their sect came together to come to an agreement concerning the principal points of the creed and of the discipline. A rehearsal of the Tripiṭaka, or even of the Vinaya and Sūtra collections, is wholly out of question[2]. Some elements of the tales connected with the first Council may, and probably will be older than the composition of the sacred writings, but they have been disfigured to such an extent that it is as yet impossible to separate the dogmatical and legendary elements from the historical facts[3].

2. SECOND GENERAL COUNCIL.

According to the universal Buddhist tradition the second general Council was held at Vaiśālī. The records of it look like copies of a genuine historical document which have been falsified as to the date and in some other particulars.

The most circumstantial account is preserved in the P. Vinaya[4]. It is in substance as follows. A century after the Lord's Parinirvāṇa the monks of Vṛji (Vajji) lineage at Vaiśālī declared as permissible the Ten Points (*dasa vatthūni*), to wit: 1. storing salt in a horn; 2. the taking of the midday meal when the sun's shadow shows two finger-breadths after noon; 3. the going to some village (or: to another village) and there eating fresh food[5]; 4. residing (in the same parish and yet holding the Uposatha separately); 5. sanction (of a solemn act in an incomplete chapter); 6. the (unconditional) following of a precedent; 7. the partaking of unchurned milk; 8. of unfermented toddy; 9. the use of a mat without fringes (not conform with the model prescribed); 10. to accept gold and silver.

At that time the Sthavira Yaśas, Kākaṇḍaka's son, came to Vaiśālī, and whilst staying in the Mahāvana, witnessed the unlawful practices of the Vṛjian monks. By addressing the laity he endeavoured to stop the iniquity of the brethren, who instead of desisting from their wrong practices, carried out against him the act of making excuses to the offended laity. Yaśas protested and demanded that a companion should be appointed to go with himself as a messenger, so that he might have the occasion of asking redress for the wrong done to him. His demand being wouchsafed, he entered with his com-

---

1 Dīpav. IV; V.

2 Cp. WASSILIEF B. 38.

3 Cp. the remarks of MINAYEF op. c. 39.

4 CV. XII. Cp. Buddhaghoṣa in S. Vibh. I, 293 ff. Saddh. S. II; Dīpav. V, 16 ff. Mahāv. IV.

5 The explanation of the elliptical terms in CV. XII, 1, 10; 2, 8, and in MINAYEF's Prātim. XXXIX, is of dubious value. Both the Points and the interpretation differ more or less in the Tibetan Vinayakṣudraka, Tār. 41; cp. ROCKHILL op. c. 171, f. The terms were obscure even to the Thera Revata, one of the chiefs of the Council. — A discussion on the interpretation of the terms in MINAYEF Recherches I, 44—50.

panion into the city of Vaiṣālī, where he laid his case before the believing laymen. He was deservedly successful in his eloquent pleading, for the laymen after hearing him declared that he alone was a worthy Śramaṇa and son of Sākya. The Vṛjian monks, being informed by their deputy of the decision, continued obstinate, and carried out against Yaśas the act of excommunication. But Yaśas rose up into the sky, and descended at Kauśāmbī. From that place he sent messengers to the brethren in the W. country, in Avanti, and in the S. country, summoning them to an assembly[1]. He himself went to Sambhūta Sāṇavāsin on the Ahogaṅga Hill, told him what had happened, and persuaded him that a lawful decision in the case was absolutely necessary. In the meantime many brethren, all Arhats, flocked together from the regions afore-named. After some deliberation they arrived at the conclusion that it would be of the utmost importance to persuade Revata, then dwelling at Soreyya, he being a man who knew the Āgamas, the Dharma, the Vinaya, and the Mātṛkās[2]. Now Revata on perceiving by his divine ear what the Sthaviras intended to do, and wishing to keep out of the quarrel, left Soreyya for Sāṅkāśya. When the brethren arrived at Soreyya and heard that Revata had left for Sāṅkāśya, they travelled to that place. On arriving they heard that he had gone to Kanauj. After many fruitless endeavours they at last overtook him in Sahajāti. There Yaśas had an interview with Revata, and submitted to him the question whether the Ten Points were allowable. The decision of Revata — as might be expected — was that they were not, whereupon Yaśas persuaded him to take the legal question in hand before the unlawful practices could become general.

Meanwhile the Vṛjian monks of Vaiśālī had heard rumours about the doings of Yaśas, and being convinced that the opinion of Revata would carry great weight, they decided upon trying to gain him over to their party. So they went to Sahajāti. Before they had had occasion to meet Revata, it happened that the Thera Sāḷha felt some doubt whether the monks of the West or those of the East were in accordance with the Law. His doubts were happily soon dissipated by a heavenly being, to whom he promised to make manifest his opinion when needed.

The Vaiśālī monks had no success in their endeavours to gain over Revata, in spite of the presents they offered to him and of their machinations to bribe Uttara, a disciple of his.

When the legal assembly had met to decide the question, Revata proposed a resolution that the Saṅgha should settle the question at that place where it arose, i. e. at Vaiśālī. The resolution being adopted, the brethren went to Vaiśālī. Now at that time there lived in that city an old Thera, Sabbakāmin by name, who 120 years ago had received Upasampadā. This venerable monk of the East was asked by Sambhūta and Revata his opinion, and he made to them the same promise as Sāḷha had done to the heavenly being.

In the subsequent meeting of the Saṅgha the proceedings did not succeed, which circumstance moved Revata to lay a proposal before the assembly that the question should be submitted to a committee. So he selected a committee of eight persons, four monks of the East, viz. Sabbakāmin, Sāḷha, Khujjasobhita, and Vāsabhagāmika; and four of the West: Revata, Sambhūta, Yaśas, and Sumana. The younger monk Ajita was appointed as regulator of seats.

---

[1] The Western monks are designed as "Pāṭheyyaka bikkhus". For Pāṭheyya and Pāṭheyyaka see ED. MÜLLER JPTS. of 1888, p. 54.

[2] This points to a previous collection of the Abhidharma.

As the place of meeting of the committee was chosen the Valikārāma, a quiet and undisturbed spot.

The proceedings of the committee[1] were conducted in this manner that Revata put the questions, and Sabbakāmin delivered his authoritative replies. All the Ten Points were declared to be against the rules, and therewith the Vṛjian monks were put in the wrong[2]. The assembly *in pleno*, in which the Vinaya was rehearsed, is said to have consisted of 700 monks. No mention whatever is made of the Suttas and the Abhidamma.

Before adducing other testimonies, we cannot help observing that the date assigned to the second Council is impossible, unless the heroes of the tale are purely fictitious. A century after the Parinirvāṇa, Sarvakāmin would have been at least 140 years of age; Yaśas, Kākaṇḍaka's son, if he be identical with Yaśas, one of the first converts of the Buddha, would have been 20 + 45 + 100 = 165 years; if he be another, then he must have been more than 120 years, and so, too, the other Theras[3]. A chronology leading to such monstrous results condemns itself. The names of the acting Theras *may* be historical, and the account of their doings, apart from some incongruities and absurdities, *may* be founded upon a genuine tradition.

The later Siṃhalese documents pretend to know much more of the Council of Vaiśālī than the canonical Vinaya. They give in substance what is found in the sacred text, but with additions which partly are not warranted by, and partly positively conflicting, with the canonical record. Thus the Dīpav. one time fixes the number of those who attended the second Council at 700, another time at 1200000[4]. It further adds that at the time of the second Council "Aśoka, the son of Śiśunāga, was king; that prince ruled in the town of Pāṭaliputra". Elsewhere[5] Siśunāga is called the immediate precedessor of the Nandas, so that Siśunāga is confounded with Kāla (v. l. Kāḷa) Aśoka. Such incongruities have nothing to surprise us in a work which is not a well-digested composition, but an uncritical collection of various older sources, chiefly memorial verses. Hence the same event is told twice with variations. The most important addition is the statement that after the second Council had been closed, another Council was held by the losing party. "The wicked Bhikkhus, the Vajjiputtakas who had been excommunicated by the Theras, gained another party; and many people, holding the wrong doctrine, ten thousand, assembled and held a council. Therefore this Dhamma-council is called the Great Council (*Mahāsaṅgīti*)." Herewith compare the statement in another work[6] that the ten thousand wicked Bhikkhus established the wrong doctrine termed the Ācariya-vāda, i. e. the doctrine of the Ācariyas, in contradistinction to the orthodox doctrine of the Sthaviras, the Theravāda. The wrong doctrine is also called that of the Mahāsaṅgha (*Mahāsaṅghika*). Hence follows, if the tradition is to be trusted, that instead of one Council, two Councils were held, the second by the condemned party[7], a short time after

---

1 Mahāv. p. 20.

2 Points 1, 2, 3, 7, 8, and 9 were in conflict with Art. 38, 37, 35, 35, 51, and 89 of Title Pācittiya; Point 10 with Art. 10 Nissaggiya; Point 4 and 5 with MV. II, 8, 3, and IX, 3, 5; the decision of Point 6 depends upon circumstances.

3 Sāḷha died before the Lord; MPS. II, 6. This fact is ignored in CV., or perhaps he had been resuscitated. Why not? We have in so serious a work as the Mil. P. a striking instance of revival in the case of the six Tīrthikas.

4 Dīpav. IV, 52; V, 20; 25.

5 Dīpav. V, 99.

6 Bodhiv. p. 96.

7 Mark that the party had not at all been condemned in matters of doctrine, but exclusively in points of discipline.

the former. Further it would appear that the majority of the Buddhists clung to the so-called schismatics. How else to explain such terms as Mahāsaṅgīti and Mahāsaṅghika? The denomination of Ācāryavāda given by the orthodox to the Mahāsāṅghika or Mahāsaṅgītika doctrine, suggests the fact that the latter cause was upheld by the more learned elements of the Order.

Now the question arises "where did the Mahāsaṅgīti assemble?" We have not been able to find a distinct statement in the Siṃhalese sources. According to a N. tradition the council of the Mahāsānghikas was held not far from the place where the first Council had assembled[1]. We are informed that the party of the Great Assembly, the Mahāsāṅghikas, derived that name from both monks and laics attending the Council, and that on that occasion a new collection of the Scriptures was made. There is no question of the Ten Points or the orthodox Council at Vaiśālī[2].

In the Siṃhalese sources the leaders of the Mahāsaṅghikas are identified with the Vṛjian monks of Vaiśālī. Now we know that these were in possession of the Kūṭāgāra Hall of the Mahāvana, as the chronicles affirm[3]. In order to obviate this difficulty, the Siṃhalese have invented a tale. The King Kāla Aśoka at first favoured the heretics — exactly as the historical Aśoka did —, but afterwards he changed his mind, thanks to the interference of the gods and to a dream of his sister. By his protection the orthodox could assemble in the Mahāvana monastery, whereas the committee had its sittings in the Vālikārāma. The canonical account knows nothing of an assembly in the Mahāvana, nor is any mention made of it in the Bodhivaṃsa nor by Buddhaghoṣa[4], though the latter, after saying that the second Council is called that of the 700, adds that it was attended by 1 200000 monks, precisely as in the Dīpav. All available Siṃhalese accounts agree in asserting that the whole collection of the Dhamma and Vinaya was revised, against the authority of the canon, which only speaks of a Vinaya Saṅgīti. In the N. tradition just alluded to there is, indeed, likewise question of a revision of the complete sacred texts, but by the Mahāsāṅghikas.

The contradictions between the canon and the Siṃhalese narratives are apt to move grave doubts anent the connection between the condemning of the Ten Points and the schismatic Great Council. Let us now turn to the N. traditions[5] about the question of the Ten Points.

When one hundred and ten years had elapsed after the Nirvāṇa some monks at Vaiśālī deviated from the Law and transgressed the rules of discipline in Ten Points[6]. In those days there lived an old Sthavira, Yaśas, in Kosala; another, Sambhūta, in Mathurā, Revata in Sahaja, Kubjaśobhita in Pāṭaliputra — all of them pupils of Ānanda[7]. Yaśas despatched messengers to summon the brethren to a gathering in Vaiśālī. When 699 monks had come together, Kubjaśobhita, perceiving by his divine eye what was going on, appeared by Ṛddhi in the midst of the assembly to complete the number. Sambhūta proposed in due form a resolution that the monks of Vaiśālī, who in

1 Voy. I, 158; III, 37.

2 No more than in the account found in a Chinese commentary on the Vinaya; WASSILIEF B. 225. As to the heretical theories of the Mahāsaṅghikas in matter of doctrine, see Kathāv. P. A. X; XI; XII; XIV; XV; XVI; XVIII; XXI.

3 Dīpav. V, 29, but Bodhiv. and Buddhaghoṣa have Vālukārāma.

4 Dīpav. l. c. again does not mention the Vālukārāma.

5 ROCKHILL op. c. 171 ff. Voy. II, 397; Tār. 290.

6 The expressions in Voy. l. s. remind one of *apagatasatthusāsana*, *ubbinaya*, CV. XII, 2, 8.

7 To whom may be added from Bu-ston (Tār. 290): Sālha and Ajita; uncertain is Vṛshabhagāmin, or rather impossible, for *Nor-can* means "wealthy".

the Ten Points had deviated from the regulations of the Master, should be censured. The resolution being adopted, "the great assembly" proceeded to severely censure the delinquents, who repented and left their bad practices.

It does not appear to which of the various sects this version of the story belongs. This much is clear that it more or less differs from the tradition of the Mahīśāsakas and from another in the Bu-ston[1]. On comparing the version preserved to us by the Chinese pilgrim with the narrative in the Pāli canon, the former makes the impression of being older, but on the whole they are much on a par. Both versions agree — and that is an important point — therein that they indirectly deny any connection between the condemnation of the Ten Points and the Council of the Mahāsāṅghikas. The expression "the great assembly", i. e. the meeting *in pleno*, positively shows that there is no question of a Mahāsaṅgīti apart from the Council on Vinaya at Vaiṣālī[2]. Such an agreement between the traditions of two totally different sects goes far to prove that the story of the Mahāsaṅgīti or Mahāsāṅghika schism as connected with the Council at Vaiśālī is an invention, perhaps suggested by such an expression as "the great assembly".

In one Tibetan source[3] we read that 110 years after the Nirvāṇa Yaśas and the pupils of Ānanda, to the number of 700, assembled in Vaiśālī, and there perfected a second collection. No such collection is spoken of in the other sources[4]. The rambling and confused narrative of Tāranātha[5] teaches us nothing.

If we wish to weigh against each other the value of the S. and that of the N. sources, we must begin with leaving out of the reckoning all unwarranted additions, either by the Simhalese or by others. By so doing and by waiving points of secondary importance, we perceive that the difference turns about ten years, the P. canon fixing the Council at Vaiśālī at 100 years after Nirvāṇa, whereas most N. traditions give 110 years. Both dates are inadmissible, and for the same reason: the impossible age of the actors. Both the P. canon and the Vinayakṣudraka, as well as Huen Thsang leave us in the dark about the king in whose reign the second Council took place. That silence has given rise to interminable controversies on the date of Buddha's death[6]. According to the chronology adopted by the Simhalese, the king reigning 100 years after Buddha's death was a certain Kāla Aśoka, whereas the N. Buddhists almost universally represent Aśoka the Maurya as having ascended the throne a century or thereabouts after Buddha's Nirvāṇa[7]. It would be

[1] Tār. 290 f.; ROCKHILL op. c. 173. In the version of the Mahīśāsakas the date is 100 years, the name of the president being Sarvakāma. This agreement with the Pali version is natural enough, because the Mahīśāsakas have branched off from the Orthodox sect after the schism of the Mahāsāṅghikas.

[2] We have seen above that Huen Thsang gives elsewhere a separate account of the Mahāsāṅghika Council.

[3] Tib. L. 309.

[4] Cp. ROCKHILL op. c. 180.

[5] Tār. 41 f.

[6] The chief papers bearing on the chronological question are TURNOUR, Pref. to his ed. of Mahāv., and in JASB. VI, 505; LASSEN Ind. Alt. II, 53; MAX MÜLLER Anc. S. L. 263; SBE. X, pp. XXIX ff.; WESTERGAARD, Über Buddha's Todesjahr; BÜHLER in Ind. Ant. VI, 149; VII, 141; XX, 299; SENART in JA. of 1879, p. 524; of 1892, p. 482; OLDENBERG in DMG. XXXV, 474; RHYS DAVIDS Ancient Coins and Measures of Ceylon p. 57; PISCHEL in Acad. of 1877, p. 145. Cp. BARTH, Rel. of India p. 107, and Bulletin des Rel. de l'Inde of 1894.

[7] It is in the Avadāna-Śataka (BURNOUF Intr. 432) that Aśoka is said to have reigned at Pāṭaliputra 200 years after Buddha's death. We may add that according to a notice in

very convenient if we could eliminate the difficulty by asserting — as has been done — that the N. Buddhists confounded two kings of the same name. Such an assertion is easy enough, but to make it good would be more difficult. In the first place, we should not speak of an involuntary confusion, for the all but general view of the N. Buddhists is intimately connected with the whole system of chronology. The Sthavira Yaśas is most decidedly and deliberately represented as a contemporary of Dharma Aśoka[1]. There can be no doubt about his identity with the Yaśas of the Vaiśālī Council. For he declares to Aśoka the Maurya that he is the oldest remaining of the Disciples of the Buddha, Piṇḍola Bhāradvāja alone excepted. The untrustworthiness of the tale remains the same, whether Yaśas showed his activity 100 years after Buddha's Nirvāṇa in the reign of a King Kāla Aśoka, or of another King Dharma Aśoka. Where two accounts are equally absurd, there is no reason to give a marked preference to either[2]. Under such circumstances any decisive choice is more a matter of taste or fancy, than of science, specially as we find no support in independent, Brahmanic sources[3].

The only indisputable fact resulting from a comparison of the different accounts is the existence of conflicting traditions, and that in comparatively ancient times. Traces of unsettled questions are found in the Siṃhalese documents. We have seen that in one of them Śiśunāga appears instead of Kālāśoka. Elsewhere we come across the following prophecy by the Buddha: "I shall reach complete Parinibbāna like the setting sun. Four months after my Parinibbāna the first convocation will be held. A hundred and eighteen years later the third convocation will take place, for the sake of the propagation of the Faith. Then there will be a ruler over this Jambudīpa, a highly virtuous, glorious monarch known as Dhammāsoka[4]". This is not the only instance. In another work[5] the date of the beginning of Duṭṭha-Gāmaṇi's reign is, in the prose text, 376 after the Nirvāṇa, but in the older and much more authoritative memorial verse following, it is 276.

If, in our helpless endeavours to find a firm support, we resort to the list of chief teachers succeeding the Master, we soon become aware of having caught hold of a feeble reed. The succession of teachers, Ācariyaparamparā, of the Theravāda down to the third Council, consists of the following names: Upāli, Dāsaka, Sonaka, Siggava, and Tissa Moggaliputta; some couple with Siggava

---

Tib. L. 309 Aśoka was born eight generations after Udayibhadra. This gives more than 200 years, and in so far corroborates the Siṃhalese tradition.

1 Divy. 381; 385; 399; 404; 406; 423.

2 The preference to the Siṃhalese account is, from a critical standpoint, the less intelligible, because ever since Turnour advocated the claims of the Siṃhalese chronology, it has been admitted on all hands that it contains an error of more than 60 years. That error has been palliated by the guess that such an error has sprung up after the period of Aśoka. But a system which contains such a blunder or wilful misstatement at a later period is *a fortiori* suspicious for more ancient times.

3 For a comparative treatment of the Siṃhalese and the Jaina chronology we refer to Jacobi, DMG. XXXIV, 185; XXXV, 667; cp. Oldenberg XXXIV, 751.

4 Dīpav. I, 24—26. The translator adds in a note: "A mention of the second convocation, which was held a hundred years after Buddha's death, is wanting in the MSS.; the third is said to have been held 118 years after the second." The first statement is true, but fails to explain the reason why the mention is wanting. The second statement is not true, for from Dīpav. VII, 37 it appears that the Council took place 236 years after Nirvāṇa. The date 218 is that of Aśoka's Abhiṣeka; Dīpav. VI, 1; Bodhiv. p. 100; S. Vibh. I, 321, where the reckoning yields 228, but evidently owing to some error in the figures.

5 Saddh-S. p. 47.

the name of Candavajjī[1]. It is well-known that Kāśyapa the Great, and not Upāli, was the head of the Order after Buddha's death, but it is admitted that Upāli was the chief of the Vinaya. Dāsaka and Sonaka are likewise designated as chiefs of the Vinaya. Therefore it is exceedingly strange that in the Council of Vaiśālī, where such important questions of discipline were treated, the chief Sonaka is conspicuous by his absence. If such a chief did exist, the great men of the committee completely ignored him. Another suspicious fact is the notice that Tissa Moggaliputta received the Upasampadā ordination in the 3d year of Candragupta's reign, i. e. 314 B. C. or somewhat earlier. He died 86 years after his ordination[2], i. e. at the age of 106 years. If, contrary to the expressed view of the Siṃhalese chroniclers, the numbers are taken as representing the years of life of the five teachers, then the sum total will yield $5 \times 20 = 100$ less, because the Upasampadā is fixed at 20 years. The interval between the Nirvāṇa and the death of Tissa M. will then be reduced with a whole century. It is by no means impossible that a similar ambiguity in the traditional numbers lies at the bottom of the difference between the Siṃhalese and the N. dates of the Nirvāṇa. The otherwise inexplicable want of agreement in regard of that date, may be accounted for on the assumption that the Buddhists of various sects were in the habit of calculating an initial date by summing up the traditional number of years allotted to the first five successive chiefs or reputed chiefs of the Vinaya[3]. The considerations which may have moved each sect to adopt their own date for the Nirvāṇa are concealed to us, but it would seem that in addition to dogmatical reasons the synchronism of ecclesiastical dates with events of local or national interest have influenced. Thus the Chinese have managed to throw back the initial date to ± 1000 B. C. It is possible, nay probable that the Siṃhalese[4] have acted upon the same principle. This would explain how they got their date of 543 B. C., which is proved to be false.

The conclusions we arrive at after comparing the various traditions or what is given as such, are extremely vague, and may be summarized in the following propositions. The Council on Vinaya in Vaiśālī has an historical base; it was held x years after the death of the founder of the Order, and a considerable time before the composition and first collection of the great bulk of the Scriptures. It preceded, but had no connection with the schism of the Mahāsāṅghikas. We leave undecided whether Kālāśoka be an ingenious invention of the Sthavira sect or not. For our part, we have a lurking suspicion that the name originally denoted the Maurya king in his black and sinful days, and is almost synonymous with Caṇḍāśoka and Kāmāśoka, as the monarch is called before his conversion, after which he became Dharmāśoka[5].

---

1 S. Vibh. I, 292; Dīpav. IV; V, 57.

2 Dīpav. V, 94; but immediately after it we find 80 years; another instance of two conflicting statements in juxtaposition.

3 Another list of five teachers (not of Vinaya) is: Kāśyapa, Ānanda, Madhyāntika, Śāṇavāsa, and Upagupta; WASSILIEF B. 225; Tār. 14. Again another has: Ānanda, Yaśas, Śāṇavāsika, wrongly identified with Yaśas, Upagupta, and Dhītika; Tib. L. 308. Cp. WASSILIEF on Tār. 290. The great man in the time of Aśoka is Upagupta, of whom the Master predicts that he will fulfil the Buddha task (*Buddhakāryam*) 100 years after the Parinirvāṇa; Divy. 350; he takes Orders under Śāṇakavāsin; 349; his feats are described 352; 359; 363; 395; he speaks like the Buddha 428. Cp. BURNOUF Intr. 377 ff.; ROCKHILL op. c. 170.

4 Properly we should say: the date adopted by the monks of the Mahāvihāra. We are not acquainted with the chronological system of the monks of Abhayagiri.

5 Divy. 374; 381 f.; Tār. 29; cp. 39.

3. COUNCIL OF PĀṬALIPUTRA.

This Council was no general Council, but a party meeting, of the Theravādas or Vibhajyavādins, as it was held after the schism of the Mahāsāṅghikas, the men of the Mahāsaṅgīti. No wonder that it is ignored by all other sects.

The account of this party meeting, held at Pāṭaliputra 18 years after the Abhiśeka of Aśoka, is so full of glaring untruths that but few of the particulars can be accepted as historical. The story[1] runs in short as follows.

The Theraș of the Council at Vaiśālī foresaw that after 118 years there would arise a Śramaṇa, who descending from Brahma's heaven, would be born in a Brahman family. His name would be Tissa, his surname Moggaliputta. After having received ordination from the couple Siggava and Candavajjī[2] he would annihilate the Tīrthika doctrines[3] and firmly establish the Faith. This would happen when Aśoka, a righteous king, would reign in Pāṭaliputra.

When *all* the 700 Theras of the second Council had attained final Nirvāṇa[4], Tissa was born, grew up, and was taught the Brahmanic sciences, until he became a convert and was received into the Order by Siggava. His Upasampadā coincides with the third year of Candragupta's reign, i. e. somewhere between 218 and 212 B. C.

When 236 years had elapsed after the Nirvāṇa, sixty-thousand monks dwelt in the Aśokārāma. Sectarians of different descriptions, all of them wearing the Kāṣāya, ruined the Doctrine of the Jina. It was then that Tissa M. convoked a Council, attended by 1000 monks. Having destroyed the false doctrines and subdued many shameless people, he restored the true Faith, and propounded the Abhidhamma treatise Kathāvatthu. It was from him that Mahendra, the future apostle of Ceylon, learnt the 5 Nikāyas, the 7 books of Abhidhamma, and the whole Vinaya.

This tale is immediately followed by a second account, evidently taken from another source, but in the main agreeing with the former; the number of monks in the assembly has increased to sixty-thousand; a difference of no value except inasmuch as it furnishes another instance of the uncritical compilatory character of the chronicle.

We have left out all the downright absurdities of the tale, but even so pruned it betrays its dogmatical and sectarian tendency. The principal object of the whole story is to prove that the Vibhajyavādins of the Mahāvihāra are the real and original orthodox sect[5]. Such a claim could hardly remain uncontested by other divisions of the orthodox, e. g. the Mahīśāsakas, who were flourishing in Ceylon when Fa Hian visited the island. Now the question arises: have we sufficient data to pronounce a judgment in the case? Let us see.

The chronicles representing the views of the Vibhajyavādins make a broad distinction between the Theravāda with its offshoots, and the Mahāsāṅghika or Ācāryavāda schism with its subdivisions[6]. The orthodox Theravāda

---

[1] Dīpav. V, 55—69; VI, 21 ff.; VIII, 34—59; S. Vibh. I, 294 ff.; 306—313; Mahāv. pp. 30—33; 42 ff.; Bodhiv. p. 104 ff. Buddhaghoṣa Sam. Pās. in S. Vibh. I, 294. Cp. Minayef Recherches I, Ch. IV.

[2] A quite extraordinary proceeding, as according to the regulations the ordination is conferred by one person.

[3] Which are wholly out of question in a Buddhist council.

[4] Consequently Siggava and Candavajjī were not among the 700. This number is canonical, but at variance with Dīpav. V, 20.

[5] S. Vibh. I, 312; Bodhiv. p. 110; Kathāv. P. A. p. 6.

[6] Dīpav. V, 39 ff.; Bodhiv. 96; Kathāv. P. A. pp. 2—5.

in course of time produced the Mahīśāsakas and the Vajjiputtakas; the latter branched off into four sections: the Dharmottarikas, Bhadrayānikas, Ṣaṇṇagarikas, and Sammitīyas; the former, into the Sarvāstivādins and Dharmaguptikas. Further offshoots may be passed in silence.

In this enumeration no sect of Vibhajyavādins occurs; naturally so, because the Vibhajyavādins themselves hold up the claim that their tenets and their canon are identical with those of the primitive Sthaviravāda. But if we turn to other documents, we cannot but feel some misgivings whether the claims put forward by the monks of the Mahāvihāra are wholly indisputable. According to the system of the schismatic Mahāsāṅghikas, who had not the slightest interest in being partial anent a question exclusively touching outsiders, we have to adopt a threefold primary division of the Saṅgha into Sthaviras, Mahāsāṅghikas, and Vibhajyavādins[1]. The Sthaviras are subdivided into Sarvāstivādins and Vatsīputrīyas, evidently the same with the Vajjiputtakas (i. e. Vṛjiputrakas) of the chronicles. This sudivision would entirely agree with the former, were it not that the Dīpav. has put the Mahīśāsakas between the Sthaviras and the Sarvāstivādins. One of the subdivisions of the Orthodox in the N., the Sarvāstivādins, consider the Mūla-sarvastivādins to be more primitive than the Vibhajyavādins, though they acknowledge the monks of Mahāvihāra, as well as those of the Abhayagiri and of the Jetavana in Ceylon, to be Sthaviras[2]. In another source[3] we read that some time after the Lord's Parinirvāṇa the Saṅgha was split up into two sects, the Sthaviras and the Mahāsāṅghikas, in the reign of Aśoka. In the third century the Sthaviras divided themselves into two sects, the Sarvāstivādins, otherwise named Hetuvādas or Vibhajyavādins, and the primitive Sthaviras, who, however, adopted the denomination of Haimavatas[4]. In a Tibetan list of comparatively late date the monks of the Mahāvihāra are entered as a distinct sect, but we may dismiss that view as erroneous, or at least as not exact[5].

The evidence adduced, if not wholly satisfactory, is sufficient to prove, not, indeed, that the pretensions of the Vibhajyavādins were unfounded, but that they were disputable, and that, consequently, it was the interest of the sect to back their claims by some weighty arguments. Hence the pains they have taken to spread the belief that the language of their canonical writings is Māgadhī; an assertion by which they have long time imposed upon European scholars. Another fiction is the prediction of the birth of Tissa M. and his descent from heaven. A third device to prove the absolute authenticity of their canon is the assertion that the Parivāra belonged to the books rehearsed at the Council of Pāṭaliputra[6], though we know that another section of the orthodox Siṃhalese did not recognize its authenticity[7].

A review of all the testimonies available leaves no doubt that the assembly at Pāṭaliputra was a party meeting, from which the Mahāsāṅghikas were excluded. Whether in those days all the Sthaviravādins formed one compact body and took part in the proceedings of the assembly, is a point which for want of data we must leave undecided. We only venture to observe

1 Tār. 271. Cp. ROCKHILL op. c. 182—196; MINAYEF Recherches Ch. VIII, IX. An exposition of the tenets of the various texts, viewed from the standpoint of the Vibhajyavādins or Theras of the Mahāvihāra, is found in Kathāv. P. A.

2 Tār. 272.

3 See WASSILIEF B. 224—226; 230.

4 In Kathāv. P. A. the Hetuvādas are implicitly represented as holding opinions differing from those of the Vibhajyavādins; XV; XVI; XVII; XIX; XX; XXXIII.

5 BURNOUF Intr. 445; Lot. 357; WASSILIEF B. 267; cp. Tār. l. c.

6 This results from Dīpav. VII, 43.

7 TURNOUR, Intr. to Mahāv. CI.

that either the Simhalese Vibhajyavādins have to some extent misrepresented the proceedings, or that the N. orthodox sects have had reason to efface the memory of that event. How else to explain that the memorable figure of Tissa Moggaliputta has totally fallen into oblivion? If we believe the Simhalese chronicles, it was "far-seeing Moggaliputta who perceived by his supernatural vision the propagation of the Faith in the future in the neighbouring countries, — sent Majjhantika and other Theras, each with four companions, for the sake of establishing the Faith in foreign countries, for the enlightenment of men"[1]. Madhyāntika being recognized as a great apostle among all Buddhists[2], it is hard to understand how his name could have survived, whereas Tissa, who sent him out, was totally forgotten. If we cling to the view that the assembly at Pāṭaliputra was a party meeting, and not a general Council, the relative obscurity of Tissa M. becomes intelligible.

4. REIGN OF AŚOKA.

The assembly at Pāṭaliputra is stated to have taken place 18 years after the Abhiṣeka of Aśoka, a date we have no reason to distrust. This king, who in his edicts calls himself Piyadassi[3], was the son of Bindusāra, and the grandson of Candragupta, the famous founder of the Maurya dynasty. His father reigned 27 or 28 years; his grandfather 24. If the notice in the Simhalese chronicles that Aśoka had reigned four or three years before his Abhiṣeka[4] be correct, this event must fall 4 + 27 + 24 after the accession of Candragupta. The exact date of the first Maurya ascending the throne is unknown, but it must lie somewhere between 320 and 315 B. C.[5], so that the date of 259 B. C. assigned to the Abhiṣeka of Aśoka by Lassen and other scholars after him must be approximately right[6].

Aśoka is described by the Buddhists as something like a monster in his youth, as an exemplary ruler after his conversion to Buddhism, and as a dotard in his old age. Their testimony is not corroborated, nor directly contradicted by his numerous edicts[7]. Those invaluable documents, so precious in many respects, afford us no real insight into the monarch's character. They show to a certain extent that he was not devoid of vanity and that he was much addicted to moralizing, but at the same time he seems to have been in earnest with his endeavours to heighten the moral standard of his subjects. His inscriptions, with a few exceptions, contain nothing particularly Buddhistic; some passages must even have been distasteful to many of his coreligionists. More than once he prides himself of his kind feelings towards all sects, his protection of the Ājīvikas and Nirgranthas[8], whereas the Buddhists in their writings, sacred and profane, never lose an opportunity to blacken those hated rivals. In so far as the edicts have no sectarian character, they

---

[1] Dīpav. VIII, 1.
[2] Tār. 12.
[3] Piyadassi and Piyadassana also Dīpav. VI, 1; 2; 14; 24; XV, 88 ff.; XVI, 5; etc.
[4] Dīpav. VI, 21; three years Mahāv. V, 34.
[5] Cp. Justinus XV, 4.
[6] Ind. Alt. II, 223.
[7] Complete translations by Senart "Les inscriptions de Piyadasi", I and II; cp. "Notes d'épigraphie indienne", 5 fascicules; Bühler, "Beiträge zur Erklärung der Aśoka-Inschriften", DMG. XXXVII; XXXIX—XLI; XLV; "Aśoka's Felsenedicte" XLIV; "Shâhbâzgarhi- and Mansehra Version" XLIII; "Nachträge" XLVI; XLVIII; "Aśoka's Rajūkas" XLVII. Cp. Ep. Ind. vol. II, 245 ff. 447 ff.
[8] E. g. Delhi Ed. VIII, dating 27 years after his Abhiṣeka.

do not here concern us; we have only to take cognizance of those inscriptions in which the King speaks as a fervent Buddhist.

The first document which has to detain us is that of the Bairat rock[1]. It is a missive from Aśoka to the Saṅgha, in token of the king's feelings of reverence and affection towards the Buddha, the Dharma, and the Saṅgha, and of his conviction that the word of the Lord Buddha is a gospel and authoritative. Then he proceeds to enumerate some Dharmaparyāyas, i. e. canonical texts, which according to his wish should be steadily heard (learnt) and rehearsed by the monks and nuns, as well as by the laics of both sexes.

This missive, which, of course, is posterior to the King's conversion, though no precise date can be fixed, proves most clearly that at the time of its being issued a body of canonical texts was existing. Among the titles only one can be identified with certainty, "the Lāghulovāda concerning falsehood"[2]. "The Questions of Upatiṣya" is identical, at least as to the title, with "The Questions of Sāriputra", only known through a Chinese translation[3]. From the circumstance that so few titles have been identified we should draw no consequences, because the same text was frequently known by several titles[4]. It is undeniable that a title like Vinayasamuk(k)a(s)sa at any rate refers to a book belonging to the class of Vinaya. Consequently the Sutta- and the Vinaya-Piṭaka are both represented in the collection, and if a work on Abhidharma is wanting, it proves nothing against the existence of that part of the Tripiṭaka, because the King recommends a selection of sacred texts, not the whole body. Of the version in which the works enumerated were existing, we cannot say anything definite; the titles are given in Māgadhī, and it is all but certain that Aśoka had in view texts in that idiom.

The second inscription, an edict issued by Aśoka when he had become a zealot, has been discovered at several places of his dominions, in slightly differing copies[5]. All the copies of the edict are unhappily replete with difficulties of every kind. The beginning of the Rūpnāth edict may be translated as follows:

"The Devānampiya speaketh thus: more than two years and a half I was a lay devotee, and I did not strongly exert myself. But it is (now) more than a year (or possibly: six years) that I have entered the Saṅgha, and that I have strongly exerted myself. Those who during this period were truly gods in Jambudvīpa, are now made false"[6]. The last sentence runs slightly different in the Sahasrām copy: "And in this time who were falsely (considered) gods, they (were) men falsely deified."

The first knotty point is the date of the edict. It is impossible to refer

1 Cunningham Corp. Inscr. Pl. XV.

2 With the Ambalaṭṭhikā-Rāhulovāda-Sutta, Majjh. N. I, No. 61.

3 Beal, Tripiṭ. p. 73.

4 This has been remarked by Oldenberg, Intr. to MV. XL, where an identification of other titles is proposed. Cp. Minayeff Recherches I, 87—91.

5 The three first discovered copies have been edited by Bühler in his paper "Three new edicts of Aśoka" Ind. Ant. 1877; second notice, 1878. The controversies to which these publications gave rise have been taken up by the same in Ind. Ant. 1893, p. 299 ff., where the papers of his antagonists are cited. The redactions found in Mysore have been published by Rice (Bangalore, 1892) and Ep. Ind. III, 134.

6 It may be observed that a man speaking in such a manner cannot have taken the word Devānampriya — a compound like Yudhiṣṭhira, and no more two words — in its etymological acceptation of "dear to the gods", a meaning which in fact nowhere occurs. Probably Aśoka attached to the compound the meaning of "harmless, pious." In later times the Jains are designated as Devānampriyas, which well accords with their being promoters of harmlessness, of Ahiṃsā, to the extreme. The transition of harmless, pious to idiot, reminds one of εὐήθης.

it to the last years of Aśoka, if the Siṃhalese chronological notices deserve unlimited credit. But they do not. To make good this assertion it will suffice to elect a few facts out of many. The oldest chronicle tells us that Aśoka was anointed king when he had accomplished twenty years, at which date he had a son, Mahendra, fourteen years. Before his anointment the monarch had reigned four years — others say: three. In the commencement of his reign he murdered his 100 — more accurately — 99 half-brothers; yet the same authority contradicts itself by telling us in another passage that the history of the brothers happened in the seventh year of his reign, two years before the ordination of Mahendra, which was conferred upon this prince when he was 20 years, consequently 6 years after the commencement of his father's reign[1]. Another authority avers that Aśoka passed the four years before his anointment with killing his 99 brothers[2]. Both authorities agree in fixing the conversion of the King at 7 years or in the 7th year of his reign, but a third confounds the beginning of the reign with the Abhiṣeka[3]. The evidence of such witnesses is for critical purposes not worth a straw, unless receiving somehow a support from another quarter. No such support is forthcoming. In the Delhi inscription, dating 27 years after Aśoka's Abhiṣeka, he prides himself of the care and benefits he bestows upon all sects, so that the Siṃhalese assertions of the King dismissing sixty thousand heretics[4] is not supported. It is not improbable that the King had already become a convert when the Delhi edict was issued, but it is manifest that he was not yet the zealot he shows himself in the inscriptions of Rūpnāth, Sahasrām, &c. Therefore these must fall between the year 27 from his anointment, and 37 of his reign, for he died after a reign of 37 years. This result is corroborated by a significant notice in the last named edicts. For the King makes known that after having been during some time an Upāsaka he has joined the Saṅgha[5]. Now it is hard to imagine how a married man can belong to the Saṅgha. It is true that, according to Buddhist notions, the king is in some respects above the law, and more than once the Master allows that his own prescriptions are infringed for the king's pleasure[6], but we are unwilling to admit that the license was illimited.

All Buddhist traditions agree in relating that Aśoka was for some time a widower before his remarriage with Tiṣyarakṣā or Tiṣyarakṣitā[7]. According to a notice in the Mahāvaṃsa the Queen Asandhimittā died when Aśoka had reigned 30 years — if we take the ordinal numbers to stand for the cardinals; otherwise the reckoning will yield 29, a difference not worth speaking of.

---

1 Dīpav. VI, 20, f. 24; VII, 27. 31.

2 Buddhaghoṣa, S. Vibh. I, 299.

3 Mahāv. p. 25; cp. S. Vibh. I, 300. It clearly follows from Dīpav. VII, 17 that the King in the 7th year of his reign became a *dāyādo sāsane*, i. e. a "pretender to the Faith," which is not the same as saying "a possessor." This is an indirect proof that his conversion occurred in a later period.

4 Mahāv. p. 28. It is a quite different question what we have to believe of Aśoka's cruelty against the Nirgranthas and Ājīvikas at Puṇḍravardhana, as related Divy. 427. This persecution is laid in the last period of A.'s reign, and may, therefore, contain a deal of truth.

5 There cannot be the slightest doubt regarding the purport of the phrase. Any other interpretation is excluded by the fact that *Saṃgha* is pointedly opposed to *Upāsaka* in the text.

6 E. g. MV. III, 4.

7 The former form is used in Kṣemendra's Avad. K. LIX, 22; Voy. II, 156, and probably also in Mahāv. p. 134, where for the abracadabra in Turner's text we have to read: "*Tissarakkham mahesitte ṭhapesi visamāsayaṃ*", i. e. (he) raised to the dignity of Queen the ill-natured Tiṣyarakṣā." Her attempt at destroying the Bodhi tree is also described Divy. 397.

We read farther on that Aśoka remarried 4 or 3 yeart afterwards. There is no reason to doubt the substantial truth of this notice, for the N. Buddhists have in the main the same tradition. Let us suppose Aśoka to have taken the vows when a widower; then the date of the edicts alluded to must lie between the years 30 and 37 of his reign, or more accurately, between 30 and 34. The date of his conversion we cannot deduce with anything like precision, owing to the ambiguity of the word *chavacchara* in the text. At any rate the date assigned to it by the Siṃhalese is wrong and perhaps the result of a confusion between the monarch becoming "a pretender to the Faith"[1] and his formal conversion. It may be, too, that the date has been falsified in order to connect the conversion with the story of Mahendra's arrival in Ceylon. Indirectly the untrustworthiness of the Siṃhalese statement is exemplified by the fact that Aśoka, 18 years after his anointment, was unaware of the existence of Tissa Moggaliputta, though this worthy had been the teacher of his son Mahendra[2]! It is barely possible that the real date of Aśoka's formal conversion is 18 years after his Abhiṣeka or 22 of his reign, the alleged date of the assembly at Pāṭaliputra. Suppose we adopt the interpretation that he had been a lay devotee "more than six years", this will carry us to the year 28 or 29 of his reign. About that period or somewhat later he lost his wife, and became a member of the Order.

On comparing these results with the opinions emitted by Bühler[3], it will appear that we agree with him in referring the edict in which Aśoka gives vent to his zealotic feelings, to his last years. We believe also that the figures 256, notwithstanding all objections, are really intended as a date of the Lord's Parinirvāṇa. But we hesitate in attaching to that date any historical value. It represents the particular view of the King, or of the party he favoured; it was not the date adopted by the Buddhist community at large. If such a date had been accepted *omnium consensu*, it is unconceivable how the great majority of Buddhists could in course of time have forgotten it. A date, once adopted, right or wrong, remains of force among all sects. There is no instance of the contrary in the history of mankind[4].

The life and deeds of Aśoka have become the subject of a series of N. Buddhist tales[5], which in few points only show coincidences with the Siṃhalese traditions. From a literary point of view those tales are highly remarkable, but the whole series has the character of an historical romance containing bits of genuine history mixed up with a great deal of fiction. It is therefore unsafe to draw inferences from such narratives. Still the traditions in various N. Buddhist works[6] regarding the last days of Aśoka's reign, tend to impress us with the belief that the once so powerful monarch, when in his old age he suffered from mental weakness, was checked in his extravagances by his ministers and the Prince Regent, and that already before his death a current of reaction had set in against his protection of Buddhism to the detriment of other communities. It is certain that a few years after his death

[1] See above p. 119, note.

[2] Dīpav. VII, 34—59; Mahāv. pp. 42—46; S. Vibh. I.

[3] Opp. cit. For the expressions *viuṭha*, *vivutha* and *vivāsa* see Minayef Recherches I, 78. *Vivāsa* has been found only in Jain writings; the same remark applies to *āsinava* Delhi Ed. III (Jain Prākṛt *aṇhava*), but that does not prove any partiality of the King to Jainism.

[4] Other speculations on the edicts, founded upon mistranslations or preconceived notions, we must leave out of discussion.

[5] Divy. XXVI—XXIX. Cp. Tār. 26—48, and the notices of the Chinese pilgrims *passim*.

[6] Cp. Tib. L. 310 with Divy. and Tār. quoted above.

his grandson Daśaratha made three grands of crypts to Ājīvika monks[1], which proves that he was at least no bigoted Buddhist. It is a well ascertained fact, too, that Puṣyamitra, who founded the Śuṅga dynasty about 180 B. C. showed no predilection for the Saṅgha; on the contrary his name has been handed down in the annals of the Buddhists as that of a persecutor of their faith.

5. PROPAGATION OF THE FAITH IN FOREIGN COUNTRIES.

During the lifetime of the Buddha he had made converts within the limits of Madhyadeśa and Prāgdeśa. This is, roughly speaking, the outcome of the data furnished by the sacred texts. This condition of things remained stationary until the conversion of Aśoka, which event inaugurated a period of zealous propaganda in distant countries. Considering the full agreement of all Buddhist traditions in this respect, we are convinced of the historical truth of the fact in general. As to the particulars the traditions disagree, and it cannot be denied that the stories of the different missions are interspersed with fables of the most transparent hue.

The most detailed account of the spiritual conquests of Buddhism in the days of Aśoka is the story referring to the conversion of Ceylon[2]. That conversion is ascribed to Mahendra, the son of Aśoka and the pupil of Tissa Moggaliputta. The Buddha, just before his final extinction, had predicted that 236 years later a man, Mahendra by name, would reveal the Faith in Ceylon. Immediately after the assembly at Pāṭaliputra, which was held in that year, Mahendra undertook the glorious task of converting the island. Accompanied by four brethren, one Śrāmaṇera and one laic, he departed from Pāṭaliputra, and travelled to Vedisagiri, where he converted his mother. During his stay in that place, he got a visit from his namesake, the god Indra, who — rather superfluously — exhorted him to preach the Law to the benighted inhabitants of Ceylon. Mahendra flew with his companions through the air, like the king of swans flying in the sky, and alighted on the mountain Missaka, now Mihintale. The king of the island, Devānāmpriya Tiṣya, happened to be a-hunting, and had a meeting with the apostle, who improved the occasion by preaching the Hatthipada Sutta, with the result that the king became a convert, along with his attendance of forty thousand men. After performing the same miracle as before, Mahendra with his companions appeared within the precincts of the palace where the princes, princesses &c. were assembled. All of them were soon converted. Meanwhile the crowd of people, anxious to hear the missionaries, had become so numerous that the preaching had to be carried on in the Nandana Park outside the town. The success was immense. At nightfall the King offered to the distinguished guests for a lodging the royal pavilion in the Meghavana Garden. The offer was accepted, and when Devānāmpriya Tiṣya came the next day to visit the monks, and heard that they were well pleased with their lodgings, he dedicated to the Congregation the Meghavana, which became the site of the Tissārāma or Mahāvihāra.

The monks of the Mahāvihāra, whose annals are the source of our information, have undoubtedly painted the conversion of the island in the brightest colours, and magnified the achievements of Mahendra. Yet we feel not at liberty to denounce the whole story as a fable, the less so because the

[1] CUNNINGHAM Corp. Inscr. I, p. 103. Cp. Ind. Ant. XX, 361.

[2] Dīpav. XII—XVII; S. Vibh. I, 318—348; Mahav. 83—183; Saddh. S. IV.

same tradition was current among the N. Buddhists, with this difference that Mahendra is called a younger brother of Aśoka, and that the conversion is said to have taken place one century after the Parinirvāṇa, quite in keeping with the usual N. chronology[1]. It is exactly the difference between the two versions which points to an historical base underlying the fabric of more or less wilful alterations, some of them of a markedly mythological character. The mythical traits recur in a later N. Buddhist tradition, which otherwise differs in some essentials[2]. All agree that Buddhism was introduced into Ceylon in the days of Aśoka. This fact we consider to be historical.

The Siṃhalese, as well as the N. Buddhists ascribe to Madhyāntika a signal part in the propaganda. The former say that it was he who conferred the Upasampadā on Mahendra, and that he became the apostle of Gāndhāra. In that country he subdued an enraged Nāga and delivered many from bondage. A later account knows the exact number of Nāgas converted; it is distinctly said that he made also converts amongst human beings[3]. The N. Buddhists, who represent Madhyāntika as a pupil of Ānanda, magnify him as the apostle of Kashmir, where he curbed the Nāga Hulunta, and preached the Law, with such an eminent success that fifty years after the Parinirvāṇa the Nāga had erected 500 monasteries[4]. The chronology is sadly disturbed. Another Thera, Majjhima, is said to have converted crowds of Yakṣas in the Himālaya[5]. He is called *sava-Himavatācariya* in a Sānchi inscription.

A third apostle was Mahādeva, who conferred the Pravrajyā on Mahendra. It was he who afterwards delivered many from bondage in the kingdom of Mysore[6]. The name of this worthy is known to the N. Buddhists also, but with them he appears in another light. He is remembered as a great sceptic, a kind of Mephistopheles, who by his destructive criticism caused dissensions in the brotherhood, much to the prejudice of the true Faith. His party was especially powerful in Kashmir[7]. The talents of this Mahādeva show, a striking resemblance to the prominent qualities of the god Mahādeva, or Śiva, for, he had destructive tendencies, and was a master in contemplation, just like Śiva, and knew the Three Piṭakas, like Śiva is Trividya. The fable of Mahādeva's pernicious activity may after all have an historical background, viz. the fact that Śivaism has been detrimental to the spreced of Buddhism in Kashmir.

The Siṃhalese mention several other apostles, as Rakkhita, Rakkhita the Great, Dhammarakkhita the Greek, and Dhammarakkhita the Great[8], the similarity of whose names is apt to move suspicion, albeit we have no right to deny the existence of those persons altogether. Still more suspicious is the duumvirate Soṇa-Uttara, that went to Suvarṇabhūmi, the Gold-land, and there, after clearing the country from Piśācas, delivered many from bondage[9]. Whether this duumvirate be identical with the Thera Soṇottara or simply Uttara, living in the time of Duṭṭha-Gāmani, is doubtful[10]. It should not be

---

1 Voy. I, 198; II, 140; cp. II, 423.
2 Tār. 44; Tib. L. 308.
3 Dīpav. VIII, 2—5; S. Vibh. I, 315; Bodhiv. 113; Mahāv. XII.
4 Tib. L. 290; 309; Tār. 8; 12; Voy. I, 95.
5 Dīpav. VIII, 10; CUNNINGHAM Bhilsa Topes, Pl. XX, Nr. 1.
6 Dīpav. VII, 25; VIII, 5; S. Vibh. I, 316.
7 Tār. 51; 293; WASSILIEF B. 38; 58; cp. 224.
8 He who ordained the Yuvarāja Tiṣya, the younger brother of Aśoka; Mahāv. p. 36; Bodhiv. 106.
9 Dīpav. l. c. Curiously enough Soṇa in Prākṛt means "gold", and *uttara* is "North"; often the Gold country is said to lie in the North.
10 Dīpav. XIX, 6; Mahāv. 172 ff.

objected that there are chronological difficulties in the way, for the Siṃhalese chronology knows no difficulties, and besides, the apostles Dhammarakkhita and Rakkhita the Great were likewise present at the consecration of the Mahāthūpa in the reign of Duṭṭha-Gāmani, something like 150 years after their mission to propagate the Faith.

The duumvirate Sona and Uttara is unknown to the N. Buddhists, unless we choose to identify Uttara with Dharmottara who founded two sects, the Tāmraṣāṭīyas and Saṅkrāntikas; a really unique performance[1]. Whether the Arhat Uttara, who is represented as living in the East[2] should be considered to be one and the same person is doubtful.

Such and similar accounts, to be gathered from various sources, have a value of their own, inasmuch as they reflect the state of mind of their framers and upholders; as historical documents they must be handled with the greatest precaution.

6. THE PERIOD AFTER AŚOKA DOWN TO KANIṢKA.

In the three centuries which elapsed between the death of Aśoka and the reign of Kaniṣka, Buddhism was steadily on the increase in the North, notwithstanding the little favour it found with the kings of the Suṅga dynasty. It extended its peaceful conquests beyond the limits of India so far as Bactria and China, whilst in Ceylon it acquired the supremacy which it has retained up to this day amongst the Siṃhalese population.

It is impossible to make out to what extent Puṣyamitra, who dethroned the last Maurya, had recourse to violent measures against the Congregation. One Buddhist tradition[3] tells us that the Brahman king Puṣyamitra destroyed by fire many monasteries from Madhyadeśa to Jālandhara, and killed several learned monks. Another tale, probably older, and certainly fuller of absurdities, contains the notice that the king, wishing to abolish the Law of Buddha, destroyed the Kukkuṭārāma at Pāṭaliputra, and afterwards killed the monks in the country about Sākala[4]. A third tradition records three persecutions of the Faith between the times of Nāgārjuna and those of Asaṅga, i. e. between $\pm$ 150 A. D. and 550 A. D.[5]. If this be true, there is no question of persecutions by Puṣyamitra.

Whatever may have been the condition of Buddhism in Madhyadeśa during the second century before our era, it flourished in N. W. India, in the domain of the Bactrian Greeks. The most celebrated of the Greek rulers, the King Menander, or as the Indians called him, Milindra, P. Milinda, seems to have had Buddhist sympathies[6], and is said to have been converted by the Sthavira Nāgasena. Our only authority for this alleged fact is the Milinda-Pañha, in which the date of Menander is fixed at five centuries after the Parinirvāṇa. This date, impossible as it is, is no argument against the substantial truth of Menander's conversion. It only proves that the book was composed or remodelled long afterwards.

As to the person of Nāgasena we know very little. In a Tibetan work

---

1 Wassilief B. 41; 42; 113; 118; 150; 233.

2 Tār. 3; 8; 291; 299.

3 Tār. 81.

4 Divy. 434. The Kukkuṭārāma was in ruins when Huen Thsang visited the place; he does not say that it had been destroyed by violence; Voy. II, 6.

5 Wassilief B. 203.

6 Strabo XI; Plutarchus Reipubl. gerendae princ. XXVIII.

he is enumerated among the sixteen apostles who after the disappearance of Kāśyapa were sent out to propagate the Faith[1]. According to another Tibetan account a schism arose in the time of the Sthaviras Nāgasena and Manoratha, 63 years before the collection of the sacred writings by the Sthavira Vatsīputra[2]. The chronology is so confused that it is unsafe to deduce from such traditions any historical fact. It may be that the monk Nāga, who caused a dissension leading to the division into four sects, is intended to be identical with Nāgasena, but if so, the obscurity enveloping his person thickens instead of being removed[3]. Certainly the Nāgasena of the Milinda-Pañha is mentioned by Vasubandhu[4].

Wholly apart from the literary documents, and exclusively relying on architectural and epigraphical texts, we arrive at the conclusion that the propaganda in the period from about 200 B. C. and 100 A. D. was successful. The foundation of the oldest Stūpas, as at Sānchi and Bharhut, may go back to the reign of Aśoka, the numerous donations of pious believers, as recorded in the inscriptions, bear the stamp of a somewhat later period. The production of Buddha images, so unmistakably betraying the influence of Greek art, must have begun somewhere in the same interval[5].

The time of fruitful propaganda was also one that was ripe in dissensions and schisms. The number of sects steadily increased, and before Kaniṣka the 18 sects of old Buddhists, the sects recognised as such in the N. and the S., had assumed their definite shape. It is moreover probable that the ideas and tendencies which led to the development of Mahāyānism in the second century of our era were slowly gaining ground already before the Council in the reign of Kaniṣka.

The progress of the Faith in Ceylon continued almost undisturbed. Devānāmpriya Tiṣya, in whose reign Buddhism was introduced, reigned 40 years, and was succeeded by his younger brother Uttiya. Regarding the subsequent rulers there is no agreement in our sources[6]. The sum total of years which elapsed between the death of D. Tiṣya and the accession of Abhaya Duṭṭha-Gāmani is given as 96 (or 106). If we accept the statement of the chronicles that D. Tiṣya ascended the throne 236 Nirv. B it follows that Duṭṭha-Gāmani began to reign 372 (or 362) Nirv. B. Another source[7] has 376. By applying the correction based upon the true, approximate date of Aśoka, we get for the commencement of Duṭṭha-Gāmani's reign 110 B. C. or thereabouts.

This ruler was a splendid patron of the Saṅgha. He erected Stūpas, monasteries and the tower Lohaprāsāda[8]; he is said to have built the Mahāvihāra, though the same authorities affirm the same of Tiṣya, while they repeat the building of the Lohaprāsāda twice over, in the reign of the later rulers Saddhā-Tissa and Srī-Nāga[9]. In the crowd of celebrities present at the solemn

1 Tib. I. 322.

2 WASSILIEF on Tār. 298.

3 Tār. 53.

4 Not by Yaśomitra, as BURNOUF Intr. 570 meant; see S. LÉVI in CC. RR. de l'Acad. des Inscr. of 1893, p. 232.

5 Questions connected with the period of Greek influence and the inscriptions have been treated by SENART, Notes d'épigraphie indienne, III; BÜHLER, Ep. Ind. II, 87; II, 366; Ind. Ant. XX, 394; V. SMITH, ib. XXI, 166; JASB. of 1892, 52; WEBER, die Griechen in Indien; S. LÉVI, Le Bouddhisme et les Grecs, in Rev. Hist. Rel. XXIII, 36.

6 Dīpav. XVII, 93 ff.; XVIII, 1—52; Mahāv. pp. 155 ff. Differently in Saddh. S. p. 47.

7 Saddh. S. l. c.

8 Dīpav. XIX.

9 Dīpav. XX, 4; 22; 36. We omit speaking of the repairs.

foundation of the Mahāthūpa we meet the Buddha, the Law and the Saṅgha, as well as the apostles Mahādeva, Dhammarakkhita and Uttara, who 150 years before had been sent out by "far-seeing Moggaliputta".

In the reign of Abhaya Vaṭṭagāmani, the reputed founder of the Abhayagiri monastery, the canonical texts were reduced to writing. This event, falling somewhere in the last century B. C.[1] is thus described in the oldest chronicle: "Before this time, the wise monks had orally handed down the text of the Tipiṭaka and also the Aṭṭhakathā. At this time the monks, perceiving the decay of beings, assembled and in order that the Law might endure for a long time, they caused the Law to be written down in books." Nothing is said of dissensions between the monks of Mahāvihāra and those of Abhayagiri as being the motive for this decision, and as having occasioned the Dharmarucika schism, as we read in later works[2]. The silence in the oldest chronicle might not be interpreted as a decisive proof against the trustworthiness of the later sources, were it not that the history of the quarrel is likewise absent from the memorial verses cited in one of those works and that the Sāsanavaṃsa[3] gives another account. However that may be, the only question which has now to detain us, is whether it be true that the sacred lore was for the first time reduced to writing in the reign of Vaṭṭagāmani. Since we have no evidence or indication of the contrary, it would be unjustified to withhold our assent to a tradition which is older at all events than the Dīpavaṃsa. The enumeration of Dharmaparyāyas in the rescript of Aśoka to the Saṅgha may be adduced as a proof for the existence of separate parts of the sacred lore; it affords no certain indication that those compositions were written books. Therefore we take the statements of the monks of Mahāvihāra to be not wholly unfounded. On the other hand it cannot be denied that the whole account in the younger sources shows a marked tendency to represent the canon adopted by the Mahāvihārians as authentic against the view of the Abhayagirians or Dharmarucikas, who impugned the genuineness of the Parivāra. Further it would seem that the Aṭṭhakathā stood in need of legitimation. That commentary — so the tale goes — was composed by Mahendra in the Siṃhalese language[4] and in the 5th century of our era translated by Buddhagoṣa. We had already occasion to remark that the translator quotes the Dīpavaṃsa by name, so that the whole of the Aṭṭhakathā cannot date from so olden times, unless the translator have taken the liberty to supply his version from various sources.

Among the successors of Vaṭṭagāmani several kings are recorded as benefactors of the Congregation. The most meritorious of all was Vasabha, who reigned at the end of the first century of our era. He constructed Stūpas, a Vihāra, an Uposatha hall, repaired dilapidated Ārāmas, held 44 times the Vaiśākha festival, was, in short, a king renowned for his pious acts[5].

---

[1] Nothing more precise can be said. The interval of time between D. Gāmani and Vaṭṭagāmani's second reign is ± 74 years; this carries us to ± 40 B. C., if we reckon from Aśoka, not if we wish to follow the Siṃhalese initial date. The event alluded to is fixed Saddh. S. p. 49 at 433 Nirv. B. Cp. Dīpav. XX; BIGANDET II, 141; MINAYEF Recherches I, 231. — The Gāmini Abaya, mentioned Inscr. in Ceylon Nrs. 1—3, seems to be Vaṭṭagāmani Abhaya, whose son was Mahācūli Mahātissa, Dīpav. XX, 22.

[2] Mahāv. pp. 207 ff.; Saddh. S. p. 48. The Dharmarucikas are not mentioned in Kathāv. P. A.

[3] The text is adduced by MINAYEF l. c.

[4] Mahāv. pp. 250 ff.; Saddh. S. 54 ff.

[5] Cp. the inscription of this king in ED. MÜLLER's Inscr. in Ceylon Nr. 7.

7. KANIṢKA. COUNCIL AT JĀLANDHARA. RISE AND GROWTH OF MAHĀYĀNISM. SCHISMS IN CEYLON.

The reign of the Indo-Scythian king Kaniṣka, or Kanēṣki, as the name is written on his coins, marks in more than one respect an epoch in the history of India. This conqueror of Śaka or Turuṣka race, from whom the Śaka era dates[1], extended his sway over a wide tract of country comprising Kabul, Gāndhāra, Sindh, N.W. India, Kashmir and part of Madhyadeśa. The N. Buddhists, who cherish his memory almost as much as Aśoka's, have a tradition that the mighty monarch was at first no adherent of their creed; they ascribe his conversion to the instrumentality of the reverend Sudarśana[2]. As a matter of fact the great majority of Kaniṣka's coins shows emblems of an Iranian religion, and only comparatively few coins of his have been discovered with Buddhist symbols. We have no single indication of the probable date of his conversion, but we shall hardly go far amiss if we assume as the approximate date of the Council held under his patronage A. D. 100. The place of the assembly was, according to one authority, the monastery of Kuvana near Jālandhara; others say that the Council met in the Vihāra at Kuṇḍalavana in Kashmir[3].

As to the proceedings at the Council the traditions are more or less at variance, and moreover very vague. Minute details are treated with diffuse loquacity, matters of importance are slurred over. The gist of one Tibetan record[4] comes to this: the dissensions which had been raging in the brotherhood for upwards of a century were ended at this Third Council; the 18 sects were all of them acknowledged as preserving the genuine doctrine; the Vinaya was put into writing; likewise those parts of the Sūtras and the Abhidharma which had not yet been written down, whereas such parts as already existed in writing were expurged. Albeit at that time some Mahāyānist writings had made their appearance, the Śrāvakas, i. e. the old Buddhists, did not deem it necessary or advisable to stir up an opposition against the tendencies of the rising party.

Another Tibetan source[5] contains the notice that 500 Arhats under Pārśva, and 500 Bodhisattvas unter Vasumitra, held the Third Council with the purpose to collect the canonical books. The information to be gathered from Huen Thsang[6] is hardly more satisfactory notwithstanding its being fuller. According to his narrative, probably based upon hear-say, it was Kaniṣka himself who, anxious to make an end to the dissensions in the Church, consulted the venerable Pārśva or Pārśvika, and upon the advice of this worthy decided to convoke a Council in which the sacred books should be commented according to the opinion of all sects. The King built a monastery where the monks, to the number of 500, held an assembly under the presidency of Vasumitra. The assembly began with drawing up a commentary on the Sūtra-Piṭaka, of 100000 Ślokas; further the Vinaya-Vibhāṣā, a commentary on the Vinaya, of as many Ślokas; finally the Abhidharma-Vibhāṣā, containing the same number of Ślokas.

---

1 N. Buddhist records fix Kaniṣka's accession to the throne — or his birth — at 400 years after the Parinirvāṇa; Voy. II, 172; Tib. L. 310.

2 Tār. 58; Tib. L. 310; cp. Rec. 34; Voy. II, 107.

3 Tār 59; 298; Tib. L. 310.

4 Tār. 61.

5 Tib. L. 310.

6 Voy. II, 172—178; cp. I, 95.

If this account were exact, the proceedings of the Council would have been limited to the composition of commentaries contenting everybody. This is highly improbable, and it is much more likely that somehow an agreement, a *modus vivendi,* was hit upon on the base of the principal truths unassailed by any of the 18 sects. On external and internal grounds we may draw the inference that the Council was only attended by the Śrāvakas or Hīnayānists, or at least that the opinions of the Mahāyānists, if represented at all, found no support. It is not improbable that the text of the sacred books underwent a revision, and it is not impossible that some parts of the canon were then written down for the first time, but it sounds strange that the whole of the Sūtra-Piṭaka and of the Vinaya up to that date only existed orally, whereas some books of the Abhidharma are said to have been already extant in written form. All accounts are silent on the idiom of the sacred texts approved or revised at the Third Council, but from that silence we must infer that the Chinese pilgrim had no notion of a canon that was written in another language but Sanskrit. It is an untoward circumstance that all the works of the old canon, the Tripiṭaka in the proper acceptation of the term, so far as they have been preserved, are only known through translations or sanskritized texts.

If many points touching the Third Council remain in the dark, one fact may be asserted with confidence, to wit, that the Simhalese branch of the Church kept apart from the Council, the authority of which is acknowledged by all N. Buddhists, the Mahāyānists not excluded. It can scarcely be matter of doubt that the subdivions of the Sthaviravāda were represented in the assembly as well as the less orthodox sects. Adherents of the Sthavira sect occur in India long afterwards[1], but we are not sure that these Sthaviras identified their sect with the Simhalese Vibhajyavādins, who claimed to be the pure and genuine Sthaviravādins.

The most significant trait of the Third Council is that it closed a period of old quarrels between the sects; it did not prevent the rise of new aspirations. Mahāyānism, which in an incipient state was already existing, ere-long boldly raised its head. Buddhist authors explain this fact in a semi-historical way by relating that the Bodhisattva Nāgārjuna, the founder of the Mādhyamika system, was born at the time of the Third Council, and became the greatest promoter of Mahāyānism. He was a pupil of the Brahman Rāhulabhadra, who himself was a Mahāyānist. This Brahman was much indebted to the Sage Kṛṣṇa, and still more to Gaṇeśa[2]. This quasi-historical notice, reduced to its less allegorical expression, means that Mahāyānism is much indebted to the Bhagavad-Gītā[3], and more even to Śivaism. One tradition assigns to Nāgārjuna a life of 60 years, when he died and went to the heaven Sukhāvatī[4]. Another gives him 100 years, whilst a wholly fabulous tradition ascribes to him a life of more than five centuries[5]. Huen Thsang calls him one of the four lights of the world, along with Deva, Kumāralabdha and Aśvaghoṣa. Considering that the Rājataraṅgiṇī represents Nāgārjuna as having

[1] E. g. in Kaliṅga; Voy. I, 185.

[2] Tār. 66; 69; 105; cp. 61; Tib. L. 310.

[3] The Lotus is full of unbuddhistic notions allied with, if not directly taken from the Bhagavad-Gītā; e. g. Lot. XXV, vss. 6; 10; 20; cp. Bh. IV, 6; IX, 17; XI, 43; XII, 7. Buddha is *sama* for all beings, Lot. V; cp. Bh. IX, 29; XII, 13; Śākyamuni's far-stretching tongue, Lot. XX; cp. Bh. XI, 30. Cp. SBE. XXI, pp. XXXI and XXXIV.

[4] Tib. L. 310. Sukhāvatī is the heaven of the Buddha Amitābha. Nāgārjuna, being a Bodhisattva, could not reach Nirvāṇa, this being only reserved for Arhats and Buddhas. He is mentioned in a Jaggayyapeṭa inscr. in Arch. Surv. S. India. III, p. 57.

[5] Wassilief B. 318; Tār. 73.

flourished immediately after the Turuṣka kings, we may hold that Nāgārjuna lived about the middle or in the latter half of the second century[1]. If Ārya-Deva, originary from Ceylon, and represented as a younger contemporary of Nāgārjuna, be identical with the Thera Deva, living in the beginning of the 3d century[2], the view here proposed would find a support in a work composed at a time not very far removed from the date of Deva.

Apart from Deva being distinctly said to be a native of Ceylon, there is another circumstance which is apt to strengthen the belief that the Thera is identical with Deva, the rival of Nāgārjuna. We are told that Deva after a protracted discussion with the somewhat older Nāgārjuna, put the latter to *terminos non loqui*. Now how could the great Mahāyānist be defeated otherwise than by an adherent of the old faith, a Srāvaka[3]?

The figure of Nāgārjuna, so prominent in the history of the rise of Mahāyānism, shows a double character. It is, on one side, the name of an influential person, the first eminent leader of a school imbued with Hinduism and the methods of Indian scholastic philosophy. On the other hand Nāgārjuna is simply a comprehensive name of the activity of Mahāyānism in the first phase of its onward course.

The activity of the rising party is exemplified, first of all, by a long series of new canonical books, many of them very voluminous. Not a few elements of the Mahāyānist scriptures are taken bodily from the Tripiṭaka, with such omissions and additions as deemed necessary. It cannot be said that the framers of the new canon have falsified the ancient sacred lore, nor that they have repudiated the old formulas of Buddhism, but by their interpretations and additions they have darkened the truths revealed by the Buddha. When the conservative Hīnayānists denounce their opponents as having set up another ideal of life, as having lowered the Arhats and extolled the Bodhisattvas, as being unorthodox in their Buddhology, they are, from their standpoint, perfectly right. It is true that the Mahāyānists despise the placid egoism, concealed under fine phrases, of the passionless Arhat, and find their ideal in the active compassion of the Bodhisattva for the weal of all fellow creatures. It is true that their Sākyamuni does not answer to the type as fixed by the orthodox sects.

Some charges[4] brought against the Mahāyānists are exaggerated or debatable. If the followers of the Mahāyāna are blamed on account of their axiom *sarvaṃ śūnyam*, they might easily retort by saying that this is the very essence of Buddhism, and that their opponents had become unfaithful to the letter and the spirit of the old Law. As to their Buddhology, it is no invention of theirs; the Hīnayānists themselves ascribe to Sākyamuni a supernatural character, and among the old sects the Mahāsāṅghikas entertained views agreeing with the Mahāyāna[5].

---

[1] The lives of Nāgārjuna, Ārya-Deva and Aśvaghoṣa are said to have been translated into Chinese A. D. 387—418; Wassilief B. 210. Cp. Waddell Buddh. of Tib. 11.

[2] Dīpav. XXII; Mahāv. pp. 255 ff. — Tib. L. 310; Tār. 83; Voy. I, 186, II, 432; 435. It cannot be true that Deva, or at least this Deva, was rector at Nalandā in the reign of the Gupta Candragupta. Cp. Beal, The Age of Nāgārjuna, Ind. Ant. XV, 353.

[3] Voy. I, 186. ff. The form in which the story is put seems to be a device to conceal the importance of the defeat suffered by Mahāyānism from orthodoxy.

[4] For a fuller account see Wassilief B. 262 ff. Cp. Rockhill op. c. 196—200. The Mahāyānists distinguish in the essence of the Buddha three bodies: the Dharma-kāya, the Sambhoga-kāya, and the Nirmāṇakāya. These are the three modes in which the universal essence manifests itself; Wassilief B. 127; Beal Cat. 134. Among the Hīnayānists the Sautrāntikas recognized the Dharma- and the Sambhoga-kāya,

[5] Waddell Buddh. of Tib. 10 characterizes Mahāyānism as a theistic doctrine

Mahâyānism lays a great stress on devotion, in this respect as in many others harmonising with the current of feeling in India which led to the growing importance of *bhakti*[1]. It is by that feeling of fervent devotion, combined with the preaching of active compassion that the creed has enlisted the sympathy of numerous millions of people and has become a factor in the history of mankind of much greater importance than orthodox Buddhism. It is by its more progressive spirit that it has succeeded finally to absorb all the old sects, barring the S. Buddhists.

This triumph, however, was not achieved without a struggle of some centuries. Both parties fought with weapons borrowed from the arsenal of Brahmanist dialectics, for the Hînayānists, conservative as they were, could not but get the conviction that they had no chance unless their philosophical training equalled that of their opponents. Before sketching the character of the four philosophical schools in which the struggle for supremacy was concentrated, and enumerating the chief actors on the scene, we will look at the state of things in Ceylon.

The Church of Ceylon kept apart from the Council at Jālandhara; even the name of Kaniṣka does not occur in its annals. Thus it would seem that the separation of the two divisions of Buddhism had become a fact in the first century of our era.

After the death of Vasabha, A. D. 110, no remarkable events are recorded during a century, but in the reign of Tiṣya, who ascended the throne A. D. 209 or 217, we hear of new heretical doctrines proclaimed by some monks[2]. That heresy, known by the name of Vetullavāda[3] or Vitaṇḍāvāda, was soon subdued by the King, who in other respects, too, was well disposed towards the Congregation, as he proved by his bounties. It was in his reign that the Thera Deva, whom we have had occasion to mention, was living.

In the middle of the third century, during the reign of Abhaya, surnamed Meghavaṇṇa or Goṭṭhaka, new dissensions arose between the monks of Mahāvihāra and those of Abhayagiri, which led to the Sāgalika schism. The Sāgalika schismatics declared the two Vibhaṅgas of the Vinaya to be apocryphal, and got the upperhand in the monastery of Jetavana, which was founded by the King Mahāsena A. D. 290 and finished by his son sometime after A. D. 302. Such is the gist of one record; other sources are somewhat at variance[4]. The Dīpav., that ends with the death of Mahāsena A. D. 302, only intimates that the Mahāvihārians had hard times in the reign of Mahāsena. Shameless persons, foremost among whom were Dummitta — a nickname of Saṅghamitta — and the wicked Soṇa, misled the monarch, and taught many unlawful things, like — *horribile dictu* — the use of ivory fans, to be allowable. The younger chronicle expatiates more in detail on the

---

"which substituted for the agnostic idealism and simple morality of Buddha, a speculative theistic system with a mysticism of sophistic nihilism in the background." It would, perhaps, be more accurate to say that it is a pantheistic doctrine with a theistic tinge, in which the Buddha takes the place of the personified masculine *brahman* of the Vedânta.

1 A good specimen of that devotional spirit is found in Bodhicary. Ch. II (Zapiski IV, 158—162).

2 Dīpav. XXII, 43; Mahav. pp. 227; 255 ff. Cp. Lassen, Ind. Alt. II, 1002; IV, 279 ff.

3 The chief heresy of the Vetulyakas consisted in their assertion: 1. that the Lord is a supernatural being, dwelling in the Tuṣita heaven; 2. that the Dharma was not preached on earth by him, but by Ânanda, who was made and deputed by him for the purpose; Kathāv. P. A. 171; other tenets of theirs mentioned 168 ff.

4 Turnour Intr. Mahāv. CI; Mahāv. p. 231; Dīpav. XXII, 66—75. Cp. Oldenberg JPTS. of 1882, p. 114. where the text of the Tīkā on Mahāv. is given.

actions of Soṇa and Saṅghamitta. It was by their instigation that the Mahāvihāra was destroyed. The monastery of Abhayagiri, on the contrary, rose in splendour, much to the detriment of the Mahāvihāra, which is said to have been reconstructed in the last years of Mahāsena, but at the same time he founded the Jetavana monastery whose inhabitants, so bitterly hostile to the Mahāvihāra, formed a new schismatic sect[1]. The conduct of Mahāsena is incomprehensible, and obviously misrepresented in the biassed annals of the Mahāvihāra monks, so that we cannot accept those tales but with the utmost reserve.

In the reign of Mahāsena's son Meghavaṇṇa, A. D. 309, the famous tooth relic was brought to Ceylon. Both Meghavaṇṇa and his successors reigning in the fourth cent. are described as benefactors of the Mahāvihāra. That may be true, but from the testimony of Fa Hian, who visited the island ± A. D. 410, we know that in his days the Abhayagiri monastery with its 5000 inmates and by its splendour ranked higher than the Mahāvihāra with its 3000 monks[2]. We moreover owe to the same traveller the notice that there were in Ceylon adherents of the Mahīśāsaka sect, for he succeeded in obtaining a copy[3] of their version of the Dīrghāgama, Saṃyuktāgama and Saṃyuktasañcaya-Piṭaka (?). The complete silence of the Mahāvihāra annals about this semi-orthodox sect in Ceylon cannot be accidental; they must have had reason to conceal the fact; what that reason was, is difficult to guess.

It was in the reign of Mahānāma, A. D. 410—432, that Fa Hian visited Ceylon, and that Buddhaghoṣa came from India to the island. The wonderful achievements of this most celebrated of S. Buddhist authors, his translation of the Aṭṭhakathā, and his composing the comprehensive Visuddhi-Magga, were such that the Siṃhalese monks hailed him as Maitreya in own person[4]. On having completed his work in Ceylon he returned to India or, according to others, went to Burma to propagate the Faith.

The history of the Siṃhalese Church, such as we find it in the partial annals of the Mahāvihāra, is made up of donations to the Saṅgha, of embellishments of sacred buildings, of the setting up of statues and the like, now and then of the renewal of petty quarrels. The King Dhātusena, A. D. 459—477, acquired merits by his pious works, and by his suppressing the Dhammarucika heresy which had revived in the monastery of Cetiyagiri[5]. In the following century, A. D. 545 or thereabouts, the old Vetulla heresy found promotors among the monks of Abhayagiri, but the King Silākala speedily put an end to it[6]. The reign of Agrabodhi, in the beginning of the seventh cent., was marked by an attempt of two monks from the Jetavana monastery to stir up new dissensions by denouncing the Mahāvihāravāsins as falsifiers of

---

[1] The Mahāvihāravāsins, Abhayagirivāsins, and Jetavanīyas are the three Ceylonese sects commonly recognized; see above p. 111, and cp. BIGANDET II, 144. A fourth schism is said to have occurred A. D. 601; TURNOUR Intr. CII.

[2] Rec. 102; 107.

[3] Rec. 111.

[4] His history with the usual embellishments is told Mahāv. pp. 205 ff.; Saddh. S. p. 52. Cp. BIGANDET II, 145; LASSEN Ind. Alt. IV, 372; FOULKES, Buddhaghosa, Ind. Ant. XIX, 105 ff. MINAYEF Recherches I, 189, ff. and the text from the Sāsanav. p. 208. In the last named source Buddhaghoṣa has become the translator of the whole Tipiṭaka into Pāli!

[5] The two Bodh-Gayā inscriptions of the Sthavira Mahānāman (Corp. Inscr. III, Nrs. 71 and 72) have given rise to the question whether this Sthavira be identical with the author of the Mahāv., the uncle of Dhātusena. The date 269 is referred by FLEET to the Gupta era, the result being A. D. 588. The identification seems highly problematic. See FLEET op. c. p. 275.

[6] Nothing of this occurs Mahāv. XLI.

the canon. By recording their own version of the Nikāyas in a form to give it the appearance of antiquity they imposed upon the people[1]. This schism it seems to have been of no consequence, for it is not made mention of in other sources[2].

The annals of the Mahāvihāra afford us an insight into the permanent state of rivalry between the inmates of certain monasteries; they give us no insight into the feelings of the Buddhists of the island at large. The information gathered by Huen Thsang, however scanty, is not entirely to be disregarded. He had heard that the Mahāvihāravāsins were strict Hīnayānists, whereas the Abhayagirivāsins studied both the Hīnayāna and the Mahāyāna[3]. There are indications in the record of Fa Hian that the Abhayagirivāsins were very partial to a pompous mode of worship, and this agrees so well with the ritualistic tendencies of the Mahāyāna that the reports which had reached the younger traveller do not seem to be wholly unfounded. Yet he adds that both sects belonged to the Sthaviras.

8. THE FOUR PHILOSOPHICAL SCHOOLS. MAHĀYĀNA IN THE ASCENDENCY. DECLINE OF THE CHURCH IN INDIA.

When the last named Chinese pilgrim stayed in India, the four philosophical schools of the Vaibhāṣikas, Sautrāntikas, Yogācāras, and Mādhyamikas had already reached their full development. The former two clung to the Hīnayāna party; the latter two supported the tendencies of the Mahāyāna.

The Vaibhāṣikas and the Sautrāntikas may be qualified as realists[4], acknowledging the real existence of the phenomenal world, but whilst the former acknowledge the direct perception of exterior objects, the latter hold that exterior objects merely exist as images, and thus are indirectly apprehended. The Vaibhāṣikas reject the authority of the Sūtras altogether, only acknowledging that of the Abhidharma. In their dogmatical system Sākyamuni is a common human being, who after attaining the qualified Nirvāṇa by his Buddhahood, and final Nirvāṇa by his death, passed into Nothingness. What may be called divine in the Buddha, is his intuitive knowledge of the truth without the aid of others.

The Sautrāntikas, in their turn, deny all authority to the Abhidharma, and keep to the Sūtras. Their Buddha is that of Scripture, possessed of the ten Powers (Daśabala), the four Vaiśāradyas, the three Smṛtyupasthānas, and of all pervading compassion. They ascribe to him a Dharmakāya and a Sambhogakāya.

The Yogācāras and Mādhyamikas, the supporters of Mahāyānism, are idealists. The former deny the real existence of all except *vijñāna*, consciousness, and are therefore often designed as Vijñānavādins. The Mādhyamikas are complete nihilists[5]. Their system is the legitimate logical outcome of the principles underlying ancient Buddhism, and in so far they are entitled to the glory of being more orthodox than the Orthodox. In their nihilism, the Buddhist counterpart, or rather adaptation of the scholastic Vedānta, of the theory of Name-and-Form, in its extreme interpretation[6], they teach that the

1 TURNOUR Intr. CII.

2 Mahav. XLII, 35 only contains the notice that a Thera, named Jotipāla, defeated the Vetullavadins.

3 Voy. III, 141.

4 WASSILIEF B. 226—286; Śaṅkara on Brahma-S. II, 2, 18 ff. Sarvad. Saṅg. 9—24; BURNOUF Intr. 447 ff.

5 WASSILIEF B. 288; 309; Śaṅkara l. c.; Sarvad. Saṅg. 22; 24; BURNOUF l. c.

6 The interpretation combated by Vijñana Bhikṣu on Saṅkhya-Pravacana I, 22.

CONTENTS.

whole of the phenomenal world is a mere illusion. Like the scholastic Vedāntins they recognize two kinds of truth, the Paramārtha and the Saṃvṛti, answering to the Pāramārthika and the Vyāvahārika of the Vedānta[1]. The second kind of truth is, properly speaking, no truth at all, for it is the produce of Reason (*buddhi*), and truth lies outside the domain of Reason; Reason is Saṃvṛti. Hence, in fact, all is delusion, dream-like. There *is* no existence, there *is* no cessation of being; there *is* no birth, there *is* no Nirvāṇa; there is no difference between those who have attained Nirvāṇa and those who have not. All conditions, in fact, are like dreams[2].

The Mādhyamikas try to avoid the usual term Māyā, and use instead Prajñā and Upāya, which answer to the Pradhāna and the Prakṛti of the Sāṅkhyas, apart from the difference between ideal and real[3].

It must be observed that morality is not jeopardized by this theoretical nihilism, for the force of illusion is irresistible, and as all distinctions are equally an illusion, the distinction of good and evil, of virtue and vice, remains unaffected[4]. The reasonable objection that if all is illusion, their idea of illusion is as non-existent as all the rest, would fail to trouble those philosophers, because, in their system, the decrees of Reason are not only fallible, but absolutely false.

The reputed founder of the Mādhyamika school is Nāgārjuna[5], whereas his contemporary Kumāralabdha is said to be the originator of the Sautrāntika system[6]. As two other celebrated contemporaries figure Ārya-Deva and Aśvaghoṣa. The former we have already met; to the latter many works in prose and verse are ascribed. He is claimed by the Mahāyānists as one of their party[7].

---

[1] Cp. the stanzas from Nāgārjuna's Mūlamadhyamaka quoted by MINAYEF Recherches I, 226. On this and other works ascribed to Nāgārjuna see WASSILIEF in Tār. 302.

[2] All this is forcibly expressed by Śāntideva, Bodhicary. IX, 2 and 150, 151:

> Saṃvṛtiḥ paramārthaś ca satyadvayam idaṃ matam,
> buddher agocaras tattvam; buddhiḥ saṃvṛtir ucyate.
> Evaṃ na ca nirodho 'sti na ca bhāvo 'sti sarvadā,
> ajātam aniruddhaṃ ca tasmāt sarvam idaṃ jagat.
> Svapnopamās tu gatayo vicāre kadalīsamāḥ,
> nirvṛtānirvṛtānāṃ ca viśeṣo nāsti vastutaḥ.

The poet is reckoned among the Mādhyamikas WASSILIEF B. 326, but he occurs also as an authority of the Yogācāra; 314.

[3] Cp. HODGSON Ess. 72; 78; 89; 104. The origin of these queer terms is not to be solved by etymology; both seem to be conundrums for *māyā*. *Prajñā* in the sense of "cunning", and *upāya* in that of "a trick" coincide with one of the meanings of *māyā*. The distinction between Prajñā and Upāya is conventional. Another explanation would be that Prajñā = Mūla-prakṛti, answers to the ἔννοια of Gnosticism, "in which", to use the words of MILL in JASB. of 1835, p. 386, "νοῦς, intellect, *buddhi*, — is the first-born offspring".

[4] In the highest truth there is, of course, no good nor evil. This is expressed by Śāntideva in the following phrases:

> māyāpuruṣaghātādau cittābhāvān na pāpakaṃ,
> citte māyāsamete tu pāpapuṇyasamudbhavaḥ.

Zapiski IV, p. 208.

[5] It is doubtful whether any of the existing works fathered upon Nāgārjuna be genuine. The Suhṛd-lekha has been translated by WENZEL from Tibetan, JPTS. of 1886. Cp. BEAL, On the Suhṛllekha, Ind. Ant. XVI, 169. According to Śāntideva, Bodhicary. V, 106 N. was the author of the Sutrasamuccaya. It is proved by his testimony that the Tib. record ascribing the Sutrasamuccaya and the Śikṣāsamuccaya to Śāntideva (WASSILIEF B. 208) is wrong.

[6] Voy. I, 89; II, 154.

[7] Tār. distinguishes two Aśvaghoṣas, one of them being confounded with Śūra, and bearing no less than 11 names, a suspicious coincidence with the 11 Rudras; 90; 216; 297; 300; 306; 311 ff. WASSILIEF B. 211 calls him a pupil of Pārśva, which would make him somewhat older than Nāgārjuna. Cp. MAX MÜLLER, India 312. A younger namesake occurs Tār. 102.

As a younger contemporary of Nāgārjuna and Deva, and their successor at the college of Nālandā, we find somewhere mentioned a certain Nāgāhvaya, otherwise named Tathāgatabhadra[1]. As Fa Hian does not speak of the college at Nālandā[2], though he visited the village, the story deserves no credit. It is more likely that Nāgāhvaya is synonymous with Nāgārjuna[3].

The school of the Vaibhāṣikas was illustrated by the Bhadantas[4] Dharmatrāta, Ghoṣaka, Buddhadeva, and Vasumitra. The first is said to have been the pupil of Ārya-Deva; if this be true, he must have flourished in the first half of the third cent. To him is ascribed the Mahā-Vibhāṣā. He is also the reputed compiler of the Udānavarga, and the author of a Saṃyuktābhidharma-śāstra[5]. Of Ghoṣaka and Buddhadeva little is known[6]. Vasumitra, flourishing in the reign of the son of Kaniṣka, is expressly distinguished from the older Vasumitra, the president of the Third Council, as well as from a younger namesake living in the 6th or 7th century, a disciple of Guṇamati[7]. As pupils of Ārya-Deva are recorded Sūra and Śāntideva. If the notice refers to the two poets whose works are known, they must have lived in the third century. Their comparatively correct Sanskrit renders this very problematical.

With regard to the condition and the peculiarities of the two great parties about A. D. 400 we possess precious indications in Fa Hian's records. Speaking of Mathurā he notices, as we have seen, that the Abhidharma- and the Vinaya-Piṭaka are worshipped by the professors of the Abhidharma and the Vinaya, severally[8]; the Prajñā-Pāramitā, Mañjuśrī and Avalokiteśvara by the Mahāyānists. When the traveller stayed in Pāṭaliputra one of the two monasteries of that city belonged to the Hīnayānists, the other, a very grand and beautiful building, to their rivals; the two together containing from six to seven hundred monks. While residing in the Mahāyāna monastery he found a copy of the Vinaya in the Mahāsaṅghika redaction, which is "the most complete" among the versions of the 18 sects. So he was told of course by the Mahāyānists, who in many respects betray a close affinity to the Mahāsaṅghikas. Yet the Mahāyānists of the monastery studied also texts appertaining to other sects, for the pilgrim got from them a transcript of the Sarvāstivāda rules, those which were observed by the monks in China. He obtained, moreover, the Saṃyuktābhidharma-hṛdaya, one chapter of the Parinirvāṇa-Vaipulya-sūtra, and the Abhidharma of the Mahāsaṅghikas.

In the sixth century Buddhist scholastic philosophy reached its apogee. The two most illustrious names in that period are Ārya Asaṅga and Vasubandhu, two brothers, from Gāndhāra.

Asaṅga, the great master of the Yogācāra, was originally an adherent of the semi-orthodox Mahīśāsakas, but became in course of time a convert to the Mahāyāna. He lived for a long time in a monastery near Oudh, and

---

1 WASSILIEF B. 202; cp. Tār. 83.

2 Rec. 81.

3 Vyu. § 177 the two names follow one another. A dubious Nagabodhi in Tib. L. 310.

4 On the title Bhadanta see BURNOUF Intr. 567.

5 Tib. L. 310; Tār. 67; 297; WASSILIEF B. 50; 270; Voy. II, 105; 119; Vyu. § 117; BURNOUF Intr. 566; ROCKHILL, Udānavarga, Introduction.

6 Tār. 4; 61; 67; WASSILIEF B. 50; 266; 281; BURNOUF Intr. 567. They do not occur Vyu. l. c.

7 Tār. 60; 68. Cp. MAX MÜLLER, op. c. 305, note. A discussion on the various authors bearing the name of Vasumitra is found in MINAYEF's Recherches I, 196 ff.

8 The S. Buddhists equally pay honour to the Sacred Books, which are literally worshipped. Upon some occasion they are put upon a kind of rude altar, near the road-side, that those who pass by may put money upon it to obtain merit; HARDY E. M. 192.

afterwards in Magadha, where he died in Rājagṛha[1]. His chief work is a book on Yoga[2].

Vasubandhu, Asaṅga's younger brother, received in his youth his lessons from Saṅghabhadra, a learned Hīnayānist in Kashmir. From Kashmir he went to Oudh, where he lived for many years. Being at first a staunch adherent of the Sarvāstivādins[3], he disapproved of Asaṅga's Yogaśāstra, but afterwards he became a convert to Mahāyānism. After his conversion he is said to have been teacher in the college of Nālandā. He died at an advanced age in Nepāl, or, as others say, in Oudh[4]. The principal work of this most celebrated of Buddhist philosophers is the Abhidharma-Kośa. He wrote besides several commentaries on Mahāyāna texts[5].

Asaṅga and Vasubandhu were followed by a series of learned authors whose names are little less famous than those of the two great masters. The most prominent among these scholars, partly Hīnayānists, partly Mahāyānists, are Dignāga, Guṇaprabha, Sthiramati, Saṅghadāsa, Buddhadāsa, Dharmapāla, Śīlabhadra, Jayasena, Candra-Gomin, Candrakīrti, Guṇamati, Vasumitra, Yaśomitra, Bhavya, Buddhapālita, Ravigupta[6].

Dignāga, from Kāñcī, a pupil of Asaṅga or Vasubandhu, is known as the author of a treatise on Logic, the Pramāṇa-samuccaya. Being a contemporary of Guṇaprabha, he must have lived from A. D. 520—600 or thereabouts[7].

Guṇaprabha, to whom a hundred treatises are ascribed, was a native of Parvata or Mathurā, and proceeded from the school of Vasubandhu. He became the Guru of the King Harṣa, and numbered among his pupils Mitrasena, who, a man of 90 years, taught Huen Thsang. In his youth a Mahāyānist, Guṇaprabha passed in riper years to the Hīnayāna[8].

Sthiramati and Saṅghadāsa belong to a younger generation than the two preceding masters. Sthiramati, who was teacher at Nālandā when Huen Thsang visited that college, is known as the author of commentaries on the works of Vasubandhu, and of notes on the Ratnakūṭa[9]. Saṅghadāsa, a native of S. India, worked chiefly in Kashmir. Nearly contemporaneous with him was Buddhadāsa[10].

1 Voy. I, 83; 114; 118; II, 105; 269; Tib. L. 310; Tār. 104; 126; 167. He reached the age of 75 years, and is said to have been 20 years older than Vasubandhu. A pupil of the latter, Guṇaprabha, died before the accession of Harṣa, i. e. before A. D. 610. The approximate date of Asaṅga may be supposed to be A. D. 485—560. Cp. MAX MÜLLER op. c. 302—312.

2 Other writings are noticed Voy. II. cc. Tār. 112.

3 His teacher, according to Huen Thsang, was Monu-ho-lita, the author of a Vibhāṣā-śāstra, Voy. I, 83, II, 105, 115. BURNOUF Intr. 567 has Manoratha; WASSILIEF B. 219 Maṇiratha. MAX MÜLLER op. c. 289; 302. Another teacher of Vasubandhu was Buddhamitra; WASSILIEF B. 249.

4 Tār. 118; Voy. II. cc. WASSILIEF B. 210; 214; 222. A Chinese biography of V., composed, they say, between A. D. 557 and 588, shows so little acquaintance with Indian customs that we disbelieve the statement of its being a translation. Cp. MAX MÜLLER, op. c. 302—312.

5 WASSILIEF B. 222; cp. 99; Voy. I, 115; II, 274; BURNOUF Intr. 563; 571; Comm. on Harṣacarita p. 490. Cp. MAX MÜLLER op. c. 308 f.

6 These and more names of teachers, not all of them Buddhists, are enumerated Vyu. § 177.

7 Tār. 127; 131; WASSILIEF B. 78; 206; Tib. L. 310. He was a contemporary of Kālidāsa, according to Mallinātha on Meghadūta vs. 14. Cp. MAX MÜLLER op. c. 305—308. D. is often quoted in the Nyāyabinduṭīkā; cp. below p. 131, note.

8 Tār. 126; 146; Voy. I, 106; cp. 109; WASSILIEF B. 78. Cp. MAX MÜLLER op. c. 309.

9 Tār. 127; 129; 135; 137; Voy. III, 46; 164; WASSILIEF B. 78. Cp. MAX MÜLLER 305; 310, note.

10 Tār. 104; 127; 135.

Among the teachers in the Nālandā college in the time of Huen Thsang is mentioned Dharmapāla of Kāñcī. If he be identical with the author of the Paramattha-Dīpanī, the commentary on the Therīgāthā — which is extremely doubtful —, he must have become a convert to Mahāyānism after his arrival in N. India. Tradition says that after he had been a teacher in Nālandā, he went to Suvarṇadvīpa[1].

Other celebrities at Nālandā between A. D. 630 and 640 were Śīlabhadra and the laics Jayasena[2] and Candra-Gomin, whose opponent was Candrakīrti[3]. Further Guṇamati, the author of a commentary on Vasubandhu's Abhidharma-Kośa[4] and the master of Vasumitra. This Vasumitra, not to be confounded with his two older namesakes, was the author of the commentary Abhidharma-Kośa-Vyākhyā. Possibly he is identical with the realist Vasumitra who about the same time flourished in Kashmir[5].

Concerning Bhavya or Bhāvaviveka and Buddhapālita, who although being both Mahāyānists were inimical to one another, we must refer to the sources[6]. Ravigupta is known as an adherent of Asaṅga and as a poet[7].

It is in the sixth and the seventh cent. that Buddhist scholasticism had its palmy days. The contention between the two great parties rather tended to stimulate the literary activity of the schools than to enfeeble the authority of the Church. The old sects, indeed, were fast losing their significance[8]. They continued their separate existence, and kept up some external marks of distinction, but in dogmatics they were either Śrāvakas or Mahāyānists. If the statistics furnished by the Chinese pilgrims are not too inexact, we must conclude that the number of monks was more considerable in the seventh cent. than two hundred years before. On the whole Buddhism was still flourishing when Huen Thsang visited India. The decline dates, roughly speaking, from A. D. 750.

The latest great champion of Buddhism, Dharmakīrti, is stated by the historians to have been the contemporary of Kumārilabhaṭṭa. That can hardly be accurate. The traveller I-tsing, who stayed in India during the last quarter of the 7th century, reckons Dharmakīrti among the recent celebrities, but does not distinctly say that he was still living. On the other hand we can hardly imagine that a celebrity like Dharmakīrtī would have been unknown to Huen Thsang. Hence we draw the inference that Dharmakīrti flourished between the stay of Huen Thsang in India and I-tsing's, and that he may have been alive, though not necessarily so, in the last quarter of the 7th century, which approaches the date of Kumārila[11].

---

1 Tār. 160; Voy. I, 123; 148; 190; II, 287; 452; III, 46; 112; 119. Cp. MAX MÜLLER op. c. 310.

2 Voy. I, 144; 152; III, 78. Tār. 205 confounds Harṣa of Kanauj with Śrī-Harṣa of Kashmir. Cp. MAX MÜLLER op. c. 310.

3 WASSILIEF B. 52; 207; Tār. 150; Zapiski IV, 29 ff.

4 Tib. L. 310; Tār. 159; Voy. II, 442; III, 46; 164; BURNOUF Intr. 566.

5 BURNOUF l. c. Voy. I, 94. Tār. calls him the contemporary of Amara-Siṃha, which is far from accurate. An elucidation of the Vyākhyā was written by Yaśomitra; BURNOUF op. c. 448; 512; 563; 566; 571; 574; Tib. L. 310; MINAYEF Recherches I, 197.

6 Tār. 135 ff.; 160; WASSILIEF B. 207; Voy. III, 112; BURNOUF op. c. 560. Cp. MAX MÜLLER op. c. 304; 311; ROCKHILL op. c. 181.

7 Tār. 146; WASSILIEF B. 207; ROCKHILL op. c. 228.

8 The sects mentioned by Huen Thsang in the course of his records are: Sthaviras, Sarvāstivādins, Sammitīyas, Mahīśāsakas, Kāśyapīyas, Dharmaguptas, Mahāsaṅghikas, Lokottaravādins; and in Ceylon: Mahāvihārians and Abhayagirians.

9 Bhavabhūti's Mālatī-Mādhava may be adduced as proving the esteem which Buddhist learning enjoyed in the 8th century at Ujjayinī.

10 See MINAYEF Zapiski IV, 31 f. and his references.

11 MAX MÜLLER op. c. 305 and 308 states that Dharmakīrti is quoted by Subandhu. That is a mistake. Subandhu in Vāsavadattā p. 235 alludes to the Buddhist work titled

Kumārila and Śaṅkara live in the traditions of the Buddhists as the most formidable enemies to their creed, as the two great dialecticians whose activity caused the ruin of Buddhism in India[1]. Albeit sober history teaches that the Faith has continued in India for more than six centuries after Śaṅkara, there is a grain of truth in those traditions, inasmuch as Budhism gradually lost ground, became more degraded, and at last died out in the land of its birth.

Our information regarding the external history of N. Buddhism from the second to the eighth century is very fragmentary. Numerous inscriptions dating from Kaniṣka, and ranging over a period of more than two centuries show that the Faith prospered at Mathurā, though Jainism would seem to have been predominant. From other sources we gather that the Church was in a flourishing condition in Kabul, Kashmir, N. W. India[2]. The epigraphic evidence from Kārli, Nāsik and Amarāvatī proves that the Faith had many fervent devotees in W. and S. India. Some of the inscriptions dating from the time of Śrī-Pulimāvi or Puḷumāvi — the Siri-Polemios of Ptolemy —, consequently from the second century, teach us that the sanctuary and monastery of Amarāvatī belonged to the Caitikas, a subdivision of the Mahāsāṅghikas; the latter possessed the shrine at Kārli, and the Bhadrāyaṇīyas a cave in Nāsik[3].

Fa Hian found Buddhism very flourishing in Udyāna, Pañjāb, Mathurā, and in a satisfactory condition more eastward. He does not mention the college at Nālandā, which in the 7th century was the chief centre of Buddhist learning[4]. The great patron of the Faith in the 7th century was the celebrated Harṣa or Harṣavardhana, surnamed Śīlāditya by Huen Thsang, who describes that king as a fervent Mahāyānist, but tolerant and benevolent towards all sects, the Hīnayānists excepted[5]. Now, it cannot be doubted that Harṣa had Buddhist sympathies. As we know from the Harṣacarita, his sister Rājyaśrī, widow of Grahavarman, had become a Buddhist nun[6]. Independently from other information tending to the same effect, the utterances of the Chinese traveller impress us with the conviction that in general the relations between the Buddhists and the various shades of Hinduism were peaceful; bitter enmity only raged between Hīnayānists and Mahāyānists. Instances like that of Śaśāṅka, king of Karṇa-Suvarṇa, who is stigmatized as hostile to the Faith, are isolated[7].

In Kashmir, one of the old centres of Buddhist learning, the Church was still powerful in the 7th century during the reign of Durlabhavardhana, though Śivaism was increasing[8]. Instances of liberality shown by one and the same person to Buddhists and to Brahmanists were frequent. As to

---

Alaṅkāra, but he does not say that the author is Dharmakīrti. It is the commentator who ascribes the Alaṅkāra to Dharmakīrti. Another work the Nyāyabindu, which has been edited by Dr. Peterson, with the Ṭīkā, is ascribed to Dharmakīrti by K. B. Pāṭhak in his paper "On the Autorship of the Nyāyabindu" (JBB. RAS. XIX, 47). The author of the Ṭīkā is a certain Dharmottara; cp. Tār. 330; Wassilief B. 290. Another Dharmottara is the one mentioned above p. 118.

1 Wassilief B. 208; Tār. 175—201; Hodgson Ess. 12; 14; 48.

2 Cunningham Arch. Surv. III, 30 ff, Rājataraṅgiṇī I, 168; Tār. 65.

3 Burgess Arch. Surv. of W. India, X, p. 33; 34; 36; of S. India, III, p. 26; 41; Bhagvānlāl Indraji, Nasik.

4 The story of the foundation is told Voy. I, 213; II, 42.

5 Harṣa was in the 26th year of his reign a Śivaite; Bühler, Ep. Ind. I, 71.

6 We know from the Harṣacarita 484 ff. that H. had a great veneration for the Buddhist teacher Divākaramitra Maitrāyaṇīya.

7 Voy. II, 349; 422.

8 Rājat. IV, 3 ff.; 80.

Nepāl, the kings and the people were no less distinguished by their tolerance[1].

The decline of the Church, as already observed, may be dated from the middle of the eighth century. It was hastened in W. India by the Arab conquest of Sindh in A. D. 712.

9. SIṂHALESE ECCLESIASTICAL HISTORY CONTINUED. PARĀKRAMABĀHU I AND HIS SUCCESSORS. TANTRISM IN INDIA. THE BUDDHISTS EXPELLED FIND A REFUGE IN NEPĀL.

The jealousies and quarrels between the monks of Ceylon subsided after the last outbreak of heresy in the reign of Agrabodhi. The repeated invasions of the island by the fierce Tamils certainly did much to foster the feeling of brotherhood among the monks, who in spite of all their dissensions were patriotic Siṃhalese and faithful sons of Buddha. More than once we hear of sacrilegious deeds and persecutions of the clergy by the enemy from Southern India, which could not but strengthen the unity of the Siṃhalese[2]. When therefore Saṅghabodhi Parākramabāhu I, reigning from A. D. 1153—1184, tried to restore the unity in the Church and to bring about a perfect reconciliation of all parties, by convoking a Council ad Anurādhapura A. D. 1165, he saw his endeavours crowned with complete success[3].

No less zealous was Kīrti-Niśśaṅka-Malla (1187—1196). This monarch, too, boasts that he had united the three Nikāyas which had been separated for a long time; he claims credit for having restored the temples and Dagobs that were destroyed in consequence of the calamities which had befallen the island[4]. Unhappily the church had soon again to endure harsh treatment at the hands of the foreign usurper Māgha from Kaliṅga, who in the commencement of the thirteenth century persecuted the true Faith[5]. This unhappy state of things lasted for twenty-one years, until Vijayabāhu about A. D. 1250 restored the dilapidations caused by the ruthless enemies and redintegrated the supremacy of Buddhism[6]. His son Parākramabāhu III (1267—1301) was not only a pious monarch, but a patron of learning, and himself a Sanskrit scholar. As there were few able teachers in the island, he invited several renowned scholars, among whom Dharmakīrti, from the Dekkhan to Ceylon[7].

The history of the Siṃhalese Church in the subsequent centuries is not marked by stirring events. Up to our days Buddhism has maintained itself against the encroachments of Śivaism, Islām, and Christianity. The clergy has lost much of its influence, and monasticism is steadily losing ground, but the Law of Buddha is still held high by the aristocracy and the people of old Siṃhalese extraction, though the popular form of religion, apart from some formulas, is extremely like Hinduism[8].

---

1 Voy. II, 407.

2 How the Tamil domination made havock in the ranks of the clergy appears e. g. from the fact that Vijayabāhu (1071—1126) sent to Rāmañña for learned monks; Mahāv. LX, 5.

3 Mahāv. LXX; 4—10; LXXVIII, 5—11; Bigandet II, 142. Cp. Ed. Müller Inscr. in Ceylon, p. 62 and Nr. 137; Taw Sein Ko in Ind. Ant. XXII, 17.

4 Ed. Müller op. c. Nr. 45 and p. 125. Cp. Mahāv. LXXX, 16 ff. Strange that this ruler denounces the great Parākramabāhu as an oppressor; Ed. Müller, op. c. p. 126.

5 Mahāv. LXXX, 58 ff. Knighton, Hist. of Ceylon 152.

6 Mahāv. LXXXI, 18 ff.

7 Mahāv. LXXXIII; LXXXV, 1—16.

8 Highly instructive for the state of religion in the 17th cent. is Robert Knox, An

The decline of Buddhism in India from the eighth century downwards nearly coincides with the growing influence of Tantrism and sorcery, which stand to each other in the relation of theory to practice. The development of Tantrism is a feature that Buddhism and Hinduism in their later phases have in common. The object of Hindu Tantrism is the acquisition of wealth, mundane enjoyments, rewards for moral actions, deliverance, by worshipping Durgā, the Sakti of Siva — Prajñā in the terminology of the Mahāyāna — through means of spells, muttered prayers, Samādhi, offerings &c.[1]. Similarly the Buddhist Tantras purpose to teach the adepts how by a supernatural way to acquire desired objects, either of a material nature, as the elixir of longevity, invulnerability, invisibility, alchymy; or of a more spiritual character, as the power of evoking a Buddha or a Bodhisattva to solve a doubt, or the power of achieving in this life the union with some divinity. There is an unmistakable affinity between Tantrism on one side, and the system of Yoga and Kammaṭṭhāna on the other. Tantrism is, so to say, a popularized and, at the same time, degraded form of Yoga, because the objects are commonly of a coarser character, and the practices partly more childish, partly more revolting.

Tāranātha informs us that Tantrism existed and was transmitted in an occult manner in the period between Asaṅga and Dharmakīrti, but that after Dharmakīrti's times the Anuttara-Yoga became more and more general and influential. Substantially his statement is certainly right[2]. He adds that during the reign of the Pāla dynasty there were many masters of magic, Mantra-Vajrācāryas, who, being possessed of various Siddhis, performed the most prodigious feats.

The kings of the Pāla dynasty, whose sway over Gauḍa and the adjacent regions lasted from about A. D. 800 to 1050, are known both from the annals and their inscriptions as protectors of the Faith[3]. It was during that period that the monastery of Vikramaśila was a renowned centre of Tantrist learning[4].

The Sena kings, who followed the Pālas in the dominion over Eastern India, though belonging to a Hindu persuasion, were not hostile to the Faith. Still Buddhism declined during their reign, and more so after the invasion of the country by the Muhammedans in A. D. 1200[5]. The monasteries of Udaṇḍapura and Vikramaśīla were destroyed; the monks were killed or fled to other countries. The learned Sākyaśrī went to Orissa, and afterwards to Tibet; Ratnarakṣita to Nepāl; Buddhamitra and others sought a refuge in S. India, whilst Saṅgama-Srījñāna with several of his followers betook themselves to Burma, Camboja, &c. And thus the Law of Buddha became extinct in Magadha[6].

---

historical relation of the island Ceylon III, Ch. 6. For the present time see HARDY E. M. 309 ff.; KNIGHTON op. c. 235.

1 Yajñeśvara in Āryavidyā-Sudhākara, p. 159. On the Tantrism of the Śākta or left-hand sects see WILSON Works I, 240 ff.

2 Tār. 201.

3 Tār. 202—252; CUNNINGHAM Arch. Surv. III, 133; XI, 172—182. To this period may belong the inscription from Koṭā, ed. by HULTZSCH in DMG. of 1884, p. 546, but the date is not certain. See further HOERNLE, The Palas of Bengal, Ind. Ant. XIV, 162, ff. and KIELHORN, Ind. Ant. XVII, 307 ff.; XXI, 253 ff. Ep. Ind. II, 370.

4 The monastery was situated in Magadha on the Northern bank of the Ganges. The superiors of the establishment were all of them Mantra-Vajrācāryas; Tār. 257.

5 Yet a Buddhist stone inscription from Srāvastī is dated (Vikrama) Saṃvat 1276 (= A. D. 1219—1220); it has been edited by KIELHORN, Ind. Ant. XVII, 61 ff.

6 The sacred spot of Gayā has up to modern times remained a place of pilgrimage. On the remarkable inscription dated 1813 Nirvāṇa, which according to BHĀGVANLĀL INDRAJI's doubtful reckoning answers to A. D. 1176, see Ind. Ant. of 1881. — Tār. 255.

Many emigrants from Magadha rejoined their brethren in the South, and founded colleges on a modest scale in Vijayanagara, Kaliṅga, and Koṅkan. The comparatively satisfactory condition of Buddhism in Dekkhan about that time is attested by the rich donations to the monastery at Dambal[1].

In Kashmir Buddhism was by most kings treated with great tolerance; those who were inimical to the Faith, like Kṣemagupta (950—958) and the talented, but licentious Śrī-Harṣa (1088—1103) were equally ruthless in their dealings with other sects. The latter's successor rebuilt both monasteries and heathen temples[2]. It was not before A. D. 1340, when Shāh Mīr got the power in hand, that Islām became predominant, and Buddhism vanished, except in Ladak.

In Bengal the Faith counted some adherents up to the 16th century. There is no reason to doubt the truth of a notice in Tāranātha, that a Bengal prince in the middle of the 15th century rebuilt the ruined monasteries and the terrace of the Bodhi tree at Gayā. In Orissa the light of the Law blazed anew for a moment about in the middle of the 16th century under the Hindu ruler Mukunda-Deva Hariścandra until, owing to the conquest of the country by the Musulmān governor of Bengal, it was extinguished[3].

The sons of Śākya, driven away from Hindustān and Bengal, sought a refuge in Nepāl. Here they found a friendly reception by their brethren in the Faith, and liberal protection by the Hindu rulers, whose tolerance extended likewise to Christians[4].

Nepāl is a storehouse of medieval Buddhist literature, both sacred and profane; the country is studded with Stūpas and other sanctuaries of ancient date[5]; the people, so far as they are no professors of Hinduism, worship Mahāyānist Bodhisattvas and Buddhas, and keep up the old formulas of the creed; but the Dharma has undergone profound modifications, and the Saṅgha has long since passed away. Nominally there is a distinction between Bhikṣus, who are bound to practice celibacy, and Vajrācāryas, married men who devote themselves to the active ministry of Buddhism. "But no one follows the rules of the class to which he nominally belongs. All the Nepálese Buddhists are married men, who pursue the business of the world, and seldom think of the injunctions of their religion. The Tantras and Dháraṇís, which ought to be read for their own salvation, they only read for the increase of their stipend and from a greedy desire of money"[6].

The four philosophical systems known by the name of Svābhāvika, Aiśvarika, Kārmika, and Yātnika, whose development seems to be peculiar to Nepāl, have only a slight tinge of Buddhism. They acknowledge, nominally, the Triratna; Buddha means with them "mind"; Dharma "matter", and Saṅgha the connection of the two former in the phenomenal world. In fact the Svābhāvikas are simply Cārvākas; the Aiśvarikas have much in common with the Naiyāyikas and theistic Mīmānsists; the Kārmikas and Yātnikas are upholders of the popular Indian views concerning *daiva* and *puruṣākāra*[7]. All these theories go back to remote times, but their superficial connection with the Buddhist Triad, and the curious interpretation of the meaning of Saṅgha render it probable that the systems have got their present shape in Nepāl.

---

1 Fleet Ind. Ant. X, 185.

2 Rājat. IV, 188 ff. 506; VI, 171; 303; VII, 1092; 1241; VIII, 2416.

3 Tār. 256.

4 A noteworthy instance of tolerance was given by the Śivaite Prakāśa-Malla in A. D. 1754. See Hodgson in JASB. XVII, 2, 226.

5 On the medieval character of Nepalese architecture see Fergusson Hist. Ind. Arch. 299 ff.

6 Hodgson Ess. 52. Cp. Bhagvānlāl in Arch. Surv. of W. India, IX, p. 97.

7 For particulars see Hodgson op. c. 23; 41; 55; 73; and cp. Bṛhat-Saṃhitā I, 7.

LIST OF ABBREVIATED TITLES.

Aṅg. N.	Aṅguttara-Nikāya, ed. by R. MORRIS; I—IV. Lond. 1885—1888.
Ann. Mus. Guimet	Annales du Musée Guimet.
Āpast.	Aphorisms on the Sacred Law of the Hindus, ed. by G. BÜHLER. Bombay 1868. 1871. Translat. by the same in SBE. II.
Arch. Surv.	Archaeological Survey, by JAS. BURGESS.
Avad. Kalp.	Avadāna-Kalpalatā by Kṣemendra. Ed. Bibl. Ind. Calc.
Avad. Śat.	Avadāna-Çataka, cent légendes (bouddhiques) traduites du sanscrit par L. FEER (Ann. Mus. Guimet XVIII. Paris 1891).
Aṣṭ. P. Pāram.	Aṣṭasāhasrika-Prajñā-Pāramitā, ed. Bibl. Ind. Calc.
BARTH Inscr. Camb.	Inscriptions sanscrites du Cambodge, par A. BARTH. Paris 1885.
BARTH Rel. of India	The Religions of India, by A. BARTH; authorized transl. by J. WOOD. Lond. 1882.
BEAL Cat.	A Catena of Buddhist Scriptures from the Chinese by SAMUEL BEAL. Lond. 1871.
BEAL Rom. Leg.	Romantic Legend of Sakya Buddha. From the Chinese by SAMUEL BEAL. Lond. 1875.
BEAL SBE. XIX	The Fo-Sho Hing-Tsan-King. A Life of Buddha by Aśvaghosha Bodhisattva, transl. from Sanskrit into Chinese by Dharmaraksha A. D. 420, and from Chinese into English by SAMUEL BEAL (Sacred Books of the East vol. XIX). Oxford 1883.
BEAL Tripiṭ.	The Buddhist Tripiṭaka as it is known in China and Japan, by SAMUEL BEAL. Lond. 1876.
Bhadrak.	Extracts from the Bhadrakalpāvadāna by S. D'OLDENBURG, in the Zapiski of 1894.
Bibl. Ind.	Bibliotheca Indica.
BIGANDET	The Life or Legend of Gaudama the Buddha of the Burmese, by the Right Rev. P. BIGANDET, 3d ed. Lond. 1880.
Bodhiv.	Maha-Bodhi-Vaṃsa, ed. by S. A. STRONG. Lond. 1891. (Another ed. by P. SOBHITA, iss. from the Lakriviḳiraṇa Press 1890).
Brahma-S.	Vedāntadarśana with the Commentary of Śaṅkara and the Ṭīkā of Govindānanda. Ed. Bibl. Ind. Calc. 1863.
Buddhac.	The Buddhaćarita of Aśvaghosha, ed. by E. B. COWELL (in Anecdota Oxoniensia). Oxford 1893.
Buddhav.	Buddhavaṃsa, ed. by R. MORRIS. Lond. 1882.
Bull. Rel. de l'Inde	Bulletin des Religions de l'Inde.
BURNOUF Intr.	Introduction à l'histoire du Buddhisme indien, par E. BURNOUF. Paris 1844 (reprint 1876).
BURNOUF Lot.	Le Lotus de la bonne Loi, traduit du Sanscrit par E. BURNOUF. Paris 1852.
Cariyā-P.	Cariyā-Piṭaka, ed. by R. MORRIS. Lond. 1882.
CC. RR. de l'Acad. des Inscr.	Comptes Rendus des séances de l'Académie des Inscriptions et Belles lettres.
CHILDERS	A Dictionary of the Páli language by R. C. CHILDERS. Lond. 1872—1875.
COLEBROOKE Ess.	Essays on the Religion and Philosophy of the Hindus, by H. T. COLEBROOKE. Lond. 1858.
Corp. Inscr.	Corpus Inscriptionum Indicarum.
CUNNINGHAM Arch. Surv.	Archaeological Survey of India. Reports by A. CUNNINGHAM.
CV.	Cullavagga (Vinaya Piṭaka II); ed. by H. OLDENBERG. Lond. 1880.
Dharma-S.	Dharma-Saṃgraha, prepared for publication by Kenjiu Kasawara, and ed. by F. MAX MÜLLER and H. WENZEL (Analecta Oxoniensia Vol. I. Part V). Oxford 1885.
Dhātuk. P.	Dhātukathā Pakaraṇa and its Commentary, ed. by E. R. GOONERATNE. Lond. 1892.

Dhp. Dhammapadam, ed. by V. Fausböll, with Latin translation. Copenhagen 1855 (Other translations by A. Weber in Indische Streifen, and by F. Max Müller in SBE. Vol. X, part 1).

Dh. Saṅgaṇi Dhamma-Saṅgaṇi, ed. by Ed. Müller. Lond. 1885.

Dīgha-N. Dīgha-Nikāya, ed. by T. W. Rhys Davids and J. Estlin Carpenter. Vol. I. Lond. 1889.

Dīpav. Dīpavaṃsa, ed. by H. Oldenberg. Lond. 1879.

Divy. Divyâvadâna, ed. by E. B. Cowell and R. A. Neil. Cambr. 1886.

DMG. Zeitschrift der Deutschen Morgenländischen Gesellschaft.

Ep. Ind. Epigraphia Indica.

Fergusson Hist. Ind. Arch. History of Indian and Eastern Architecture. Lond. 1876.

Frankfurter Handb. Handbook of Pali, by O. Frankfurter. Lond. 1883.

Gautama Gautama Dharmaśāstram. The Institutes of Gautama, ed. by A. F. Stenzler. Lond. 1876. Transl. by G. Bühler in SBE. Vol. II.

GGA. Göttinger Gelehrte Anzeigen.

Hardy E. M. Eastern Monachism, by R. Spence Hardy. Lond. 1860.

Hardy Legends. The Legends and Theories of the Buddhists, by R. Spence Hardy. Lond. 1866 (a second ed. 1881).

Hardy M. of B. A Manual of Buddhism, by R. Spence Hardy. Lond. 1860 (a second ed. 1880).

Hodgson Ess. Essays on the Languages, Literature, and Religion of Nepál and Tibet. Lond. 1874 (reprint).

Ind. Ant. Indian Antiquary.

Inscr. in Ceylon Ancient Inscriptions in Ceylon, ed. by Ed. Müller. Lond. 1883.

JA. Journal Asiatique.

Jaeschke Dict. A Tibetan-English Dictionary by H. A. Jaeschke. Lond. 1881.

JASB. Journal of the Asiatic Society of Bengal.

Jāt. The Jātaka together with its commentary, ed. by V. Fausböll. Lond. 1875 seq. (in progress). Transl. of Vol. I, Buddhist Birth stories by F. W. Rhys Davids. Lond. 1886; another transl. by Chalmers 1895.

Jāt. Mālā Jātaka-Mālā, ed. by H. Kern (Harvard Oriental Series I). Boston 1891. Translation by J. S. Speyer (Sacred Books of the Buddhists). Lond. 1895.

JBB. RAS. Journal of the Bombay Branch of the Royal Asiatic Society.

JPTS. Journal of the Pali Text Society, by T. W. Rhys Davids.

JRAS. Journal of the Royal Asiatic Society of Great Britain and Ireland.

Kār. V. Kāraṇḍa-Vyūha. Calc. 1873.

Kathāv. P. A. Kathāvatthu-ppakaraṇa-Aṭṭhakatha, ed. by J. Minayef, in JPTS. of 1889.

Koeppen Rel. des B. Die Religion des Buddha und ihre Entstehung, und die Lamaische Hierarchie und Kirche, von C. F. Koeppen. Berlin 1857. 1859.

Lal. V. Lalita-Vistara, ed. by Rájendralál Mitra. (In Bib. Ind. Old series). A French transl. after the Tibetan version by Ph. E. Foucaux, Rgya-cher-rol-pa ou Développement des Jeux. I, II. Paris 1847—1848; and Le Lalita Vistara traduit du Sanskrit (Ann. Mus. Guimet VI, 1884. XIX, 1892).

Lassen Ind. Alt. Indische Alterthumskunde, von C. Lassen. Bonn 1847 seq.

Mahāv. Mahāvaṃsa, ed. by G. Turnour. Ceylon 1836. From Ch. XXXVII ed. by H. Sumangala and Andris de Silva Batuwantudawa. Colombo 1877. Transl. titled: The Mahâvaṃsa, Part II, containing Chapters XXXIX to C. Transl. by L. C. Wijesiṃha, Mudaliār. Colombo 1889.

Majjh. N. Majjhima-Nikāya, I, ed. by V. Trenckner. Lond. 1887.

Manu. Manu-Saṃhitā, with the Comm. of Kullūka; ed. by Vidyānanda Vidyāsāgara. Calc. 1874.

Max Müller India. India what can it teach us, by F. Max Müller. Lond. 1883.

Mhv. Le Mahāvastu, ed. by E. Senart. Paris, I, 1882. II, 1890.

Mil. P. Milinda-Pañho, ed. by V. Trenckner. Lond. 1880.

Minayef Recherches Recherches sur le Bouddhisme par J. P. Minayef traduit du russe par R. H. Assier de Pompignan (Ann. Mus. Guimet, 1894). The Russian title is Новыя Изслѣдованія о Буддизмѣ.

Minayef Prātim. Prātimokṣa-Sūtra ed. by J. P. Minayef. St. Petersburg 1869.

MV. Mahāvagga (Vinaya Piṭaka I), ed. by H. Oldenberg. Lond. 1879.

OLDENBERG Buddha	Buddha; his Life, his Doctrine, his Order. Transl. from the German by W. HOEY. Lond. 1888.
Par. Dīp.	Paramattha Dīpanī, Part V. Commentary on the Therīgāthā. Ed. by ED. MÜLLER. Lond. 1893.
Peta-V.	Peta-Vatthu, ed. by I. P. MINAYEF. Lond. 1889. Partially transl. by the same in Zapiski VI, 335.
Pugg. P.	Puggala-Paññatti, ed. by R. MORRIS. Lond. 1883.
Rec.	A Record of Buddhist Kingdoms; being an Account by the Chinese monk Fâ-Hien of his Travels in India and Ceylon (A. D. 399—414). By J. LEGGE. Oxford 1886.
Rev. Hist. Rel.	Revue de l'Histoire des Religions.
RHYS DAVIDS B.	Buddhism; being a Sketch of the Life and Teachings of Gautama, the Buddha, by T. W. RHYS DAVIDS. Lond. 1878.
ROCKHILL L. of B.	The Life of the Buddha and the Early History of his Order; by W. W. ROCKHILL. Lond. 1884.
Saddh. Puṇḍ.	Saddharma-Puṇḍarīka (French transl. by E. BURNOUF, Le Lotus de la bonne Loi; an English transl. in SBE. XXI).
Saddh. S.	Saddhamma-Samgaha, ed. by NEDIMALE SADDHAMANDA. Lond. 1890.
Sam. Pās.	Samanta-Pāsādikā, by Buddhaghosa (in Sutta-Vibhaṅga I, 283).
Saṃy. N.	Saṃyutta-Nikâya, ed. by LÉON FEER. Lond. 1884 seqq.
Sarvad. Saṅg.	Sarvadarśana-Saṅgraha, ed. Bibl. Ind.
Sāsanav.	Sāsanavamsa and Sāsanavaṃsa-Dīpa by Vimalasāra Thera. Colombo A. B. 2424 (Only known from quotations).
SBE.	Sacred Books of the East, transl. by various Oriental scholars and ed. by F. MAX MÜLLER. Oxford.
SENART, Not. Ep.	SENART, Notes d'Epigraphie indienne.
SMITHER	Architectural Remains, Anurādhapura. By J. G. SMITHER. Ceylon.
S. Nip.	Sutta-Nipāta, ed. by V. FAUSBÖLL. Lond. 1884. Transl. by the same in SBE.
Sum. Vil.	Sumaṅgala-Vilāsinī, by Buddhagosa, ed. by T. W. RHYS DAVIDS and J. EASTLIN CARPENTER.
S. Vibh.	Sutta-Vibhaṅga (Vinaya Piṭaka III. IV), ed. by H. OLDENBERG. Lond. 1881—1882.
Tār.	Târanâtha's Geschichte des Buddhismus in Indien, aus dem Tibetischen übersetzt von A. SCHIEFNER. St. Petersb. 1869.
Therag.	Theragāthā, ed. by H. OLDENBERG. Lond. 1883.
Therīg.	Therīgāthā, ed. by R. PISCHEL. Lond. 1883.
Tib. L.	Eine Tibetische Lebensbeschreibung Çâkyamuni's, des Begründers des Buddhathums, im Auszuge mitgetheilt von A. SCHIEFNER. St. Petersb. 1848.
Trans. 9th. Cong. of Or.	Transactions of the ninth Internation Congress of Orientalists. Lond. 1893.
Ud.	Udāna, ed. by P. STEINTHAL. Lond. 1885.
Versl. Meded. K. Akad.	Verslagen en Mededeelingen der Koninklijke Akademie van Wetenschappen. Afd. Letterkunde. Amsterdam.
Vim. V.	Vimāna-Vatthu, ed. by GOONERATNE MUDALIYAR. Lond. 1886.
Vis. M.	Visuddhi-Magga. Printed Colombo 1890 (in progress).
Voy.	Voyages des Pèlerins Bouddhistes, III volumes (I. Histoire de la Vie de Hiouen Thsang et de ses voyages dans l'Inde. II. III. Mémoires sur les contrées occidentales) trad. par STANISLAUS JULIEN. Paris 1853—1858.
Vyu.	Mahāvyutpatti, ed. by I. P. MINAYEF, in his Буддизмъ. St. Petersburg 1887.
WADDELL Buddh. of Tib.	The Buddhism of Tibetan Lamaism, by L. A. WADDELL. Lond. 1895.
WASSILIEF B.	Der Buddhismus, seine Dogmen, Geschichte und Literatur. (From the Russian). St. Petersb. 1860. A French transl. by COMME. Paris 1865.
WILSON Works	Works of the late HORACE HAYMAN WILSON. Lond. 1862 seq.
WINDISCH Māra und B.	Māra und Buddha, by E. WINDISCH. Leipzig 1895.
WRIGHT Hist. of N.	A history of Nepal, by D. WRIGHT. Cambr. 1877.
WZ.	Wiener Zeitschrift für die Kunde des Morgenlandes.
Yājñav.	Yājñavalkya-Dharmaśāstram, ed. A. F. STENZLER. Berlin 1849.
Yoga-S.	Patañjala-darśanam, ed. by JĪVĀNANDA VIDYĀSĀGARA. Calc. 1874.
Zapiski	Zapiski Vostočnago Otdêleniya Imperatorskago Russkago Archeologičeskago Obščestva.

INDEX
OF INDIAN NAMES AND TERMS.